Digitalized Finance

Studies in Critical Social Sciences Book Series

Haymarket Books is proud to be working with Brill Academic Publishers (www.brill.nl) to republish the *Studies in Critical Social Sciences* book series in paperback editions. This peer-reviewed book series offers insights into our current reality by exploring the content and consequences of power relationships under capitalism, and by considering the spaces of opposition and resistance to these changes that have been defining our new age. Our full catalog of *SCSS* volumes can be viewed at https://www.haymarketbooks.org/series_collections/4-studies-in-critical-social-sciences.

Series Editor
David Fasenfest (SOAS University of London)

Editorial Board
Eduardo Bonilla-Silva (Duke University)
Chris Chase-Dunn (University of California–Riverside)
William Carroll (University of Victoria)
Raewyn Connell (University of Sydney)
Kimberlé W. Crenshaw (University of California–LA and Columbia University)
Heidi Gottfried (Wayne State University)
Karin Gottschall (University of Bremen)
Alfredo Saad Filho (King's College London)
Chizuko Ueno (University of Tokyo)
Sylvia Walby (Lancaster University)
Raju Das (York University)

Digitalized Finance

Financial Capitalism and Informational Revolution

Edemilson Paraná

Haymarket Books
Chicago, IL

First published in 2018 by Brill Academic Publishers, The Netherlands.
© 2018 Koninklijke Brill NV, Leiden, The Netherlands

Published in paperback in 2020 by
Haymarket Books
P.O. Box 180165
Chicago, IL 60618
773-583-7884
www.haymarketbooks.org

ISBN: 978-1-64259-069-2

Distributed to the trade in the US through Consortium Book Sales and Distribution (www.cbsd.com) and internationally through Ingram Publisher Services International (www.ingramcontent.com).

This book was published with the generous support of Lannan Foundation and Wallace Action Fund.

Special discounts are available for bulk purchases by organizations and institutions. Please call 773-583-7884 or email info@haymarketbooks.org for more information.

Cover design by Jamie Kerry and Ragina Johnson.

Printed in United States.

10 9 8 7 6 5 4 3 2 1

Library of Congress Cataloging-in-Publication Data is available.

For Bela

There is some kind of necessary relationship between the rise of postmodernist cultural forms, the emergence of more flexible modes of capital accumulation, and a new round of "time-space" compression in the organization of capitalism.
    DAVID HARVEY (2013a, p. 7)

While capital must on the one hand strive to tear down every spatial barrier to intercourse, i.e. to exchange, and conquer the whole earth for its market, it strives on the other to annihilate this space with time, i.e. to reduce to a minimum the time spent in motion from one place to another. The more developed the capital, therefore, the more extensive the market over which it circulates, which forms the spatial orbit of its circulation, and the more it strives simultaneously for an even greater extension of the market and for greater annihilation of space by time.
    KARL MARX (2013b, p. 445)

Contents

About *Digitalized Finance* IX
   Alfredo Saad-Filho; Leda Paulani
Foreword XI
   Maria de Lourdes Rollemberg Mollo
Preface XIII
   Luiz Gonzaga de Mello Belluzzo
Acknowledgements XIX
List of Illustrations XX
List of Abbreviations XXI

1 Introduction 1
   1.1 Methodological Considerations 15

2 Capitalism at the Beginning of the 21st Century: Globalized Finance 18
   2.1 A Brief Review of the Theories of Financialization 18
   2.2 Interest-Bearing Capital and Fictitious Capital 23
   2.3 Globalization of Capital: Neoliberalism and Finance-dominated Accumulation Regime 29

3 Technics, Capital and Society: The Material Bases of Technological Development 40
   3.1 Investigating the Technological Practice from Its Social Content 40
   3.2 Technological Development and Financialization of the Economy: Theoretical Starting Points 50

4 Digitalized Finance: Informatization at the Service of Financial Dominance 60
   4.1 The State of the Art of Digitalized Finance at the Beginning of the 21st Century 60
   4.2 The Consequences of Digitalization in the Capitals Markets 77
   4.3 Recent Trends: The Next Steps for Digitalized Finance 101

5 **Digitalized Finance in the Brazilian Context**   105
   5.1   A Brief Overview of the Technical-Operational Development of the Capitals Market in Brazil   112
   5.2   The Development of the ICT and the Transformations of the Brazilian Capitals Market: Elective Affinities   129

6 **Final Considerations**   143

References   149
Index   157

About *Digitalized Finance*

Edemilson Paraná offers the reader a rich overview of the impact of financial globalization. In the current Age of Neoliberalism, finance controls the intertemporal allocation of resources (the relations between consumption and investment), its sectorial allocation (the composition of output, investment, labor and consumption) and international distribution (the pattern of specialization between countries). Digital finance is the outcome of the convergence of new technologies and the expansion of financial logic: the quest for tiny gains in millions of transactions performed in milliseconds, often reversed almost immediately, without any real effects except the enrichment of a few.

Digitalized Finance lies at the intersection of economics, politics and society: by seeking instantaneous speculative gains, finance declares its support for, or rejection, of political decisions in real time whilst, also, establishing the limits of social wellbeing at every moment. Social and political activity can no longer exist separately from finance and its effects; nor can they ignore the shifts in economic and ideological structures dominated by finance.

Financialization has also fostered a generalized rise in rates of exploration. This book shows in detail how these processes take place, and how the application of the most advanced information and communication technologies have supported the rise of new ways of exploiting people, poor countries and nature, including a detailed and unique analysis of the restructuring of the relations of control and domination in Brazil. This book is essential reading for anyone wishing to understand the distinguishing features of contemporary financialized capitalism.

Alfredo Saad-Filho
SOAS University of London

The relationship between technological progress and capitalist development is symbiotic. The paradigmatic example of this mutualism is the industrial revolution in the mid-18th century. Ushered in by the advance of the very capitalist relations that it started, it ultimately determined the victory of this means of social organization over all others. Within this same social shift, it forged a kind of technological advance that, if it does indeed contribute so greatly to the destruction of the material barriers holding back the development of the human spirit, then it does so with the parameters found in the logic and the imperatives of the accumulation of capital. But just as the commodity – the "maternal cell" of this economic system – seems natural, so too does the permanent advance of the technology.

The constant celebration of technological virtuosity is therefore explained as though it were independent, neutral and linear, responding solely to man's incredible capacity to create. This is not the case, however, with the book you have in your hands. Fully aware of all the issues that are involved here, and following this methodological principle to the letter, Edemilson Paraná has provided an astute and solid analysis of the role of Information and Communication Technologies (ICT) in the intensification and strengthening of the financialization process of the global economy.

Exploring what he calls the "Cycle of Operation of Digitalized Finance", Paraná introduces us to the unbelievable world of the creation of abstract wealth, bolstered by sophisticated mathematical models, automated robots and trading software that seeks unimaginable revenues in a matter of milliseconds. Enormous investments, in the region of hundreds of millions of dollars, are made by companies looking to gain two or three milliseconds in the period between a trading order being made and its actual application (to get some idea of what this means, the blink of an eye takes around 400 milliseconds).

Faced with such an incredible scenario, the author only manages to resist the fetishistic temptation of seeing financialization as the result of the development of the ICT by staying true to his firm methodological discipline. The result of his analysis is, therefore, formidable: he demonstrates that, just as the machinery of the industrial revolution made the already formally existent subordination of labor to capital a reality, the untiring development of the ICT over the past few decades, by firmly establishing the compression of the space-time that is the nature of capital, has meant the increasing and very real subordination of the logic of productive accumulation to the logic of financial accumulation (that the crisis of the 1970s had already set in motion). This is, therefore, a book that is essential for anyone wishing to understand contemporary capitalism.

Leda Paulani
University of São Paulo (USP)

Foreword

For those, like me, who see capitalism as a historically dated form of production, with its own productive forces and social relations of production that evolve with it, Edemilson Paraná's book provides an important illustrative example of this evolution.

Based upon interviews with those involved in the operationalization of the Brazilian capitals market, the author seeks inspiration in Marx and specialized literature to understand the influence of Information and Communication Technologies (ICT) in the emergence and consolidation of the process of financialization of economies or the predominance of finance over the production that characterizes current capitalist development. Under Marx's terms, this predominance of finance over production is no more than the development of fictitious capital. Over the course of this book, there are certain aspects of his analysis that are of special note and to which I pay particular attention in this introduction, not only to give them added value, but to stress the importance of their continued development over the coming years.

For Marx, capital is money that valorizes when, upon purchasing the labor force as a commodity, it is able to generate a value that is greater than its own, the surplus value, from which profit arises, that is realized when the produced commodity is sold. This is the complete reproduction cycle of capital, which requires both the circulation of commodity and its production, as necessary steps of the same social process. The faster the movement of purchase of the labor force, production and sale, the greater the rhythm of production, increasing the profit made and allowing a new cycle to begin.

Marx also defines another capital, said to be fictitious because, without passing through the manufacturing process and, therefore, without purchasing the labor force and producing surplus value, it manages to increase its value. For this, it is necessary to make gains in operations involving the purchase and sale of assets, when sale prices, the fruit of the simple capitalization of prospective earnings, are greater than purchase prices. In this case, this concerns valorization that is merely speculative, since there is no return on the capital for investment in the real production where the labor force, the only thing likely to generate new value, is purchased. It can be seen here that the faster the turnover of purchase and sale, the greater the possibilities of development of the fictitious capital, because the possibilities of speculative gain are greater.

And that is why, as Edemilson Paraná in his Introduction quotes Marx himself as saying, "capital (...) has to strive to tear down every spatial barrier to intercourse, i.e. to exchange, and conquer the whole earth for its market". This happens with economic globalization, and the neoliberalism that sustains it, to free up transactions, thus expanding the space in which markets can operate. But he also then says that it is necessary "to reduce the time that the movement from one place to another costs". If this is relevant to any capital, as we have seen, purchasing labor force, producing surplus value and transforming it into profit through sale, then for the development of fictitious capital this is especially important, since its valorization, in order to become concrete, requires the sale of assets at prices that are higher than the purchase prices. Its development, therefore, can only take place if there is an increase (and the more the better) in the purchase and sale transactions. Paraná's book describes in detail how technology, and in particular ICT (Information and Communication Technologies), allows for a reduction in this time, since it provides for transactions that are faster and faster, thus increasing the possibilities of fictitious gains. This is the first thing to note about the analysis the author has undertaken. What the book shows, in this respect, is how these transactions were able to increase when "the closure of trades on the stock exchange stopped being measured in minutes and seconds, and started being accounted for in 'milli', 'micro' and even 'nano' seconds, as can now be seen".

The second point of note is how the book discusses and illustrates the biased nature of technical progress. It serves for the development of capitalism and is fundamental in the competition that characterizes it – a process that, instead of praising it as a means of guaranteeing efficiency, as the economists of the so-called "mainstream" do, is criticized by Marx for creating greater inequality. In particular, it is the very success in the competition process that leads to the concentration or centralization of the capital, another tendency that the book describes and that is intensified by the development of finance.

A reading between the lines of the interviews presented in the book also demonstrates the excessively vain tone of the operators, who seem to see the technical progress of the ICTs as all-powerful and self-sufficient, capable of providing unlimited and permanent profits, as long as it is leading the competition. The delight with which the operators, for this very reason, greet the commodification of the technology is also clear. The factual dismantling of these illusions came with the crisis which started in 2008 and that the whole world is still dealing with. The analysis of what Paraná calls the "technical fetishism" involved in this concept, is the third point that I would like to highlight from amongst the contributions made by the book, which provides far more than this presentation is able to cover.

Maria de Lourdes Rollemberg Mollo
Professor, Economics Department at the University of Brasília (UnB),
Associate Fellow of the World Academy of Arts and Science (WAAS)

Preface

This book by Edemilson Paraná carries out a rare feat. It deals with the promiscuous relations between "financialization" and the nature of technical progress in the recent period. Edemilson analyzes the acceleration of time and the shrinking of space, twin phenomena that Marx unveiled in the movement of *real abstraction* generated in the bowels of the capital regime.

In *Grundrisse* and in *Capital*, Marx performs the works of the negative dialectics: the negation of direct exchange; the negation of the generalized exchange of commodities in the absence of the commodification of the labor force; the negation of the valorization process in the absence of the capitalist productive forces.

At the same time, in their unfoldings, the implicit negations in the transmutation of the simplest or elementary relations constitute new positivities that move in an admirable dialectic of forms. The more developed forms subordinate and rearrange the position and meaning of the most elementary forms. The positions of the categories change: the realization of the value form, in the affirmation of its empire, is assuming more concrete configurations throughout the process of *real abstraction*. It is not a conceptual game engendered in the mind of the investigator. The movement of *real abstraction* accompanies the theoretical "construction" of Capital. This mode of exposure is exemplified in Marx's treatment of the development of money as a form of value and universal expression of wealth.

A careful reading of *Grundrisse* and the three volumes of *Capital* will show that money turned into capital – the origin and purpose of capitalist circulation and production (Money-Commodity-Money) not only requires real submission of labor to the domain of productive forces but also imposes on workers (and on owners of capital-value) the dictates of the incessant process of accumulation of abstract wealth. The accumulation of more money through the use of money to capture more value in the form of money is at the same time a movement of *real abstraction* that culminates in the "developed" (and more concrete) forms of interest bearing capital, of credit money and fictitious capital. In these forms, money-capital performs its concept of "value which valorizes" and tries to add its value without the mediation of the commodity labor force. M-C-M' converts to M-M'.

Karl Marx treated interest-bearing capital and fictitious capital as the most developed forms of capital. Most developed because the most abstract. Marx works within the simultaneity of two movements: the reiteration of the basic mechanisms of economic and social reproduction of capitalism and the transformation, the change, driven by the incessant impulse to overcome these limits.

Financialization is not a deformation of capitalism, but a "perfectioning" of its nature. This "perfectioning" exacerbates its contradictory movement: in the ceaseless pursuit of "perfection", that is, the accumulation of money from money, the capital regime is bound to devalue the labor force and to expand fixed capital beyond the limits allowed by the relations of production, which not only engenders the periodic crises of realization and over-accumulation, but also transforms, in its inexorable dynamics, the labor on "a miserable basis" of the process of creation of value.

It is through the financial form that capitalist competition takes place, that is, it becomes possible to "thaw" the immobilized capital in the various spheres of production, in search of the best opportunities and the most profitable applications. Competition must be understood as the imposition of rules governing production methods, the labor process, imposing on workers the dictatorship of socially necessary labor time and, at the same time, dictating to the capitalists the compulsion to reduce it. Capital, Marx says, is the contradiction in process.

The Finance of the Neoliberal Era

The typical precautions of the so-called Keynesian era, the stage of "financial repression", was aimed, in particular, to attenuate the instability of the markets for the negotiation of securities representing wealth and income. Monetary and credit policies were oriented toward securing favorable conditions for the financing of productive expenditure, public or private, and to mitigate the effects of the fictitious valuation of wealth on the current spending and investment decisions of the capitalist class. The aim was to avoid over-valuation cycles and catastrophic devaluations of *existing financial wealth stocks*.

Sociologist and economist Wolfgang Streek, director of the Max Plank Institute, points to the origin of the "transfer of power to the markets" in the stagflation of the 1970s. At this point, the social and economic arrangement of the previous decades was broken up in the name of removing barriers to free operation of the markets.

The financial deregulation of the neoliberal era has allowed the demarcated borders after the crisis of the 1930s between commercial banks, investment banks, insurance companies and savings and loans to be erased.

Transformed now into financial supermarkets, banks took care to advance the securitization of loans and engage in the financing of positions in the capital markets and in off-balance sheet operations involving derivatives. This was accompanied by a spiral of leverage and increasing interpenetration of debt and credit relationships in the "food chain" of finance.

The advancement of these interrelations was supported by the expansion of the global interbank market and by the improvement of payment systems. Investment banks and other shadow banks have moved closer to the monetary functions of commercial banks, fueling their liabilities in the "wholesale money markets", backed by short-term investments by companies and households. In the 2000s intra-financial debt as a proportion of US GDP grew faster than household and corporate indebtedness.

Without pretending to be exhaustive, it is necessary to enumerate the trends that have since defined the metamorphoses of global finance: (1) the greater weight of financial wealth in total wealth; (2) the increasing power of managers of the mass movable assets (Mutual Funds, Pension Funds, insurance) in defining the ways of using "savings" and credit; (3) the free movement of capital between financial markets and the adoption by national economies of floating rate regimes and inflation targets; (4) risk rating agencies assume the role of courts, with a view to judging the quality of national assets and policies; (5) the expansion of futures markets and the generalization of the use of derivatives give greater elasticity to credit.

In the genesis, development and configuration of the expansion cycle that culminated in the crisis of 2008 is the rearrangement of portfolios, a financial phenomenon: the gross flow of private capital from Europe and the Periphery to the United States. Financial interpenetration led to the diversification of assets on a global scale and thus imposed the "internationalization" of wealth managers' portfolios.

The United States, benefited by the attractiveness of its broad and deep financial market, has absorbed since the mid-1980s a volume of foreign capital that has surpassed the current account deficits.

In a world where capital mobility prevails, the determination does not range from the current account deficit to "external saving". It is the high liquidity and high "elasticity" of the global financial markets that sponsor the exuberant expansion of credit, asset inflation and the indebtedness of hyper-consumer households.

At the epicenter of the transformations of the last decades is the exceptional growth of the gross capital flows destined for the United States and intermediated, above all, by the European banks. This means that the changes in debit and credit relationships, and therefore in the assets of banks, companies and households, were much more intense than those reflected in the current account deficit.

In the context of the new "Sino-American" relations, the production-income-consumption circuit can be presented in the following stylized form: gross capital flows – expansion of domestic credit in the United States – acceleration of US consumer spending – additional generation of employment and incomes in emerging China – Chinese trade surplus supported by exports of manufactures – accumulation of reserves (financial savings) – "final financing" of the US current account deficit.

Financial innovations and the global integration of credit institutions promote the exuberance of household consumption financing, which leads to reckless indebtedness and, obviously, the deterioration of the quality of the balance sheets of financial institutions and debtor households. It is this "arrangement" that generates the current account deficit in the balance of payments, not the other way around.

The dominance of the financial sphere was associated with the incessant search for new "competitive" areas by the block of leading companies and their suppliers. This alliance imposed on the global economy a dramatic increase in the productivity-wage ratio in the manufacturing of emerging Asians. The capital movement irrigated the American financial market and allowed the maintenance of low interest rates on long-term securities. The offer of cheap funds was important to finance the productive metastasis of the great American, European, and Japanese enterprise to the Pacific of "small tigers" and "new dragons".

The new manufactures are produced in the economic space built by the Asians around the "big Chinese automaker". The huge reserve of labor, devalued foreign exchange, and abundance of foreign direct investment allow China to establish a virtuous division of labor with its neighbors. At the same time, the shifting of American, European, and Japanese subsidiaries in search of global sourcing forces the US national economy to expand its degree of trade openness and generate a growing trade deficit. It becomes imperative to accommodate the manufacturing and commercial expansion of the new partners, produced largely but not exclusively by the displacement of large American capital in the pursuit of greater competitiveness.

The chronic imbalance of current account balances between China and the United States was therefore not an "anomaly" of the Sino-American model, but a constituent factor in the dynamism of the global economy of the Third Millennium.

The global competitiveness game has aligned itself with new corporate governance standards to focus power in the hands of shareholders and financial wealth managers. Companies have significantly expanded the ownership of financial assets, not as a capital reserve for future fixed investments, but as a way of altering the strategy of managing retained earnings and indebtedness.

The objective of maximizing the cash generation determined the shortening of the business horizon. The expectation of variation of the prices of the financial assets began to play a very important role in the decisions of the companies. Financial profits outperformed operating profits. Corporate management was thus subject to the dictates of short-term "patrimonial" gains and financial accumulation imposed its reasons on investment decisions, those generating employment and income for the masses.

Treasury and Central Bank in the Financial Crisis

In the aftermath of the crisis, the carnal relations between money, public finances and private financial markets in contemporary capitalism came to light. The modern credit system, when creating deposits, that is, means of payment – whose unit of account is defined by the State – operates as a private monetary administration center. Banks (and other non-bank institutions that supply their liabilities in the wholesale money markets) define the rules for access to liquidity, credit and the payment system. Such rules impose constraints on the conditions of production and competition of undertakings.

In the period of euphoria that preceded the crisis, commercial banks, investment banks, pension fund managers, mutual funds, private equity funds, not to mention sophisticated hedge funds, escaped the standards of rationality and risk assessment proclaimed by the Efficient Markets Hypothesis. They succumbed, in fact, to the impersonal forces of competitive mimicry, referred to in the vulgar language of merchandising as "herd behavior". They all consolidated their conviction that they were armored against market, liquidity and payment risks.

The "confidence" climate, as usual, spread the systemic risk that the "wise men" imagined had been diverted by the use of derivatives. In recent years, the decline in asset and currency price volatility and increased liquidity have fueled the exasperation of "leverage", from demented consumers to hedge funds based on bank lending.

This is the crucial paradox of contemporary finance: the "private centralization" of money and credit in "too-big-to-fail" institutions has spread – in the wake of the global integration of financial markets – the competitive process of generation and distribution of assets backed by real estate (asset backed securities) whose enigmatic pricing was supported by the infamous Risk Rating Agencies.

Euphoria causes collapse. When the wheel of fortune turns falsely, the collapse of asset prices imposes state "centralization", under penalty of destruction of credit and currency, that is, of the market infrastructure.

The stability of the monetary economy therefore depends on the complex relationships between the collective funds administered by the private credit assessment committees and the state's ability to guide the behavior and expectations of private agents engaged in the field of abstract wealth accumulation. These works of the state are executed by the monetary policy of the central bank in conjunction with the management of public debt by the Treasury. In a financial crisis, such as the one we are going through, government bonds in the dominant countries reveal their nature as "assets of last resort", a shelter where the anguish that seizes the souls of private owners and controllers of wealth is cooled.

The crisis was triggered in the United States has seriously affected its financial markets. However, the bailout sponsored by the Federal Reserve and the Treasury to institutions "too big to fail" has elicited a "flight to quality". This avid quest for quality denounces the exorbitant privilege of the managing country of the reserve currency and the hierarchy of currencies in the international system.

Until yesterday damaged in their credibility by their own exploits, the "markets" were reinvigorated by formidable cash injections, a spectacular "inflation" of central bank monetary liabilities. The money was distributed generously in an "atypical" form of cooperation between the once independent central banks and the formerly austere national treasuries. The former housed the subprime financial scum and its surroundings, set up programs for the exchange of bad debts for liabilities of their issue, that is, money, while treasuries issued public bonds to protect private wealth in a perilous state.

At the height of the crisis, the central banks of the capitalist cusp fulfilled their mission. In addition to their classic lender-of-last-resort functions, central banks promoted the implicit transfer of ownership of debt-credit relationships, without allowing the principles of private wealth ownership to be violated, even though individual owners had been sacrificed.

Luiz Gonzaga de Mello Belluzzo[1]
Professor, Economics Institute at the University of Campinas (Unicamp) and Faculties of Campinas (Facamp)

---

[1] Luiz Gonzaga de Mello Belluzo is included in the *Biographical Dictionary of Dissenting Economists* (2001) as one of the world's 100 most important heterodox economists. Recognized as the Brazilian Intellectual of the Year – Juca Pato Award (2005).

Acknowledgements

The content of this book is drawn from a master's dissertation presented to the Sociology Department of the University of Brasília (UnB) in September 2014, and published in book form in Brazil in May 2016. For the publication of this book in English, a number of alterations, as well as updates, have been made, but the initial argument and conclusions, however, remain unchanged. Wherever possible, series of data which, in the original version, provided figures up to 2013, were updated to 2016.

Throughout the process which has allowed the publication of this book, first in Portuguese and now in English, for the critical dialog and encouragement they provided, I would like to thank professors Michelangelo Trigueiro and Maria de Lourdes Mollo, from the University of Brasília (UnB), Alfredo Saad-Filho (SOAS – University of London), Leda Paulani (University of São Paulo – USP), Marcos Antônio Macedo Cintra (Institute of Applied Economic Research – IPEA) and Luiz Gonzaga Belluzzo (University of Campinas – Unicamp). Obviously, none of them should be held responsible for any errors that may possibly be found in this publication. I also thank the UnB Postgraduate Program in Sociology for the material support given to this publication.

Illustrations

Figures

1. Fictitious wealth (world stock of financial assets) and global real revenue (GNP) US$ trillions   20
2. Co-location (number of trades) – Bovespa segment   71
3. HFT (daily number of trades) – BM&F segment   72
4. HFT (daily financial volume) – Bovespa segment   77
5. The rough timeline of the events spanning decades that led to the current market penetration of high-frequency trading   83
6. The spiral of complexity of digitalized finance   88
7. Cycle of operation of digitalized finance   93
8. Participation by type of investor (volume of trades) – Bovespa segment   135
9. Participation by type of investor (contracts volume) – BM&F segment   136
10. Share of the stock market in the hands of the five biggest brokerage firms (as a percent of the total)   137
11. Number of registered brokerage firms operating in the stock market   138
12. Average daily number of trades made in the stock market   139

Tables

1. Sudden events relating to the operation of HFTs and/or incorrect functioning of automated trading mechanisms and systems   82
2. Measures for regulation and risk control in the financial markets   95
3. Time line of technological innovations in the Brazilian capitals market   130

Abbreviations

AT	Algorithmic Trading/Trader
BM&F	Bolsa de Mercadorias e Futuros (Brazilian Commodities and Futures Exchange)
Bovespa	Bolsa de Valores de São Paulo (São Paulo Stock Exchange)
CATS	Computer Assisted Trading System
CFTC	Commodity Futures Trading Commission
CMN	Conselho Monetário Nacional (Brazilian National Monetary Council)
CPF	Cadastros de Pessoa Física (Registry of Taxpaying Individuals)
CVM	Comissão de Valores Mobiliários (Brazilian Securities Commission)
DJI	Dow Jones Industrial Average
DMA	Direct Access Market
FBI	Federal Bureau of Investigation
Febraban	Federação Brasileira de Bancos (Brazilian Federation of Banks)
FIX	Financial Information Exchange Protocol
FP	Productive Forces
GDP	Gross Domestic Product
GNP	Gross National Product
GTS	Global Trading System
HFT	High Frequency Trading/Trader
IBGE	Instituto Brasileiro de Geografia e Estatística (Brazilian Institute of Geography and Statistics)
ICT	Information and Communications Technologies
IPO	Initial Public Offering
IT	Information Technology
NYSE	New York Stock Exchange
PQO	Programa de Qualificação Operacional (Operational Qualification Program)
R&D	Research and Development
S&P	Standard and Poor's
SEC	Security and Exchange Commission
SRP	Social Relations of Production
UNCTAD	United Nations Conference on Trade and Development
USA	United States of America
WTr	Web Trading

CHAPTER 1

Introduction

Since the controls on the reproduction and circulation of fictitious capital (Marx 1988)[1] (the establishment of which began in the 1930s as part of the response to the structural crisis of the capitalist system that occurred in 1929) started gradually being dismantled in the 1970s, a set of structural changes in the world economy have become more established and consolidated as a result.

Widely discussed in literature (Guttmann 1999, Serfati 1999, Stockhammer 2000, Epstein 2002, Giffin 2007, Langley 2008, Eckhard and Treeck 2008, Braga 2009, Foster 2009, Mollo 2011, Guillèn 2014), the financialization of the economy,[2] resulting from the freeing of hindrances on the reproduction and circulation of financial capital on a global scale, has found in the globalization of production, circulation and consumption of commodities, assets, services and information, a fertile ground for advancement, producing effects in the most diverse areas of social life.

This process of globalization, advanced thanks to an intense advance in technology, cannot, however, be seen as the material antecedent that produced the conditions for the financialization of the global economy, since neither, based upon the theoretical framework that we have assumed, can exist as such, unless they are dialectically related, as integral parts of the same systemic process. As Chesnais (1996, p. 11) states, "the financial sphere represents the spearhead of the movement of globalization of the economy".

If, as we intend to demonstrate, in its operating dimension and logic, the financialization of the economy, as such, anchored in the hegemony of speculation – or in other words, in the process in which decisions on the purchase and

---

[1] For a definition of fictitious capital see Chapter 2, Section 2.
[2] Understood here, primarily based upon the formulations of François Chesnais (1996, 2005, 2014), as being a general logical reordering of the accumulation of capital in favor of financial accumulation, or in other words, submission of the productive process as a whole to its own objectives and modes of operation. This process can be explained in contemporary terms by: (i) the autonomization of the financial sphere in relation to the sphere of production and to the state control; (ii) the fetishism of the forms of valorization of financial capital (due to its highly abstract and fictitious character); and (iii) the growing power of the "financial operators" to trace the contours and directions of the economy as a whole, and to decide which agents, from which countries, and which types of transaction can enter into the financial globalization and those which cannot.

sale of stocks driven by the expectation of resale/repurchase with profits in secondary markets of stocks, properties, currencies, credits, commodities and various other assets (Bastos 2013) – is a phenomenon that has developed more forcefully since the 1970s and 1980s, then the gains of autonomy and influence of fictitious capital on the group of capitalist economies as a whole date from long before. In *Capital*, written in the 19th century, Karl Marx noted the oppositional nature of "bank capital" or "money capital" in relation to "real capital" – the latter being submitted to the first; and in 1917, Lenin (2011) presented his thesis on imperialism, describing the function of financial capital as being to create profits under imperial colonialism.

This process of separation of the "real" economy and the financial economy, as an expression of the autonomization of financial capital in relation to real capital, however, assumes profiles that are considerably different over the different phases of development of the capitalist system; presenting extremely particular characteristics during the last quarter of the 20th century. As Chesnais (2014) explains:

> Every Marxist and indeed heterodox economist is obliged to propose a definition of "financialization". I see it as an epoch in the history of capitalist development starting in the mid-1980s, inextricably linked to the globalization of capital in its industrial, financial and commodity capital forms, in which the traits of "interest-bearing capital" taken *in toto* have pervaded the process of capital-extended reproduction and accumulation in its entirety (verbal information[3]).

These economic changes, in line with an increase in quality, volume and intensity in the exchange and circulation of goods, people and information, enhanced by an intense process of scientific-technical development, that activates and is activated by these economic transformations, allows a countless number of alterations, new configurations and possibilities in contemporary societies, influenced by new political, institutional, cultural and identity dynamics.

To conceptually describe and organize the changes which societies undergo at the end of the 20th century and beginning of the 21st, various authors

---

3   Information provided by François Chesnais during a discussion held at the IIRE Economy Seminar 2014, in Amsterdam, Holland, on February 14, 2014. Hosted by: IIRE – International Institute of Research and Education. Available at: <http://www.4edu.info/index.php/IIRE_Economy_Seminar_2014>. Accessed on Nov 24, 2017.

suggested terms and concepts that address these transformations in the productive forces, such as, for example, digital capitalism (Schiller 2000), virtual capitalism (Dawson and Foster 1998), high-technology capitalism (Haug 2003), informatic capitalism (Fitzpatrick 2002), communicative capitalism (Dean 2005), cognitive capitalism (Negri and Vercellone 2008), and informational capitalism (Castells 1999). Despite the controversy that these formulas have given rise to, what is important to us here is the focus of these definitions on their desire to understand the dialectic relationship between technological development and mode of production, or, in wider terms, between technology and society, a subject that has attracted the attention of many scholars.

In an era in which the discussion around the relationship between information technologies and society, and its many different developments and consequences in various areas, is gaining weight in the public debate, a closer look at the technics may help us to avoid the traps of technological determinism that puts forward the destruction of the environment, privatizations, and the reduction of social protection, unemployment, the increasingly flexible and precarious nature of work, the intensification of the working day, outsourcing, and so many other political-social steps backward as the natural and inevitable consequences of the process of digitalization of society. A qualified evaluation of these phenomenon, in their interaction with technological practice (which, as we intend to demonstrate in this book, maintains a social and, therefore, political content) will allow us to confront the approaches that treat technical progress as a direct and automatic synonym of regression or social progress.

We will therefore take a close look at the relationship between the mode of production and technical development, with a view to contributing to the expansion of the critical reading and comprehension of the economy and society of our age. As part of this work, we are looking to clarify the relationship between the development of the Information and Communication Technologies (ICT) and the intensification of the process of financialization of the world economy. The underlying intention is to investigate the possible affinities between the two phenomena, in order, ultimately, to understand the influence of the ICT on the emergence and consolidation of a new global financial system in a network connected twenty-four hours a day.

To do so, as well as a specialized bibliography, we use interviews with specialists in information technology and the financial system, as well as economic data. The analytical approach concentrates on the years between 1980 and 2008, a period widely pinpointed in economics literature as the period of acceleration and consolidation of the financialization of the international economy. However, due to the restrictions on the sources of primary data and due to the particularities of recent Brazilian economic history, the starting point for our study, the historical series of data start in 1994, the year the Real Plan was adopted, and run through to 2016.

In addition to the general discussion provided by Karl Marx (1988) in relation to the capitalist economic-political system, especially the operating and reproduction logic of fictitious capital, and the evaluation of the phenomenon of financialization of the economy in David Harvey (2005, 2011, 2013a) and François Chesnais (1996, 1998, 2005), we resurrect in Louis Althusser (1979a), and his formulations surrounding the concept of over-determination, or over-determined contradiction, an important theoretical reference for the understanding of the dialectic relationship between technological development and structural transformation of the capitalist economy. Supporting this perspective, our references are the technology-critical authors (Aronowitz 1978, Braverman 1977, Bukharin 1971, Burawoy 1978, 1990, Chesnais and Serfati 2003, Cohen 1978, Feenberg 2002, Goonatilake 1984, Hobsbawn 1996, Mészáros 2002, Noble 1979, 2001, Therborn 1980) who provide support for the discussion on the (inter)relationships between technology, economy and society.

As we noted, there are a great many works that discuss the process of financialization of the world economy based upon the approach of Political Economy. Far from denying them, we praise some of these contributions as important theoretical references for the expansion of the understanding of the socio-economic problem that we propose to investigate.

However, as a complement to these readings, we argue that an understanding of the logic of the technical-operational functioning of the financial system based upon a sociological approach can open up new levels for the reading of the contemporary economy in its financial dominance, as well as the role that technological development, as a complex social process and subject to disputes and clashes between different players, agents and classes has had, and continues to have, on the expansion of a reconfigured capital; to the extent that, as Chesnais (2014) argues, (verbal information[4]), we can no longer look at the process of financialization simply as the product of a growing dominance of fictitious capital in relation to productive capital, but, above all, for the transformations of the "capital as a whole", restructured in the wider sense as interest-bearing capital.

Behind everything, this involves an investigation of how the advance of the ICT, by participating in the overcoming of the space-time frontiers and other technical constraints on free circulation and management of the accumulation of capitals on a global level, has both contributed and continues contributing

---

4 *Ibid.*

(through its objective and subjective, material and ideological dimensions) to the intensification of this process of structural reconfiguration of the capitalist system in our age. At the core, and the central impetus for this work, are, therefore, the following questions: what is the role that technological development has played in the changes capitalism has been through over the past 40 years? More specifically, what is the relationship between the development of the ICT and the intensification of the process of financialization of the economy on a global scale? What problems, dilemmas or possibilities can these transformations bring to our attention? How can these elements be observed in Brazil's reality?

Laborious, and in some ways limited in its efficiency, is the methodological objective of isolating certain aspects (in our case, the development of the ICT) in the comprehension of complex phenomenon with various causes, as can be seen in the process of financialization of the world economy. Once we have understood this limitation, we can turn to an investigation that is always inspired in political-economic, social-historical and cultural questions concerning this problem, dialectically articulated in the dimension of the totality. This epistemological topography (the search for an understanding of particular phenomenon based upon their articulations with the social whole) is implicit throughout this work, motivating and being motivated by the object of study we undertake to investigate.

Maintaining this observation intact, however, we take a careful look, just as an eyeglass magnifies one's view of the small parts of a vast object, at the sociotechnical dynamics involved in the operation of the international financial system from 1980 – a date widely cited in economic literature as the verifiable start (including statistically) of this process – to 2008, when a serious economic crisis erupted, having started in the financial sphere and spreading to the other sectors of the economy, and being recognized as one of the greatest since the crisis of 1929, for reasons that stretch back, according to the authors we adopt as part of our theoretical framework, to the structural transformations that were started in more earnest in 1980. In relation to the Brazilian capitals market, to which we will be paying special attention, our evaluation extends through to 2016.

More specifically, based upon an understanding of the logic of the technical-operational functioning of the Brazilian financial system, we will venture to understand whether (and, should the answer be in the affirmative, in what way) the development of the ICT reconfigured the operational dynamic of the capitals market (speed, quantity, quality, institutional arrangements, and nature of the financial operations and products) or if it simply deepened or triggered processes that had already been identified as a trend by the capitalist system's development dynamic itself, as a response to its constant need to find new ways to encourage the accumulation of capital.

As a guiding basis in this discussion, we will defend the argument, confirmed by our investigation, that, far from being the cause or principal responsible factor, the development of the new Information and Communication Technologies can be seen as the transmission vehicle that aims, by means of technical-logistical support, to intensify and expand the functioning logic of the finance-dominated accumulation regime, making it faster, urgent and essential. The intense technological development, is not, therefore, a source of the economy's financialization process, and nor is it a fundamental explaining reason, but rather an integral part of the same phenomenon (of productive restructuring and transformations in the area of the accumulation regime) which has many causes and is made up of various dialectically articulated social aspects, policies and technologies.

Behind this argument is also our agreement with readings of the process of technological development as being not neutral and partially autonomous, a product of our historical time, the conveyor of a social content and, as such, in our reality, the result, in the final analysis, of a capitalist context as the structural enabling factor of its material reproduction.

The idea of cutting-edge technological development being intimately connected with the dynamics of expansion of capitalist accumulation, despite being an extremely plausible reading of the current situation, is not exactly a historical revelation. It is enough to simply remember the role that nascent modern science, and the technical apparatus connected to it, played in the industrial revolutions of the 19th and 20th centuries. Going back a little further, it is also even possible to notice a parallel with the great colonial discoveries, intimately linked to the techniques used for navigation and war at the time.

If this is true, it seems evident, however, that the peculiarities of the process of technical evolution which humankind has experienced over the last 40 years, focused on the dynamics of production, exchange, processing, storage and communication of information, point the way to new scenarios. In the financial sector there are numerous indications of this, especially in the creation of new financial products and new mechanisms of credit management and its risks (Lapavitsas and Dos Santos 2008). It is at the frontier of understanding this phenomenon, therefore, that we are exploring in this book.

This does not mean, however, that its importance is being artificially inflated, whilst ignoring that, as integral parts of the same reality, technological advances and productive restructuring are interconnected by a two-way channel. The celebrative support of the idea that we will be seeing the birth of a new economy and, as a consequence, a new society, tending toward being freer in nature due to the possibilities of overcoming the exploitation of labor by capital that have appeared in our age, do not appear to have any grounds in reality.

On the contrary, as Antunes (2012) noted, we suspect that in present day capitalism, steered by the financial logic that restructures, re-conceives and reworks the senses and notions of time and space, as well as production, we have witnessed an increase in the means of extracting surplus value.

> It seems to us that there are new ways of creating value which are capable of articulating highly advanced machinery – of which Information and Communication Technologies are an example – that have invaded the world of commodities manufacture, be this commodities tangible or not, at the same time as capitals search the world of labor for "new qualifications and skills" using all the different forms of labor, whether they have a specifically manual profile or whether they develop together with the communication technologies of the information era, which in a certain way offer greater intellectual or intangible potential, but which form part of the complex process that is common to production as a whole, and is ruled by social labor that is complex and combined. Labor these days therefore combines dimensions that are both tangible and intangible. And this is something that, instead of bring down the theory of value, has been contributing to it. These new forms of labor, in fact, hide means of exploitation and self-exploitation of labor. Our hypothesis is that these new forms of labor, both apparent or "invisible", are, in fact, a phenomena-based expression that covers a real creation of surplus-value in practically every sphere of the world of labor, where it can be performed/preserved/expanded. Capital was, therefore, masterful in taking the exploitation of surplus value into spaces where it had not previously existed (verbal information[5]).

In accordance with this interpretation, it is essential, as Chesnais (2014) argues, that we do not see finance as an artificial part and, therefore, separate from the real economy. Financialization is intimately related to the process of productive restructuring – which we could define as a process of organic development of renewed forms of exploitation of labor by capital.

---

5 Information provided by Ricardo Antunes during a speech delivered at the University of Brasília on the afternoon of October 19, 2012, at the round table entitled: "Theory of Value, Labor and Crisis", that formed part of the I International Meeting on the Theory of Value, Labor and Social Sciences. Hosted by: Research and Study Group on Labor of the Sociology Department of the University of Brasília. Available at: <https://www.youtube.com/watch?v=fD5K5lXbimg>. Accessed on Nov 24, 2017.

Within this context, finance plays a central role in the reordering of capitalist relations of control and domination and, therefore, of seeking the continual increase of profitability. This movement is intimately related to the process of oligopolization of the world economy, with its growing number of mergers and acquisitions. This does not involve a simple opposition between industry and finance, or between production and usury, as some approaches suggest, but rather a systematic reconfiguration of production itself as a whole.

As such, it is possible that the increasingly concentrated migration of the industrial productive capital to countries with cheap labor costs (once it is hyper-exploited) such as those in south-east Asia, will not be the result solely of financialization *strictu sensu*, arising from a neoliberal financial "coup", but rather an integral and inseparable part of this process of structural change of the capitalist economy. As Chesnais (2014) argues:

> [...] capital as a whole has no "new frontier", nor any new fields or "provinces" of accumulation (Rosa Luxemburg). Technological investments, with the partial exception of China, are highly focused on labor saving innovations and geared to surveillance and control. They cannot lift the world economy out of slow growth and very high global unemployment. (Verbal information[6]).

It is also of interest to note that processes of financial expansion in the capitalist economy are nothing new in history, even if the size and quality of their occurrence at the moment requires that we take a much closer look. As we mentioned earlier, thinkers from the beginning of the 20th century, such as Hilferding (1981) and Lenin (2011), as well as Karl Marx (1988) in the 19th century, were already concerned about the power of finance, as well as its importance as the spearhead for the process of imperialist internationalization of capitalist exploitation.

Furthermore, we should also remember, as David Harvey (2013a) argues, that the current "regime of flexible accumulation" is also characterized by resuming and re-stimulating primitive dynamics of accumulation, typical of the beginnings of capitalism, as a means of redirecting the search for profit and restructuring, with the same objective, production in the wider sense in

---

6 Information provided by François Chesnais during a discussion held at the IIRE Economy Seminar 2014, in Amsterdam, Holland, on February 14, 2014. Hosted by: IIRE – International Institute of Research and Education. Available at: <http://www.4edu.info/index.php/IIRE_Economy_Seminar_2014>. Accessed on Nov 24, 2017.

response to a crisis of over-accumulation of capital, evidenced by the collapse of the fordist regime of accumulation.

Supporting, therefore, our thesis that the advance of Information and Communication Technologies actually operates as a transmission belt for logic that makes financial domination in the economy imperative, and based upon the investigation into research from which this book results, we defend the idea that, on the structural level, cutting edge technology operates in three dimensions, corresponding to three evolutionary trends observed in the financial system: (i) the shortening or shrinking of the space-time flows in which capitals circulate and appreciate; (ii) the consequent increase in the difficulties of controlling and regulating the markets by societies, governments and their administrative bodies, and; (iii) local and overseas concentration in the markets – amongst its players, yes, but also amongst the different global financial marketplaces.

Together, these tendencies, at the level of circulation, control and accumulation of capitals, consolidate and intensify the process of strengthening interest-bearing capital as a predominant means of extracting value in the economy, in relation to which the others will be in service in the dynamic conformation of the regime of accumulation with financial dominance. Interconnected in their functioning logic, these three tendencies feedback on themselves in such a way that they drain and keep capitals in the financial sphere, reinforcing and increasing instabilities and tendencies toward crisis in the global economy.

In the first of the dimensions, we can see that the shortening of the space-time flows, due to the digitalization of finance, reduces the objective barriers on the circulation of capital, allowing more transactions to be performed in an unimaginably shorter period of time. Operating via the Internet or their own networks, with the help of cutting-edge infrastructure and high-performance information technology, capitals invade and abruptly abandon markets, regions and countries, arbitrating currencies, stocks and securities based upon the best opportunities for gain in the short-term. Processes of speculation and arbitration reach the speeds of "milli" and "micro-seconds", operated by automated negotiating systems that buy and sell thousands of stocks literally in the blink of an eye. Such possibilities, opened up by the advances produced by the informational revolution,[7] expand the possibilities of previously inviable

---

[7] For Lojkine (2002, p. 14, author's highlights), "[...] the transfer, to 'machines', of a new type of abstract cerebral functioning (which essentially defines automation) is at the heart of the *informational* revolution, since the fundamental consequence of this transfer shifts human labor from *manipulation* to the handling of abstract symbols – and, therefore, shifts it to the 'handling' of information. Considering this, the informational revolution was born from the opposition between the machine-tool revolution, based upon the objectification of manual

financial gains, and allow an increase in the number of financial operations and transactions through large-scale aggregated gains.

This scenario of increasing innovation and speed, makes the already inglorious task of regulating, controlling and inspecting the markets that much more complicated. Be it by means of innovations, subterfuge or exploration of new frontiers of gain through mechanisms anchored in intensive technology, or be it due to the growing power of financiers in the definition of the economic and monetary policies of governments and central banks at the judicial-institutional level, the difficulties imposed upon the forces of regulation and control of the markets by societies, governments and inspection organs can be added into this scenario. If it is in the nature of regulation to always be one step behind the object of its control, then maybe we are entering a scenario in which this vacuum is, at least, increasing substantially, that is also a product of historical decisions of liberalization and deregulation of markets, as we will see. This is because, with the deregulation, flexibilization and liberalization of the financial markets having been concluded to a certain extent at global level, the tendency is that technological development is increasingly becoming one of the few frontiers remaining in the tireless search for increased freedom for capitals and competition between investors.

As a result of this *modus operandi*, in which intensive investment in technology is established as a frontier of competitiveness between the players in the market, the tendency toward a concentration of gains is expanding considerably. The rising sums being traded on the stock exchange, even (or above all) in times of crisis, are concentrated in the hands of a few, large operators, anchored in a few, large financial marketplaces (even though they are interlinked by global connectivity). Such concentration sets out an exclusive scenario, making the economic inequalities between regions, countries, classes and individuals that much worse, and increasing the social tragedy of economic crises. Also (but not only) because of the high cost that this technological race imposes, the number of brokerage firms, banks, financial institutions and large investment funds is reduced in relation to the growth of their gains, through alliances, mergers and acquisitions.

---

functions, and the automation revolution, based upon the objectification of certain cerebral functions developed by industrial machinery". For Lojkine, the Technological (or "Digital") Revolution carries the same magnitude as that of the machine-tool revolution, given that "the computer information, when connected to other new techniques of telecommunication, can allow the creation, circulation and storage of an immense amount of information that was once monopolized, and partially sterilized, by a small elite of intellectual workers" (p. 15).

INTRODUCTION

If setting out this *cycle of operation of digitalized finance*[8] – composed of acceleration, lack of discipline, and the growing concentration of accumulation, valorization and circulation of large-scale capitals that was previously unimaginable – helps us to understand what occurs in the relationship between the "real" and "fictitious" economies, and between the financial markets and the productive sector, it is a fact that, together or separately, these dimensions do not indicate any tendencies that are exactly new in what is referred to as the capitalist mode of production as a whole.

As Marx (2013a) pointed out in Chapter IV of Volume I of *Capital*, the constant search for "valorization of value" is part of the constitutive nature of capitalism. If the paths, modes and forms of achieving this goal undergo processes of reconfiguration in our time, as we aim to demonstrate, the end of this chain, however, still remains exactly the same. As a result of this structuring axis, the automaton of capital, via technical development, subverts the frontiers and barriers that would prevent its valorization, amongst which, as we strongly stress in our reading of the scenario, are even, and above all, the barriers of time and space.

> While capital must on the one hand strive to tear down every spatial barrier to intercourse, i.e. to exchange, and conquer the whole earth for its market, it strives on the other to annihilate this space with time, i.e. to reduce to a minimum the time spent in motion from one place to another. The more developed the capital, therefore, the more extensive the market over which it circulates, which forms the spatial orbit of its circulation, and the more it strives simultaneously for an even greater extension of the market and for greater annihilation of space by time.
> MARX 2013b, p. 445

If this can be verified in the reality of the financial markets, as we will seek to demonstrate in this book, the same can be said of the tendency to concentrate gains, and the number of players and financial marketplaces in the globalized market, that find solid support in the same theoretical reference. Thus, in its more advanced form, and using the tools of digitalized finance in the

---

8 This will be a term that will recur repeatedly throughout this book, and which, we hope, will be properly clarified as the text unfolds, with presentation of the necessary examples and contexts. In general, we define *digitalized finance* as being the technical-operational compound of the management of the circulation, accumulation and valorization of financial capital through cutting edge automated technological resources that accelerate the compression of space-time flows for the exploitation of financial gains through the speculation and arbitration of securities, currencies and other assets.

21st century, capital behaves in a manner which reinforces the tendency that had already been noted in the 19th century.

> To the extent that capitalist production and accumulation develop, so too do the two most powerful levers for centralization, competition and credit. In parallel, the progress of the accumulation increases the material capable of being centralized, that is, the individual capitals, at the same time as the expansion of the production on the one hand creates a social need, and on the other creates the technical means of those powerful industrial enterprises that are connected to a prior centralization of capital. Today, therefore, the mutual power of attraction of the individual capitals and the tendency toward centralization are stronger than at any other time.
> MARX 2013a, p. 702

In this way, and noting the reality of industrial capitalism at the time, Marx, in Chapter XXII of Volume I of *Capital*, whilst in the midst of theorizing upon the process of the expanded reproduction of capital, described the general trend toward the concentration and centralization of the capitalist economy in periods of expansion and economic crisis, respectively. It can be seen, therefore, that from this theoretical point of view, regardless of whether we are evaluating financial wealth or not, capitalist expansion always tends toward the centralization and concentration of capitals. By highlighting competition and credit as the "two most powerful levers for centralization", Marx also provides us with a solid starting point for the investigation of the submission of productive capital to fictitious capital in our present reality. We will develop this discussion, along with the others, later on.

All in all, this technological development, in many ways prompted by financial wealth itself, and by means of the abovementioned tendencies, ends up accelerating and strengthening the financialization process of the economies or, more accurately, providing sustenance for the functioning of the finance-dominated accumulation regime, which does not exist as a result of the development of the Information and Communication Technologies, but which could not, within this scenario, operate as such without their support. By shortening time as a means of increasing the number and volume of operations in the markets, and expanding their short-term gains, the development of the ICT creates a scenario that is considerably more favorable for the maintenance and imprisonment of capitals in the financial sphere. As we will discuss further on, this growth reinforces the trend toward concentration of the markets. In this way, wealth, concentrated in the financial sphere, and enjoying the full freedom guaranteed for capitals institutionally and technically, ends up increasing the tendencies of detachment between the real and fictitious economies (or, better, of the dominance of the latter over the other), in a scenario of increasing financial instability and crisis. Displacement of the space-time flows, an increase in the technical vacuum between the regulator and regulated, and a concentration of gains in the financial sphere are, as such, mutually joined and reinforced in the configuration of what we call the *cycle of operation of digitalized finance*.

Discussion of this point, however, does not end here. Contradictory as it is in terms of its production, use and interaction in societies, since it is marked by a social content that is equally contradictory and permeated by social conflict, technology ends up contributing to the conformation of tendencies that counter those we have mentioned. One example of this is its use in the conception and evolution of means of regulation, control, supervision and governance in the markets as well as in the construction of systems for the evaluation and control of risks. This reading is defended especially by those who support stricter regulation of the markets as a means of resolving the central dilemmas brought into play by financialization. We will come back to this discussion later on.

Finally, as we have mentioned, we will be endeavoring to discuss the ways in which (in its contemporary relations) technological development has influenced the changes that capitalism has undergone over the last 40 years and, more specifically, the role that the development of the Information and Communication Technologies (ICT) plays in the conformation of the finance-dominated accumulation regime on a global scale.

Having briefly outlined the general overview of our argument, that will be presented with all relevant context, explored more deeply, and argued over the following pages, we would now like to explain a little about the structure of the book. Afterwards, we will provide a brief description of the methodological options and actions in the research field that have provided a basis for this book.

In summary, as we have explained, the research is grounded on: (i) published works on the subject; (ii) investigative interviews with academics and specialists for the construction of panoramas surrounding the debates that exist in their areas and to better outline the object of the investigation; (iii) in depth interviews with many of those involved in the financial market (brokers, stock exchange directors, members of financial institutions, those responsible for technology companies focused on the financial market and some of their specialized professionals, amongst others); and, finally, (iv) financial, accounting and economics data that reinforces, in some way, the trends observed in the field, in interviews, conversations and specialist talks in this area in which we have participated as part of this immersion process.

In Section two we will discuss globalization as financial *mondialisation*,[9] from a historical and theoretical perspective. In the development of this discussion, we will make reference to various authors, above all to the formulations of François Chesnais and David Harvey that have already been mentioned. By outlining a panorama of neoliberalism as a general movement of liberalization of markets and capitals in accordance with the post-fordist productive restructuring, we intend to contextualize the background as well as the current state of the regime of accumulation with the dominance of financial accumulation.

In the chapter that follows, we set out a panorama of the discussion over the relationships between technics, capital and society, that inspire, in the outlining of its sociological core, the discussion that guides this book. Here, supported by arguments critical of technology, we discuss the technological factor in light of the economic factor, in what ways they interrelate in the configuration of the technological practice, as well as their role in the social dynamic.

In the fourth and fifth sections, based upon the data and conclusions obtained from the supporting research, we present the book's central arguments, grounded in practical evidence and theoretical discussions, within the international and domestic contexts. In addition to what we have observed in the field, this is where we will present the most up-to-date information and data on the broad use of the ICTs in the operation of the financial markets.

Finally, in the last part of the book, we will highlight a number of general conclusions on the discussion to understand the manner in which this

---

9 In the publication *The Globalization of Capital* (1996), Chesnais presents a discussion of the differences between the terms of globalization and *"mondialisation"* of capital, that he himself has proposed. In the introduction to the book *La mondialisation financière* (1998), which he himself also edited, there is an explanatory note that summarizes this discussion. We reproduce it here: "We should recall that the expression '"*modialisation*" of capital' is what most closely corresponds to the meaning that is hidden by the English term 'globalization' (Chesnais 1994). Relating to the production and commercialization of material and non-material ('goods and services'), the term globalization covers the strategic capacity of the large oligopolist group in its 'global' behavior and reach, which are simultaneously relative to the solvent demand markets, the sources of provision, the localization of industrial manufacturing, and the strategies of the main competitors. The same applies, in the financial sphere, to those operations that financial investors make and to the composition of their portfolios of assets (currencies, bonuses, shares and derivatives), as well as to the decisions they take, be this in matters of 'arbitrage' between different financial instruments or compartments of the markets, both in the choice of the countries whose currency they purchase or whose titles they hold" (Chesnais 1998, pp. 12–13). That said, in the absence of a better English word for the concept, we maintain the use of "globalization".

mechanism has strengthened the detachment (contradictory and incomplete) of the fictitious economy from the real economy, contributing to the occurrence of the great financial crisis of 2008, the worst since 1929.

1.1   Methodological Considerations

All the organization of the research that guides this book is based upon an extensive bibliography focused on the process of financialization of the world economy, and the nature of technological development in contemporary society. It is also supported by interviews with specialists in the areas of Economics, Sociology, Computer Science, Information Technology and with investors, operators and professionals in the financial market,[10] as well as financial, accounting, economics and macroeconomics data and additional information relating to the subject matter.

As primary data, we have used the mentioned interviews, by means of which we were able to obtain valuable information that has guided the book's investigations and subsequent conclusions. In the first phase of the investigation in the field, as part of the search for this primary data, we performed an important set of exploratory interviews that were more open and less directed, with academics in the areas of Economics, Sociology, Computer Science and Information Technology to establish the framework of the analysis and understand, in addition to their specific languages, the issues and discussions in question concerning the subject we will venture to describe, understand and discuss. By means of an analysis of the most pressing questions in the mentioned areas, we were able to draft an investigative map, which we could use to create a general guide for the research work subsequently performed, both in relation to the interviews and study of the literature available.

Following on closely from this, in the second phase, we focused on interviews with stock exchange directors, investors, operators, and professionals from companies specializing in technology for the financial market. The aim was to investigate the operating dynamics and economic and technological operation of the stock exchanges and the global markets of financial assets, as well as, based upon this, to obtain detailed data and information on other

---

10   Despite the processes of automation, electronification and computerization generally extending into every sector of financial activity, the scope of this investigation is restricted to the capitals market in Brazil. For more information on the history of the automation of banking in Brazil, see Pires (1997), Diniz (2004), Diniz, Meirelles and Fonseca (2010), Dantas (1988) and Dantas (1989). For a critical compilation and systematization of this discussion, using as its context the development of the Internet in Brazil and elsewhere, see Horta (2017).

aspects that they involve. Here we were working with directed interviews, with support from base-questionnaires, produced from the mapping performed in the previous interview stage.

With a more detailed approach, to understand the dynamics of technological development and operation of hardware, software and orgwares connected to the international business market, we sought to establish information on the means of operation and the technical functioning of networks, programs and supercomputers that allow the stock exchanges to operate on a global level, with 24-hour interconnectivity, at the level of those that deal directly with these resources. What technology tools are used, how do they work, and what are their objectives? What have been the great advances in Information and Communication Technologies that have most significantly altered the way the markets operate over recent years? In what ways do these technologies increase the possibilities for gain in the markets?

The resource used in the execution of this field research work was the methodology technique known as "snowball sampling", also referred to as simply "snowball". This involves the construction of a sample that uses chains of reference – a type of network. This non-probabilistic sample is used in social studies, and involves the initial participants in a study indicating other participants, who in turn indicate other new participants and so on successively, until the proposed objective has been achieved, or a "saturation point" is reached, when the new Interviewees start to repeat the content already obtained in previous interviews, without adding new information that might be relevant to the investigation; all this based upon a list of questions, relating to the hypotheses previously alluded to. One potential advantage to the use of this technique lies in its ability to access the most visible, known or representative Interviewees, as references, in certain spaces/processes.

In total, 25 people were interviewed (four of them on more than one occasion) in four important Brazilian cities, totaling almost 37 hours of recorded material. Of these, 8 were academics from the areas of Sociology, Economics, Computer Sciences and Information Technology, and the other 16 were from the financial market, who, at the time the interviews were conducted, were working in various areas, and included directors from BM&FBovespa, representatives of stock brokerage firms, banks (ex-employees), financial institutions, technology companies focused on the financial market, operators, regulators and other professionals from the area. In addition to this, we took part in five talks directed especially toward investors that related to the issue of the financial market and technology in the cities in question.

In terms of secondary data, we analyzed documents, figures, tables, graphs and other financial, accounting, economic and macro-economic information from different sources, amongst which we can cite the Central Bank of Brazil, the Brazilian Institute of Geography and Statistics (IBGE), and the Brazilian Securities Commission (CVM), as well as international consultancies and multilateral organs, whilst the most frequently consulted source was the BM&FBovespa, from which we obtained important data on financial volumes, investor profiles, and the balance sheets of companies listed on the exchange, amongst other information.

Despite using the analytical approach employed from 1980 to 2008, above all in relation to that pertaining to the discussion on the conformity of the finance-dominated accumulation regime, the majority of our data actually refers to the period between 1994 and 2016. Since the observation of this global phenomenon is performed, in this book, from the perspective of the context and reality of the Brazilian financial market, it was the adoption of the Real Monetary Plan, in 1994, that ended up conditioning not only the discussions and readings of the issue in Brazil, but also played a determining role in compiling and establishing the parameters of the financial and economic data, in this case being that of the Brazilian stock exchange, that offers more detailed data only in the historical data series that started that year. Compared with an analysis focusing on the period between 1980 and 2008, in that which relates to the broader aspects, we felt that the historical data series used in this book, the majority of which started in 1994, were by and large relevant to the objectives of this investigation.

In parallel, and concurrent to this work, the theoretical contributions in the economic field, in relation to the general operating mechanisms of the international economy, to the internal development of fictitious capital, and to the process of financialization, were, ultimately, of most importance to the general reading of the situation in which we have sought to locate ourselves, and to the adjustment of our position for the reading of the technological phenomenon based upon these references.

Furthermore, the critical approach in relation to technological development, in terms of its social content, helped us in the prevention of deterministic or unidimensional analyses concerning the relationships between technics and capital, and economic and technological development. Creating a sociological map, based upon this reference point, of the complexities and disputes that are present within this dynamic, helped us to develop our understanding of the process of financialization of the economy during the period analyzed as being multi-causal, and susceptible to its understanding being based upon other interpretative keys through contributions from the Social Sciences on the phenomenon.

CHAPTER 2

Capitalism at the Beginning of the 21st Century: Globalized Finance

2.1 A Brief Review of the Theories of Financialization

As has been widely discussed in literature, in *Capital*, Karl Marx outlines a strong systematization of the operating dynamic of the mode of capitalist production as a product of the growing reproduction and accumulation of capital. According to his formulations, the fundamental contradictions of this form of production that are anchored, above all, in the relationships of exploitation of human labor in order to obtain surpluses, are recurrent crises of over-production, that contribute to the instability of capitalism, due to its conflicting and contradictory nature, as a means of organizing economic and social life.

If this is true, it is also a fact that history has shown that in every crisis, be it big or small, capitalism has demonstrated, as Marx himself forecast, an incredible capacity to revolutionize in order to reconstruct itself, reestablishing its predominance as such based upon complexification processes, that introduce new forms of exploitation and extraction of surplus value. Far from being set out as some sort of automatism of historical inexorability, guiding this movement are disputes of an economic, political and cultural order, that make up an open field of possibilities in the social universe, even though they are submitted to a hegemonic trend of operation established by means of this relationship.

In this way, capitalism found, above all through the state, but also through the employment of ideological and cultural resources, ways of surviving the serious crises that it went through in the 19th and 20th centuries. For the French Regulation School or the Regulation Theory (Aglietta 1999, Boyer 1990), the capitalist system manages to survive the systemic crises and, as such, continue reproducing, through the creation of a regulatory apparatus that, once established, tends to act anti-cyclically, avoiding or softening them. Such regulatory apparatus, or regimes of accumulation, presuppose certain political and institutional configurations that "organize" productive activity in such a way as to suit the production to the consumption, with the aim of avoiding crises of over-production and other economic problems, such as inflation, for example, with the capitalist means of production remaining upright and fully operational.

These regimes of accumulation are established by means of a set of laws, regulations, social values and customs (forms of regulation) that articulate structural elements or forms of integration, in order to produce a context that is favorable to capitalist accumulation, such as: form of adhesion to the international system, a monetary standard, a form of competition, a form of state and salary/labor relations. From the systemic relationship between these structural forms, in a given regime of accumulation, will result a certain form of economic development.

Since the 1970s, and more acutely since the 1980s, a set of changes have been seeking to provide an answer to the crisis of over-accumulation of capital, produced by the post-war "golden years" of Fordism. These transformations, politically established using neoliberal and specific measures in different spheres of social life (political, economic, techno-productive, cultural, etc.) achieved a scale to the point where, for some players, they configured a new regime of accumulation, the "finance-dominated accumulation regime" (Chesnais 1996, 1998, 2005).

The reading put forward by Chesnais, that supports one of the most profitable contemporary theories on the process of financialization of the world economy, combining Marxist, regulationist, post-Keynesian and economic sociology contributions, highlights the fact that, in this current phase of capitalism, financial valorization is not only more important than productive valorization, but imposes itself as a structuring logic for the entire process of capitalist accumulation and reproduction. This is because, being over-accumulated in the productive sphere, and experiencing, as a result, recurrent drops in the general rate of profit, this capital will look for ways of freeing itself from the constraints on accumulation, venturing, to an extent as yet unobserved, into accumulation in the financial sphere, by means of titles, stocks, commercial papers arising from financial innovations, and even speculation with national currencies. This process of releasing capital on a wide scale does not occur automatically or without any resistance, but based upon important political-institutional changes, performed at the heart and on the peripheries of capitalism, with serious consequences for those dependent upon labor.

Within this process, that which Marx (1988) named "fictitious capital" – basically composed of the valorization of stocks and securities in secondary markets – is expanded in unprecedented quantity and quality, seeking to become increasingly autonomous, by means of its own assets, in the face of the real economy; thus achieving growing importance for the economy as a whole (Mollo 2011).

Within the sphere of this discussion, Paulani (2009) offers data (Figure 1) that demonstrates the growth of the global stock of financial assets (fictitious capital) in relation to the real global revenue, as of 1980. In 2008, fictitious wealth (not including the enormous number of derivatives) in financial assets,

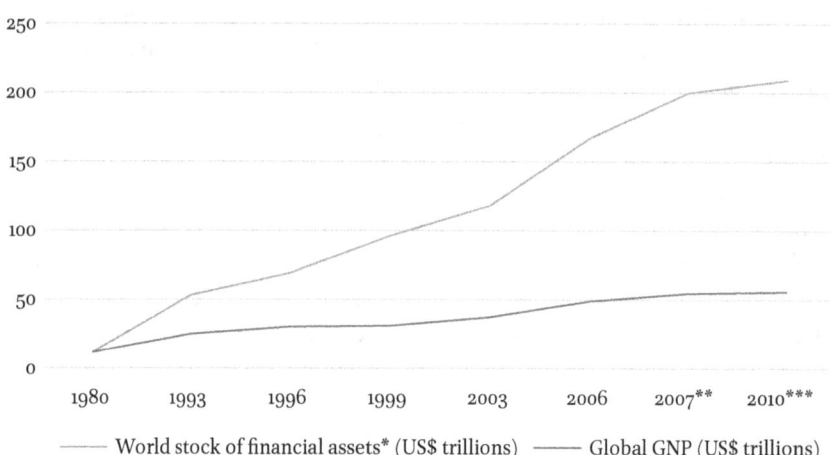

FIGURE 1 Fictitious wealth (world stock of financial assets) and global real revenue (GNP) US$ trillions.
SOURCE: MCKINSEYS GLOBAL INSTITUTE (ASSETS) AND IMF (GNP); DATA GRAPH CREATED BY LEDA PAULANI
N.B.: FOR CONSTRUCTION OF THE GRAPH, THE GLOBAL STOCK VALUES OF FINANCIAL ASSETS CORRESPONDING TO THOSE YEARS WITHOUT AVAILABLE DATE WERE ESTIMATED AS INCREASING IN ACCORDANCE WITH THE CONSTANT
* Includes shares and debentures, private and public debt securities and bank applications; does not include derivatives.
** Estimation
*** Projections

amounted to four times the sum of all the revenue accumulated by the real production of the world economy.

It is important to stress that, to the extent that it appropriates the revenue generated in the productive sector, by means of the simple ownership of assets, financial accumulation is closely tied to "rentism".[1] Since it obtains gains without being directly tied to productive activities, anchoring itself in the constant maintenance of liquidity, such logic puts long-term investments in check, to the detriment of short-term gains, and stimulating and increasing the processes of speculation in various areas, that result in impacts in the form of the reproduction and accumulation of capital as a whole. As Paulini (2006) put it:

> The invasion of this logic by all areas of the reproduction of capital is what is responsible for the diffusion of the large transformations in the manufacturing processes inherited from the Fordist era. The need to

---

[1] Understood here as the obtaining of revenues through the simple ownership of the production factors (land, capital) or assets and financial products, rather than directly through the manufacture of commodities, goods or services.

customize production, make labor more flexible, reduce stocks and the number of management levels, and outsource services and the stages of the manufacturing process, all obey the imperatives of financial logic: dividing the risks of capitalist production with the workers and the consumers, ensuring that capital is not tied up in fixed assets, stocks of raw materials and products, and preserving and seeking liquidity wherever it may be.

PAULANI 2006, p. 20

As such, we can relate the financialization of the economy or, more precisely, the transformation of the structure of capitalist accumulation, now dominated by financial accumulation, with the intense productive restructuring which the capitalist system undergoes, most acutely from the 1980s on, especially in the robotization and informatization of the productive processes.

Following the diagnosis that we would be experiencing the unfolding effects of a crisis of over-accumulation of capital, Harvey (2005) highlights that capitalism has returned to processes that are typical of the primitive accumulation of capital as a form of freeing itself from structural restraints. For him, processes of primitive accumulation, despite never having completely left the scene, have become more intense in times of crises of over-accumulation.

These processes – originally described by Marx as the intrinsically violent foundations of capitalism, in the sense that they expelled producers from their lands, and looted territories and colonies by means of fraud, theft and war, and serve as a political-economic basis for the foundation of the modern state – whilst at the same time that these processes were made possible thanks to its appearance and centralization – , are currently characterized by what Harvey describes as "accumulation by dispossession".

As expressions of this process, capital and state, structurally aligned, open new dimensions for accumulation, through privatizations and fiscal adjustments, cuts to social and labor rights, the growth of the importance of government securities, property speculation and the social-spatial reconfiguration of cities for financial accumulation. This is what Harvey (2013a), in opposition to the "rigid" form of accumulation of Fordism, calls "flexible accumulation", or in other words, an arrangement that reinforces the overcoming of space-time boundaries, as well as the legal, social, geo-spatial and economic constraints on the present-day accumulation of capital.

Although there is no direct and structured dialog open between Chesnais and Harvey on this matter, there is a clear interface between the two authors,[2] going beyond the sharing of references on the Theory of Regulation, to provide

---

2 For more information on this subject, see Lapyda (2011).

a complementary diagnosis concerning the process of financialization of the economy as a product of the unfolding effects of a crisis of over-accumulation of Fordist capitalism, that ends in the economic and political-institutional changes that we are now seeing as a means of overcoming the constraints on the accumulation of capital.

Different to the evaluations presented above, the post-Keynesian approaches (Crotty 1990, Pollin 2007, Epstein 2005) have centered on the concept of "rentier", and, in particular on the money lender as a "rentier", to explain the process of financialization of the economy. The aim is to evaluate the damaging effect of the expansion of finance in relation to the productive process. In this sense, the weak performance of the real economics would, according to those versed in this approach, be caused largely by an expansion of the financial sector.

As such, as noted by Lapavitsas (2011, p. 615) in a didactic review of the current theories of financialization, in a post-Keynesian approach:

> The re-emergence of the rentier – partly due to neoliberal economic policy – has fostered financial at the expense of industrial profits. Consequently, financialization has induced poor performance in investment, output and growth in developed countries. Policy intervention is required to regulate finance – for instance, liquidity reserves of banks, direction of credit, limits on investment banking activities and so on – resulting in improved output, employment and income.

For Arrighi (1994), and his historicist-leaning World-systems theory, capitalism can be understood as successive cycles that were initiated at the start of the modern era. The hegemonic capitalist formations, according to the author, follow a cyclical pattern of evolution, one following on from another. Financialization would therefore represent the twilight of a hegemon, when its productive power is in decline and the sphere of finances expands. Genoa, Holland, Great Britain and currently the United States all entered into processes of financialization when they lost their prominence in global production and trade. Once in decline, they became lenders, particularly to the emerging powers that would come to overtake them. Currently under way, however, is a discussion over the verification or not of the evidence of the fall from prominence of the United States as a hegemonic power, that would make this reading valid and applicable for modern times.

Supported in the readings of Hilferding (1981) and Lenin (2011) on imperialism at the beginning of the 20th century, that highlight the structural relationship between bank capital and industrial capital in the systematic organization of imperialistic capitalism, Lapavitsas (2011) stresses the importance that contemporary configurations or reconfigurations of this relationship (especially in the transformations of the role of the banks considering the empowerment of financial institutions and the companies, who start to trade commercial papers on the financial markets themselves) have in the organization of the process of financialization of manufacturing activity and the economy as a whole.

This interpretation – that sees the current phase of capitalism as a product of a reorientation in the role of the banks, financial institutions, companies and citizens, in line with the advance of financialization – leads Lapavitsas (2011) to believe that there is little evidence that capitalism has actually undergone a crisis of over-accumulation in its recent history. In explaining the 2008 financial crisis, for example, the author confirms that it started in the area of finance and spread to manufacturing, partially through financial mechanisms. Its global character, the author explains, was basically due to large-scale securitization that encouraged the aggressive activities of investment banks and commercial banks. For the author, the origin of the crisis also (and above all) lay in the insolvency of the mortgage loans to the poorer strata of the working classes in the US. None of these factors, Lapavitsas argues, would serve as evidence in the theories that defend that we would be dealing with the effects of a crisis of over-accumulation of capital.

Following this brief review, and without going into the polemics that these different approaches raise, we would like to focus, based, above all, on the contributions, briefly summarized above, made by François Chesnais and David Harvey, as well as other authors and contributors who, along the same lines, help us to understand this issue/problem, on starting a discussion of the concept of financialization and, more broadly, on the regime of accumulation that has been consolidated and worsened in the present crisis. Further on, we will briefly return to the history of its process of conformation, particularly during the last 30 years of the 20th century, together with the configuration of what has come to be known as neoliberalism. Finally, we would like to start a debate on the role of technological development within this process, that will be explored in more detail in the next section.

2.2 Interest-Bearing Capital and Fictitious Capital

As part of this discussion, we should first present the theoretical starting points shared by the abovementioned authors and their approaches, especially some of Marx's theories and concepts, such as money capital, bank capital, interest-bearing capital, fictitious capital and financial capital (the authorship of which some authors attribute to Hilferding and, later, to Lenin), that will recur from time to time during this book. The most suitable definitions of these concepts are part of an intense debate in the Marxist tradition, that does not end with the technicality of the terms, but with their connections, articulations and variants explained in the reading of different economic, social and/ or political phenomenon, in such a way that, far from exhausting them, we venture to simply take a general shot at the subject in question.

Simply put, money capital, as its name suggests, different to productive capital or commodity capital, is that which is constituted of money in its cash form and which can, therefore, circulate, being maintained or appreciated in this state thanks to the process of productive intermediation or, as we explained earlier, thanks to the "illusory" mechanism of capitalization. Bank capital, in turn, corresponds to the assets (usually monetary assets, many of which are fictitious, as we will see) that banks hold as capital. These terms will be better clarified when properly positioned and contextualized within our discussion. For now, we will be looking at interest-bearing capital and fictitious capital, these being especially important for the purposes of this book.

As we explained earlier, it is in Volume III of *Capital*, edited by Friedrich Engels, that Marx presents his ideas on what he calls fictitious capital; an understanding that, for him, derives directly from the so-called "interest-bearing capital". These two forms of capital, presented together in the mentioned publication, are, according to the author, the most alienated and fetishistic that capital can assume, and are by far – and not by accident – the dominant forms in processes of financialization, as the one we intend to look at in more detail.

Most usually made available in its monetary form, interest-bearing capital is at the basis of those operations involved in credit systems, that is, in the amount of money capital expected to be used in production, and expected to return, following accumulation due to the subsequent manufacture of commodities with the extraction of labor and surplus value, into the hands of its owner. Its fundamental reason for being, as with any form of capital, is its own valorization, which, in turn, can only actually occur after the effective production that allows the creation of interest as a part of the surplus value obtained in the manufacturing process. Expressed in its outward M-M' form, and thereby hiding its real form of M-[M-C...P...C'-M']-M',[3] makes the manufacturing

---

3 Being M = money; C = commodities; P = production.

process appear unnecessary (as though it were possible to produce money out of money) (Marx 1988).

Directly connected to this, as a derivative produced by extrapolation from the credit system, is fictitious capital that, through its promissory notes, letters of credit, and exchange, is characterized as a secondary level of interest-bearing-capital, with no direct connection to the real material valorization (and, as such, has relative autonomy[4] in relation to such), or in other words, the production of goods: hence the name "fictitious". As Mollo (2011, p. 9) explains:

> This type of rationale is what lead Marx to distinguish interest-bearing loan capital from fictitious capital (Mollo, 1989). First, he says, it has as use-value its ability to "function as capital" (Marx, 1974, p. 392) and, "as potential capital, as a means of producing profit, it becomes commodity, but commodity of a particular type" and "it is bursting with surplus value" (Marx, 1974, p. 396), because the "loaning of money as capital – assignment conditional upon restitution following a certain period – assumes that the money is really applied as capital, effectively returns it to its starting point" (p. 404), and "interest-producing capital is only sustained as such in the sense that the money loaned is effectively converted into capital, producing a surplus of which the interest is a fraction" (p. 439).

Further on, the author states that:

> With fictitious capital, things are different, because "first the monetary revenue is converted into interest, and with the interest one finds the capital from whence it comes" (Marx, 1974, p. 534). Or in other words, the evaluation of the capital loses its relationship with the process of real production or the generation of surplus value. As examples, Marx cites public debt securities, "because the sum loaned to the state not only no longer exists", but "was never planned to be used [or] employed as capital, and only invested as such would it have the ability to be transformed into value that could be maintained" (Marx, 1974, p. 535). This also refers to

---

[4] It is necessary for us to emphasize the relative nature of this autonomy, since full autonomy of circulation in relation to production, or of fictitious capital in relation to real production would be impossible, since it is from real production that the remuneration from interest-bearing-capital arises and, therefore, from fictitious capital, always as a fraction of the surplus value extracted through overwork. And it is precisely the mismatch between the two areas or, better, its failure to become real in the production, that leads to financial crises, as we will see.

the price of stocks, "the market value [of which] is established differently to the nominal value, without the value being altered (even though the valorization of the effective capital is modified)" (Marx, 1974, p. 537).

MOLLO 2011, p. 9

As Mollo (2011) points out at the end of this passage, Marx highlights three forms assumed by fictitious capital: letters of credit and currency exchange, the public debt, and company shares. In the first of these forms, the author cites as an example the duplication of means of secondary payments between two points, between Britain and its colonies, due to the lengthy period of time necessary for the transport of commodities. In this way, it was possible, in both locations, to circulate means of payment in various other transactions, at sums greater than those corresponding to the original goods, until such forms could be liquidated after the arrival of the products.

In the case of company shares, made possible thanks to the advent of the stock exchanges and joint-stock companies or corporations, its fiction is not necessarily in the sum obtained from the opening of its capital for the financing of its manufacturing activities (that, in this manner, represents a real fraction of its capital), but in the secondary circulation and negotiation on the stock market, which is subject to variations in price and speculation, both capable of "multiplying" this capital without being directly connected to the company's corresponding real productive capacity – its means of production or labor force, for example.

Finally, the public debt is a dimension that is even more evident in the fiction of capital. As this concerns a commitment that is related to an expenditure made by the state, which should, in turn, perform its payment by means of future collection of taxes (made up, basically, of fractions of surplus-value and salaries), there is no tie to any duplicate/trade bill of any manufacturing capital and, as such, it is not – and never has been – capital of any sort. Its conversion into "capital" is performed by means of a process which Marx called "capitalization", that, due to the establishment of a basic interest rate in the economy, allows all money to have the power to provide some sort of interest, which thus allows anything, even if it is not capital, to act as such in terms of "return". Therefore, by means of capitalization, interest-bearing capital becomes generalized across society, providing for extrapolation in the form of interest beyond situations in which it is possible or supposedly justifiable as such.

Whatever the situation, in any of these cases, this fictitious capital that, as we have shown, is independent in a way that is always relative, depends directly on the equivalent (future) production of commodities or realization of subsequent value. When this, for various reasons, does not happen, the tendency is for there to be a "readjustment" in the dynamic of this distancing, that generally tends to lead to the creation of crises. As Mollo (2011, p. 14) summarizes by citing Marx:

> Fictitious capital, as we have seen, is a typical case of disjunction or autonomy in circulation in relation to production, which is different to interest-producing loan capital and to the initial public offering of shares that can provide the potential for production and even delay crises, by synchronizing steps and bringing forward production and consumption. But the development of fictitious capital, by unnecessarily increasing the disjunction mentioned by Marx, is found at the base of the crisis, in particular the financial crisis, defined by Marx (1971, p. 152) as a "particular type of money crisis that can appear independently, with repercussions on commerce and industry. They are crises in which the driving center is money capital, exercising their immediate action on the banking sector, stock exchanges and finances". As he also said (Marx, 1980, p. 84), and which can be associated with production and circulation as stages of the same social process, "it is absolutely essential that the elements separated by force, that essentially go together, manifest themselves in the form of violent explosions as a separation from something that essentially goes together. The unit is established by violence".

One clarification that will be valuable in the discussion that will follow in relation to the regime of accumulation with financial dominance is therefore clear: fictitious capital is only capital for its individual owner, who (temporarily) obtains revenue from its possession, whilst the mechanism of financial valorization in the markets is capable of supporting itself thanks to the correspondent injections of liquidity, drawn, primarily, from real production, in such a way that the regular functioning of the markets is capable of guaranteeing its conversion into money and, therefore, into effective wealth. That said, the fetishistic and contradictory nature of this "entity" becomes clear: not being capital from the social point of view, in the sense that there is not sufficient wealth to make it fully material, the fictitious capital can only exist, as such, as long as all or a great many of its owners do not try to convert it into money at the same time.

As such, it is worth noting, as Marx concluded, that for capital, the production that allows for valorization of value becomes simply "a necessary evil" in pursuit of this end. It seems evident, therefore, that the search for expanding autonomy of valorization in relation to production, that, as we intend to show, is becoming notably more sophisticated in our time, with the assistance of the highly developed Information and Communication Technologies, is positioned itself as a trend within the evolution of the capitalist mode of production as such, always focused as it is on the search for the greatest freedom possible for the accumulation, valorization and circulation of capitals.

In this way, overcoming the costly and difficult "barriers" involved in real production (obtaining raw materials, capital management, exploitation of labor, etc.) for a quick valorization of value means substituting the process of valorization measured by production of commodities (M-C-M') with another that is essentially a "rentier" process, dominated, at all its stages, by interest-bearing-capital (M-M'). This search, however, simply deepens even more the contradictory nature of the capitalist mode of production, due to the fact that, as we will show, this autonomy can never be truly established without producing serious crises. As Paulani (2016, p. 526) points out, "these considerations indicate the presence, in capitalism today, of a strong rentist strain. Such rentism is now formative in the process of accumulation, and not a 'sin against accumulation', as it was interpreted by the Political Economy when it was born".

The search for an understanding of this movement that is highly evident in our current reality, is not, however, exactly new. As mentioned previously, back at the beginning of the 20th century, Hilferding and Lenin were interested in developing a definition of financial capital that would help decipher the relationship between monopolistic capital and imperialism.

As noted by Chesnais (2006, p. 90), "Hilferding is the first theorist, after Marx, to be truly dedicated to an analysis of finance, and it remains practically alone". According to the author, in addition to the accepted socio-political definition of financial capital as the alliance between commercial, industrial and bank capital under the direction of "high finance", it is still possible to find in Hilferding a second definition of the concept, that is equally anchored in the idea of unification of capital, derived from Marx's formulations.[5] This concerns the

---

5 In presenting an alternative definition for the concept of financial capital, Mollo (2011, p. 482) problematizes the formulations of Hilferding with respect to this concept. In the author's words: "It is this need for capital to obtain the maximum amount of profit, and to be accumulated for such, which leads, on the one hand, to any money that has not been applied being used in capitalism, and flowing into the banks' coffers, and on the other, to the banks returning it into the process of accumulation via loans. By means of this process, certain capitalists develop a specialization in the trading of money, giving rise to what Marx called financial capitalists and financial capital. Marx's vision, which we adopt here in relation to financial capital, is different to that of Hilferding (1970), despite his Marxist tradition. After Hilferding (1970) and Lenin (1916), financial capital came to be associated with the merger of bank capital and industrial capital (Bidet 1982). Hilferding's monetary approach, however, is different to that of Marx, since 'he initially considers currency not as a problem, but as

centralization of capitals (not only in relation to the different sectors of capital, but also the joining of small sums of money capital, that, separately would not have had conditions to valorize to any great extent) under the dominance of the form of valorization typical of interest-bearing capital, or in other words, D-D'.

Despite disagreeing with its characterization, in relation to the reality observed at the end of the 20th and beginning of the 21st century, that delineates a more confused and even conflicting relationship between industries, banks, funds and other agents in the market that are guided by financial valorization, Chesnais (2010) seems to be highlighting two dimensions for the definition of financial capital, both of which were also observed by Harvey (2005) – who names them "visions": a particular form of circulation of capital, defined by the prominence of the interest-bearing capital with the consequent increase of fictitious capital, and the arrangement of blocks of power within the bourgeoisie; "the finance".

Using this debate as a base, critically articulating the formulations of Marx and Hilferding concerning interest-bearing capital, fictitious capital and financial capital, as well as theoretical constructs developed by the French Regulationist School, Chesnais produces a wide reaching concept of financialization that, from amongst various aspects, points most emphatically toward the centrality and dominance of financial capital in the globalized economy.

2.3 Globalization of Capital: Neoliberalism and Finance-dominated Accumulation Regime

According to Chesnais (2005, p. 35), "the contemporary world presents a specific configuration of capitalism, in which interest-bearing capital is located at the center of economic and social relations". This capital, "that seeks to

---

a solution' (Brunhoff 1979, p. 42). Given this, his perception of financial capital privileges its functional character, preventing him from truly comprehends the financial crisis (Mollo 1989). Thence because, for him 'the Stock Exchange makes the mobilization of capitals possible' (Hilferding 1970, p. 206), as Marx had considered, but given the growth in the size of companies and joint-stock companies, and the seizure of control of credit by cartels, he considers that 'the overthrow of credit is not as complete as the crises during the period at the beginning of capitalism' (p. 393). Furthermore, he says that 'the evolution of the credit crisis to the financial crisis becomes difficult due to the changes that have taken place in the organization of credit, in the first place, and the relations between commerce and industry' (p. 393). The idea is that the concentrated bank system allows for a reduction in the risks and a drop in speculation (Brunhoff 1974). He cannot therefore see that the same credit system that creates the potential for accumulation also develops fictitious capital, which lies at the basis of financial crises".

'make money' without leaving the financial sphere, in the form of loan interest, dividends and other payments received by way of the possession of shares, and, ultimately, profits born of successful speculation" (Ibid., p. 35), can only acquire the condition of dominance thanks to a set of policies incorporating liberalization, deregulation, and flexibilization that expand the freedoms for the broad accumulation and circulation of capital, above all for financial capital on a global scale.[6] This process, related to the movement of political rearrangement, that started in the developed countries in the mid-1970s and then expanded to the other economies, widely known as neoliberalism, thus allowed for the emergence of a "global financial space", that, in line with other policies and measures, created a fertile base for the advance of financial valorization.

The roots of this movement are found, in the opinion of both the authors – Chesnais and Harvey (as well as the cited commentators), as we have pointed out, in the crisis of over-accumulation of capital that developed during the previous period – the 30 "golden years" of Fordism-Keynesianism following the war – that formed perspectives for decreasing rates of profit (or, at least, rates that would not grow as substantially as they did in the preceding years) in the core capitalist economies. As a response to this unfolding scenario, such measures were – not without political resistance – applied together with a broad process of productive restructuring, that repositioned the operation and functioning of large industries and their productive chains, intensified the exploitation of labor, and redesigned the standards of consumption in line with the so-called financial globalization.

In this manner, the end of the gold standard and other Bretton Woods agreement measures, with the subsequent devaluation of the dollar and adoption of a floating exchange rate regime, are some of the elements that marked the start of the downfall of Fordism-Keynesianism as the management model for the systemic contradictions of capitalism. The excess of production and stocks, or in short, the capacities of companies, accumulated during the "golden years", led them to start a process of productive restructuring, marked, above all, by the rationalization and intensification of the control of labor. The crisis of 1973, made worse by the oil crisis, would be the decisive factor in unlocking an ugly process of economic, social and political adjustment in the 1970s and 1980s.

---

6 "Classically, authors distinguish three constituent elements in the implementation of financial globalization: monetary and financial deregulation or liberalization; the decompartmentalization of the domestic financial markets, and disintermediation, that is, the opening of loan operations, previously reserved for banks, to any type of institutional investor" (Chesnais 2005, p. 46).

This process took shape in many different forms. In addition to the broad liberalization of the economies under the all-controlling guidance of financial predominance, a factor considered here to be of key importance, it flexibilizes and geographically shifts industrial manufacture (especially through the migration of large European and US factories to China and South-east Asia), increases technological development for the economy of time, raw materials and labor in the manufacturing process (which would lead, as we have mentioned, together with other factors, to an increase of concentration and monopolization in the global economy) and redesigns, above all through its homogenization, the patterns of consumption, now increasingly internationalized. Together, these elements have shaped a new form of management for capitalist accumulation at the end of the 20th century and the beginning of the 21st century. Systematized by Chesnais in the construction of the scenario defined as the regime of accumulation with dominance of financial valorization (in which a specific configuration of private capitalist ownership, ownership of equity, enshrined in our time by the symbolic figures of owner-shareholder and institutional shareholder owning company securities, has come to dominate), these factors are described by David Harvey as part of a new "flexible regime of accumulation".

> This flexible accumulation, as I will call it, is marked by its direct confrontation with the rigidity of Fordism. It finds support in the flexibility of the labor processes, the labor markets, products, and consumer patterns. This is characterized by a sharp increase in the number of entirely new manufacturing sectors, new means of supply from the financial services, new markets and, above all, highly intensified rates of commercial, technological and organizational innovation.
> HARVEY 2013a, p. 140

In this way, flexibility involves quick changes in the patterns of unequal development, growth of the services sector, and what Harvey defines as a "compression of space-time", something that we will expand upon in more detail later on. Forming an equal part of this movement is the process of reconfiguration of the role of the state.

This is because neoliberalism applied profound changes in countries' economic, fiscal and social dimensions, amongst which we can highlight cuts in spending (above all social spending), reductions in taxes on capital and great wealth, flexibilization of the exchange rate, as well as, in the institutional-legal area, privatizations, flexibilization of labor legislation and relations, and liberalization of the markets and flow of capitals. Furthermore, in the political sphere, these measures were part of a broad process of weakening the power of the unions and workers' organizations. The privatization of the social security systems that came under the control of financial institutions and large pension funds ended up placing those who were retired and wage earners in the illusory condition of "investors" and "shareholders", injecting an enormous sum of resources and liquidity into the markets, thus stimulating financial valorization.

The end of Fordism-Keynesianism, that conferred on the state the attribute of mediator between capital and labor, based upon mechanisms of regulation, supervision and control in an attempt to guarantee social cohesion, was intended to take away its redistributing power to impose limits on private capital and make social welfare payments. This movement is aggravated by its allegedly fiscal crisis and the weakening of its institutions.

As such, being restructured, the state increasingly directs itself to guaranteeing the maintenance of financial valorization. Whilst at the same time as it maintains its ability to regulate labor and boost the flow of assets on the financial markets (through the issuing of debt and other mechanisms guaranteed by its function as the central tax collector in society), it privatizes various sectors and services, exempting itself from many of its social attributes and, when in debt, is relieved of its macroeconomic intervention instruments such as its control of the flow of capitals and the exchange rate, thus finding itself more vulnerable to fiscal crises and international monetary pressures. Faced with great difficulties in dealing with issues that are increasingly internationalized, and in regulating the functioning of the markets and the global flows of capitals, the state is put in a thankless situation: at the same time as it should be regulating capital in an attempt to guarantee the improvement of the quality of life of its people, in both the domestic and international contexts, it is pulled into creating an attractive environment for international financial capital, that is increasingly concentrated in fewer and fewer global financial marketplaces.

In summary, this highlights a coincidence of neoliberalism with the imposition of financial dominance in the configuration of financial globalization (Chesnais 1998), that has become especially intensified over the last three decades. Harvey and Chesnais are in agreement over the diagnosis that, in so far as it has increased the possibilities of valorization of financial capital, the deregulation of financial activity and the flow of capital was a determining factor in the process of neoliberalism. As Harvey (2008, p. 41) has pointed out, "neoliberalism means the 'financialization' of everything. This further established the dominion of finances on all areas of the economics, as well as on the apparatus of the state and [...] everyday life".

Along this same line of rationale, this "shift of power from manufacturing to the world of finances" (Harvey 2008, p. 42) can be equally understood as the result of the pressures by the representatives of interest-bearing capital on the governments, which, in turn, in embracing financial deregulation as the answer to the negative effects of the mentioned crisis of over-accumulation, ended up empowering them even more. The process that establishes this financial roundabout within the patterns of accumulation of capital is, in this sense, closely related to the forces of the neoliberal movement to reduce the power of labor and reorganize the dynamics of power within the economically dominant groups.

This new category of rent seeking capitalists, that are "owners who are located in a position outside production and who are not creditors" (Chesnais 2005), are strengthened by the accumulation of "equity ownership", the primary purpose of which is "neither consumption, nor the creation of wealth that increases manufacturing capacity, but rather 'income'", in search of "sterile hoarding". This characterization is closely connected, as Chesnais accepts, to what David Harvey defines as accumulation by dispossession.[7]

Based upon the ideas of Rosa Luxemburg and Marx, especially in that which relates to "primitive accumulation", the concept of "accumulation by dispossession", developed by David Harvey (2008), is defined by processes that make use of violent mechanisms for the direct appropriation of resources or the imposition of new conditions for the expanded reproduction of capital. Amongst the examples of this type of accumulation, cited by the author, are: the monetization of the exchange rate and taxation, usury, the national debt, and the use of the credit system, the exploitation of the land and natural resources, and real-estate speculation.

Despite being defined as mechanisms that run in parallel with production (of commodities, with extraction of surplus value), they are absolutely vital for the reproduction of capitalism, mainly in situations of over-accumulation of capital. In this way, they figure just as much as direct effects of the crisis of over-accumulation that occurred in the 1970s; because, by opening up opportunities that are advantageous to new investments, and avoiding devaluations by means of the rapid centralization of capital, accumulation by dispossession becomes a central element in the expansion of the frontiers for valorization.

The author also defines the four main characteristics of this type of accumulation: (i) privatization and commodification, with a view to the opening of new spheres for the accumulation of capital (almost always under the

---

[7] In Chesnais (2005, p. 21) words: "The institutional system of globalization opened up (to concentrated capital in its different organizational forms) increasing possibilities for the appropriation of value and surplus, but very often also of reactivated or new forms that David Harvey regroups under the name of 'accumulation by dispossession'. Other forms rest on mechanisms such as the new system of intellectual property established within the framework of the WTO".

leadership and management of the financial market); (ii) financialization itself, defined by the speculative logic of money capital, especially from the 1980s on, which, by means of the deregulation already discussed, turned the financial system into one of the main centers of reallocation of global wealth; (iii) the exploitation of crises, which uses speculative bubbles and manipulation of countries' public debt to intensify the transfer of wealth from poor countries to rich ones; and, finally, (iv) the redistributions controlled by the state that, once restructured and submitted to financial power, become an important agent in wealth ("counter") transfer policies. The close relationship is therefore evident between accumulation by dispossession and financialization, in which the first becomes a determining component of the latter (and vice-versa). What these and other neoliberalism strategies have in common, therefore, is their exploitative quality.

When we speak of the conformation of "patrimonial capitalism" (Chesnais 2005), we do not wish this to suggest the end of the importance of the manufacturing process of commodities, as the debate over the definition of the concept of fictitious capital denies, but of its submission to the objectives and modus-operandi of the financial sphere by means of the mechanisms mentioned earlier. As such, even though, ultimately, financial capital cannot reproduce itself without productive valorization, this new arrangement – defined by the deregulation of the flows of capital at a global level – ends up putting it in a central place.

This incredible rise of the financial sector can be understood, according to Chesnais (2005), within three basic dimensions: (i) growing autonomy of the financial sector in relation to the manufacturing sector and to control of the monetary authorities; (ii) the fetishistic character of the "values" created by the financial markets (due to its highly abstract and fictitious condition, as can be seen in the appearance of new financial products and innovations); and (iii) the increase in the power of the financial "operators" to define which agents, countries or even which types of transactions can or cannot enter into the internationalization of finance.

This restructuring of the power of finance has at least two fundamental systemic results: (1) the expansion of the centralization and concentration of capital; and (2) the accommodation of the operating logic of finance (positioned outside production) at the heart of the industrial groups.

With regard to the first point, this concerns a general tendency of the expanded process of reproduction of capital, as we noted in the introduction to this book, described by Marx in *Capital*, that highlights the centralization and concentration of capital during times of expansion and crisis, respectively. Put simply, it can be noted as an effect of competition amongst capitalists.[8] In the context of financial globalization, this process, that occurs both domestically and internationally, is intensified by mergers and acquisitions (through the mass purchase of shares) driven by financial investors and their boards.[9] The race for technology, as we will discuss later on, provides this particular point with a central role.

The financialization of industrial production and the administration of the businesses, tied to the second aspect, is one of the effects of this new type of relationship between the industrial and financial sectors, no longer defined in terms of a simple alliance that is commanded by one of them (Hilferding 1981), but as a real subsumption of industry to finance, in which the first submits itself in what is most fundamental to its administrative cognition to meet the seconds' increasing demands: sizable, short-term returns for its investors. With this perspective, businesses end up subjecting other productive needs to the movement that the value of their shares and dividends represent on the stock exchanges, as well as to their ability to guarantee returns that can fuel the markets' continual need for liquidity.

By means of the regulations and standards of "corporate governance", shareholder councils and their representatives, who come to command these

---

8   As Marx explains: "The competitive struggle is waged by means of lowering the prices of commodities. The low price of commodities depends, *caeteris paribus*, on the productivity of labor, but this, in turn, depends upon the scale of production. The larger capitals therefore overpower the smaller ones. We should recall, moreover, that with the development of the capitalist mode of production, the minimum volume of individual capital required to conduct business under normal conditions increases. Smaller capitals therefore seek the spheres of production in which large-scale industry seizes control only sporadically or incompletely. Competition flourishes there in direct proportion to the quantity, and in inverse proportion to the size of the rival capitals. It always ends with the collapse of many small capitalists, part of whose capitals pass into the hands of the victor, and part of which is lost" (Marx 2013a, p. 702).

9   As Plihon explains in the article *Au nom des entreprises?*, published in February 1999 in the Le Monde Diplomatic newspaper: "If they do not truly contribute to the financing of companies, what then is the economic use of the financial markets and, in particular, of their principal players, the pension funds? Essentially it is to facilitate the restructuring of modern capitalism through operations of external growth, public offerings and merger-acquisitions. By purchasing and selling stocks, pension funds circulate capital and accelerate the evolution toward a new configuration characterized by the taking of control of productive capital by investors (pension funds, investment funds and insurance funds) and, simultaneously, by the creation of a class of rentiers amongst wage earners themselves". Available at <http://www.monde-diplomatique.fr/1999/02/PLIHON/2759>. Accessed on: Nov 27, 2017.

companies (the majority of CEOs are remunerated with company shares – stock options), finance hosts the foundations of interest-bearing capital (which, due to its "external" status in relation to the production, is focused on establishing growing autonomy from such production) at the heart of industrial administration, which, as well as operating in the short-term, starts to speculate on the markets with assets and securities, as a way of making more gains (especially in scenarios with waning returns in the productive sphere). As such, the large industrial conglomerates become part of the chains of financial valorization, in order to strengthen the previously mentioned tendency toward centralization.

As a result, there is a reduction in the amount relating to the salaries in the composition and division of the revenue, through countless mechanisms of intensification of the exploitation of labor, that have already been mentioned, with a consequent increase in the levels of social inequality and the rising indebtedness of families. As such, whilst there is an expansion of the profit concentrated in the hands of smaller and smaller global industrial-financial groups, which operate in a very small number of international financial marketplaces, it is possible to see real global economic growth advancing slowly[10] – in opposition to neoliberal promises of reestablishment of economic growth out of the supposed injection of dynamism into the economies.

Along the same lines, the vocation of interest-bearing capital to constantly demand of the economy more than it is capable of providing, which is a direct consequence of its position outside the productive sphere, in a very important way increases the systemic tendencies to produce crises. It is in this sense that Chesnais, in connection with the various factors described in this chapter, points to a "systemic fragility", in order to suggest that within this context, the crises are not just cyclical, but are even more recurrent and abrupt, as they unfold within a framework of chronic economic instability, in which the conditions for the occurrence of crises are inseparable from such operational logic. This systemic fragility is, as we will see, highly connected with the increase in complexity and opacity, made possible by the development of liberalized markets and the adoption of advanced operational technologies.

Put more simply, it is enough to understand such crises (using the outstanding example of the 2008 financial crisis) as results of the expansion of freedoms for fictitious capital in its trajectory of empowerment in relation to the real economy. Initially offered on a large and growing scale, fictitious capital needs to find some sort of objective correspondence capable of nourishing its dynamics of valorization. Circulating and reproducing at speeds and scales much

---

10   For data and information on this issue see Chesnais (2005), pp. 56–60.

greater than the corresponding productive capacity (which, on the contrary, is depressed as the fruit of the draining of capitals with the subsequent fall in investments in production, despite the same thing occurring when the productive capacity rises quickly without the consequent increase in demand or spending power), fictitious capital leads to the production of financial "bubbles". Since the interest on fictitious capital can only be paid by means of the finalization of the cycle of valorization, or in other words, on the purchase/sale of commodities, if it is not made concrete it leads to the bubble bursting, highlighting the crisis that it had been hiding. Without any profit, therefore, there is no payment of interest. This demonstrates the fictitious nature of this capital.[11] As Mollo (2011, pp. 19–20) demonstrates within the context of a discussion of the crisis of 2008:

> Despite being inherent to the logic of capitalism, the credit system has developed enormously with the so-called neoliberalism because, on the one hand, it has stimulated the competition between capitals, an important force in the definition of the laws of movement within capitalism. On the other, it has deregulated the financial system in general, allowing financial innovations that have significantly amplified the fictitious nature of the capital. The development of fictitious capital was possible, for a long time, as though the circulation-production autonomy had no limits, considering the opening for movement of capitals and an inflow of capital arising from the privatization of public pensions. This enormous mass of resources, applied in very few developed and emerging markets, meant an enormous increase in demand and a sizable appreciation of the number of securities negotiated in them. But over time the real production started to resent the new investments that grew at a lower proportion, and the revenue responsible for the demand for the securities fell, or at least decreased. Increasingly risky innovations, encouraged by legislation and fraud, bolstered the detachment of production from circulation all the more. But the crisis arrived, brutally demonstrating that this autonomy is always either relative or limited.

---

11   Put another way, "the development of fictitious capital has to have a limit, since its valorization arises from demands supported by sales proceeding from the productive process (the profits and high salaries which such generates). If the growth of production is delayed in relation to the valorization of the fictitious capital, there will be a lack of demand to sustain new appreciations and new gains, which ends up with their owners being required to sell their commercial papers, thus unlocking the spiral of deflation that highlights the crisis. The consequent crisis, therefore, is a brutal way of establishing limits on the autonomy of circulation in relation to production" (Mollo 2011, p. 19).

Due to this brief and summarized systematization of financial globalization, that demonstrates its economic, political and social roots, we should, along the lines that we have thus far argued, question the readings that confer the rapid development of the Communication and Information Technologies on the structural origins of the process commonly known as globalization. As Chesnais rhetorically asks:

> Could it be that the transformations that have taken place over the last fifteen years, under the conditions of remuneration, hiring and work of salaried workers (with the salary relationship being that of the Regulation Theory), with the generalization of precarious contracts, the subordination of companies to the requirements of flexibilization, the relative drop in salaries, all based upon high and continually rising unemployment, after it had never existed before (in Japan), are solely attributed to the effects of the changing technology? Or could they also be connected to the increasing weight of finances and to the demands of the new, non-banking financial institutions?
> CHESNAIS 1998, p. 19

Within a discussion of the global markets as a single unit being one of the elements responsible for the creation of a globalized financial marketplace, the author drops clues to his understanding of the secondary character reserved for the technologies of connectivity in the setup of the broad picture of the regime of accumulation with the dominance of financial valorization.

> It is wrong to attribute the singularity of the financial markets essentially to the technologies (telecommunications, computerization) that provide a solid basis for the interconnection of the financial marketplaces (see also Helleimer, 1995, in the book by Boyer and Drache, 1996). This interconnection arises from the operations that transform technical potential into economic fact. [...] The international integration of the financial markets became a possibility due to its regulatory opening and its interconnection in real time. But the effective context of this integration arises, more firmly, from the decisions taken and the operations performed by the managers of the most important and most internationalized portfolios.
> CHESNAIS 1998, p. 12

If, in the end, we do not necessarily disagree with his formulation in which it refers to the negation of "technological fetishism", we do believe its careful investigation and questioning to be fundamental, whilst such concern makes little appearance in the author's work. Moving in a different direction, we should ask some counter-questions, with the aim of shifting the attention toward a more restrained evaluation concerning the relationship between the technical phenomenon and the misfortunes of the capitalist economy: could the technological development be a mere appendix to its material basis? And, even if it were, how is such domination established and maintained? Is the technics truly a smaller element within capital or does it possess contradictions and counter effects that, in an interaction with other dynamics and social practices, allow for the objectification and materialization of unforeseeable scenarios, contexts and situations? This is what we intend to discuss in the next chapter.

CHAPTER 3

Technics, Capital and Society: The Material Bases of Technological Development

3.1 Investigating the Technological Practice from Its Social Content

As we have seen, the current period of development of capitalist production, characterized by a finance-dominated accumulation regime (Chesnais 1996, 1998, 2005), can be read as an extremely tight interdependence of the financial markets, which spread and establish their logic of accumulation in other spheres and sectors of the global economy.

In one way, going beyond the wide range of political, social and economic measures that have allowed for the establishment of this logic since the neoliberal offensive in the 1970s and 1980s, and have only established themselves even more firmly ever since, this dynamic is made viable, from a logistical perspective, thanks to the massive advances in the area of computer technology, that have, through automation, considerably expanded the capacity of fictitious capital to condition the manner in which the global economy operates.

This form of regulation of capitalist accumulation, managed twenty-four hours per day in internationally connected financial markets, operating in "real-time",[1] allows for million-dollar transactions to take place in a matter of thousandths of a second. The deregulation of the financial markets and the liberalization of international transactions, allied with the creation of a technological infrastructure, that uses advanced telecommunications, interactive information systems and powerful computers, capable of high speed processing of the models necessary to handle the complexity of the transactions, allows capital (as well as savings and investments, interconnected throughout the world by means of banks, financial institutions and stock exchanges) to be

---

1 In relation to operations on the capitals market, the term "real time" should always be used with caution, since it is just a rhetorical/explanatory abstraction used to identify the meeting of intention, interaction and perception of a given event in time. In practice, however, there are always temporal differences between these dimensions and this is especially important in the reality of the capitals market, since, as we will see, it is in precisely this exploitation of milliseconds that technically defines these differences, that an important frontier for the exploration of financial gain through arbitration with commercial papers is to be found.

transported from one side of the world to the other, crossing different economies, in very short periods of time. As such, the flows of finance observe impressive growth in terms of volume, speed, complexity and connectivity, increasing technological empowerment and the prominence of the fictitious economy, to the detriment of the real economy, at the same time as it has raised the interdependency between the markets submitted to this way of operating. This phenomenon produces drastic consequences in the configurations of the national states and their institutions, private companies and the manufacturing sectors, as well as of civil society, establishing a series of new political and social dilemmas and complexities.

It therefore seems important to us, based upon this diagnosis, to think about the role that the technological phenomenon plays in the structural changes which the economies and society have undergone during our times. Far from diving into the celebration of technology that characterizes many contemporary approaches, maintaining, at their root, a greater or lesser degree of analytical determinism, we believe the technological dimension to be an important interpretative key, amongst many others, to an understanding of the processes of structural transformation of the capitalist economy.

This is because the capitalist economy was born and is increasingly legitimized as a technical economy (as if it were possible to talk of an economy as being "non-technical") of domination of nature by man, through work and, as a consequence, of man by man (Marcuse 1979), based upon the distinct forms of social organization of this work. Supporting itself in the fetish of interminable, rational-instrumental, neutral and autonomous progress, the form of organization of social life created by capitalism, is legitimized, along this path, as being inexorable, as an automatic result of the human need to transform nature, in a desire to reproduce human existence as comfortably and securely as possible. Countless critics working in the western tradition, have turned their thoughts toward analyses of this phenomenon and its various consequences. Far from attempting to summarize this enormous debate, or provide a superficial opinion on it, we intend here to present a review that aims to show the reader the following objectives of this work: an investigation into the various relations between technology and capital and, more specifically, between the development of the Information and Communication Technologies (ICT) and the process of financialization of the capitalist economy in our time.

One of the biggest challenges to our research on technology, from this point of view, is to avoid the temptation of technological determinism, or in other words: the understanding that, ultimately, technology is autonomous and determines the direction of social dynamics. Put this way, the idea seems extremely rudimentary. However, it is important that we make it clear that it is within this orbit, that is tentatively linked to this understanding, that academic tradition will construct the debate on the relations between technology and society.

In the wake of the discussions on theories of cyber-culture, as a means of systematizing the debate, Rüdiger (2011) provides a simplified look at those individuals dedicated to thinking about the technical aspect, dividing them into "Faustians" and "Prometheans", figures drawn from western literature who respectively represent "technophobes" and "technophiles". If, on the one hand, technology is seen as a process relegated to the disintegration of the ties of solidarity between men and the production of a self-destructive bent – so well represented by the image of the "Luddite" and "neo-Luddite" movements – , then on the other, it is proclaimed as the kingdom of freedom of man from nature, as the emancipating sign of progress and evolution of the species.

This positioning provides us with an understanding that, despite their being apparent opposites, it is possible to observe in both positions the same technological determinism which we seek to distance ourselves from, or in other words, a belief in the autonomous force of technology to both break up and self-destruct society and to elevate ourselves into the realm of progress.

We have seen classic social theory authors turn their attention to this issue, amongst whom we can highlight Karl Marx and Max Weber. Dedicating his work to an evaluation of the relations between economy and culture, in the conformation of western rationalism and the predomination of an instrumental rationality, that will characterize the wide process of rationalization and autonomization of social spheres, Max Weber sees technology as part of a process of domination of the world. At the base of his Theory of Social Action is a technical understanding of rationality that, ultimately, is related to the human technical making and acting, cognitive bases of the mechanization of the productive process and the industrialism of his era.

Just as in Weber's work, one cannot speak of a study of technology as such in the work of Karl Marx. Different to Weber, for whom modern technology is somehow limited to the wider process of rationalization of the world, for Marx, the question of technology is, above all, a problem relating to the world of work and production. From this perspective, it should be considered from the point of view of capital, or in other words, of the social relationship of production of which it forms a part. In light of this method of analysis, modern technology can be related to the exploitation and domination of man, the sophisticated forms of intensification of extraction of surplus value, the control of labor by capital and, consequently, the suppression of the subjectivity of the worker who, removed from his role as an intellectual force in the production process, sees himself as being cheated into being the operative appendix to the machine.

From a brief overview of the contributions these two classic thinkers have made in relation to modern technology, a series of disagreements between them can be seen. Whilst Karl Marx understands it as a dimension of the mode of production and, therefore, of capital, Max Weber sees in the transformations in culture and in thought, the predominance of a given Western rationalism as a means of controlling the world. Whilst Weber theorizes on the growing rationalization of labor and society through maximum economy or minimum spending, Marx outlines a rationalization of oppression, through a science apparatus focused on the control of labor by capital, in the struggle between the classes. If, on the one hand, Weber points out the autonomization of social spheres as a result of the cognitive instrumentalization of life that transforms means into ends, then on the other, Marx is concerned about the hijacking of the worker's subjectivity, as he is subsumed as a mechanical appendix of the machine. Whilst Weber sees technics as an essential dimension of social action, Marx, in turn, presents it as an instrument of inversion of the relationship between man and tool, in the transformation of nature. The technics that is conformed and affirmed for reasons of cognitive order in Weber's work, is opposed in that of Marx as a specific technic of a given mode of production that materially relieves and separates man from his "human essence".

These counter-positions – derived from different perspectives of understanding of the social reality and structurally distinct approaches from the philosophical and theoretical points of view – present questions that could, as they were and still are, be the objects of complex debate and thought. We still know that this separation defines epistemological divisions, which are the object of serious criticisms of Marx by Weber, who he calls an economic determinist.

It is, however, possible to find a number of converging areas in the two authors' perspectives on this point, since, in our opinion, Marx and Weber have – albeit using different lenses and explanations – diagnosed the same problem, such being: the imprisonment of man by the technological apparatus which he himself has produced. This conclusion has much in common with a dimension that Martin Heidegger (2006) situates as part of the *ontological* configuration of technology (*techné*): the availability or disposal (*disposition*) as control of the world and domain over the forces of nature, the "bringing-forth", a "way of revealing" [the truth] (even though Weber's definition of technics as a means, rooted in the tradition of Western thinking, is one of the main targets of the criticism presented by Heidegger).

Be it the technical control through the rational instrumentalization of social life, or be it the technical control of labor in manufacture for the domination of class, we can see in both a certain concern over freedom in relation to nature and society, and the role of technology in this relationship as an instrument of domination of nature to despotically convert itself into an instrument of domination over man. How can tools that could free man from the hardships of material existence and lead him toward a better life be transformed into tools of domination and control? This is a question which, despite moving toward different answers, both are committed to answering.

In relation to the role of the economic structure in the formation of the technological apparatus, some of the thoughts developed by these two authors are surprising in their similarity. Despite negating, through his multi-causal epistemology, that the economic is a determining factor in the configuration of the technological sphere, Max Weber points out that:

> [...] throughout time, and especially today, the principal factor for technological development is economic conditioning; without rational calculation as a basis for the economy, that is, without the extremely concrete historical-economic conditions, rational technics would not have come into being.
> WEBER 1994, pp. 29–30

In his *General Economic History* (1980), Weber describes in detail the process of machination of modern economic technics. Just as Karl Marx did, he sees in the factory the space in which tools or instruments are effectively transformed into machines, in the sense that they bring together, in a single location, sources of energy, workers, labor processes and businesspersons. In one passage that could be confused with a part of the explanation of the concept of subsumption in Marx, Weber stresses that "the difference is seen in the fact that the devices are in the service of man, whilst in the modern machine precisely the opposite occurs" (Weber 1980, p. 139). As Sell (2011) explains, Weber demonstrates here that he was able to see much more than a simple quantitative or qualitative development of new technologies, also demonstrating a concern, as did Marx, with the machine's estrangement from man, its creator.

> Between today's technology and that of previous times, there was a qualitative rupture. This break in continuity therefore allows us to speak of 'modern' technics. Its most central and specific characteristic is its independence from the natural and human cycle. There is an inversion at work here, since pre-modern technics still behaves within clear limits set

within the natural and human world, whilst in modern times this limit has been pierced, with the functions of man and nature being reordered by technics. The notion of "independence" from the technical complex points not only in the direction of the systemic character of technics within the context of modernity (demonstrating its *autopoietic* character), but also reveals an important contradiction or social pathology of our time – the alienation (*Entfremdung*) from the means, created by man, of its own creator.

SELL 2011, p. 576

It is true that there are elements that Weber saw as being positive in the process of rationalization of societies and disenchantment of the world, that would have freed man from of the yoke of unquestioned tradition, from a previously defined destiny, and from the material dependence on nature. This enthusiasm can also be found in Karl Marx, in relation to the ability of capitalism to produce goods and innovation in quantities and quality never before seen in history – technical conditions, materials and objectives that, based upon the political overcoming of its model of social organization, allow the production of a society in which freedom reigns.

In order to evaluate and study the technical apparatus in capitalist society (and as an important part of its influence on the discussion that will follow amongst other thinkers), we should highlight, however, the dystopian images found in the writings of Weber and Marx in relation to this: the iron cage and the subsumption of man to the machine, respectively – in relation to which the following summary provided by Weber is especially clear:

> An inanimate machine is a mind made concrete. Only this fact provides the machine with the power to force man to operate it, and the power to dominate their daily working lives so completely as occurs in the reality of a factory. Firmly established intelligence is also an active machine, one of bureaucratic organization [...] Together with the inanimate machine, firmly established intelligence is occupied in the construction of the shell of bondage that man may one day be forced to inhabit, making him as impotent as the peasants of Ancient Egypt.
>
> WEBER 1994, p. 25

Leaving behind the dichotomy of utopia vs dystopia, we find in Trigueiro (2008) a program of systematic and structured analysis of the technological practice in complex societies, based upon the understanding that he, following many other authors, calls "the social content of technology". Based on a critical analysis of technological thinking sustained upon the contributions from the Theory of Knowledge, the Sociology of Science and the Philosophy of Technology, with special emphasis on the critical and constructivist approaches to technology, Trigueiro extends the discussion to consider technology in its structural, ideological and pragmatic aspects, with the intention of theorizing on the process of creation of technology. In defense of a non-autonomous, socially conditioned, understanding of technology, his work presents a broad review of the literature on the subject, which, because of this broadness, it will not be possible to analyze to a very great extent in this book.

In the Marxist tradition, with which we establish a direct dialog, this intense debate is centered, above all, on the objective and subjective role of the productive forces and their development in the form of capitalist production, as well as in their characterization as an obstacle or stimulus for this to be overcome, or on the relevance of their use in the construction of a post-capitalist society. At the base of these discussions, naturally, are the discussions surrounding the autonomy versus non-autonomy, of technology and neutrality versus conditioning by values in the process of technological development or the productive forces (PF). Romero (2005) and Novaes (2010) provide expansive panoramas in relation to this discussion, both in the work of Marx, and in that of other thinkers in the area of technology in the Marxist tradition.

Romero (2005, p. 28) presents the concept of real subsumption in the works of Marx, based upon an analysis of the industrial revolution, as well as, derived from this reading, the way:

> […] in which capital creates a science identified with its interests, in so far as it develops technology focused on the extraction of relative surplus value and control over labor, seeking to suppress the workers' subjectivity as much as possible (even though it is never completely effective) and concentrating the intellectual forces of the production process on capital.

Based upon an extensive bibliography, Novaes (2010) questions the orthodox Marxist interpretation and its defenders, in relation to the technological development of the productive forces of capitalism, as well as how to overcome it. Centered on a mechanical and deterministic reading of the contradiction between the social relations of production (SRP) and productive forces, described by Marx in the preface to his *Contribution to the Critique of Political Economy*, this tradition will, according to the author, in the hyper-development of the PF, perceive the opportunity of structural overcoming of the capitalist SRP and, along with this, a political horizon to be sought as part of the attempt to construct the objective conditions for the destruction of capitalism, as well as the construction of socialism.

Still according to Novaes (2010), this reading consciously or unconsciously suffers a certain "technological fetishism", in so far as it ignores the fact that the technical artifacts are not neutral or autonomous, nor are they mere technical-instrumental products designed to rationally articulate ends and means, but carry within themselves, as part of the objective and context for which they were developed, elements of the selfsame capitalist SRP, that are committed to the control and domination of labor by capital.

Quoting passages from speeches and texts by Lenin and Stalin (Novaes 2010), and supported by the critical analyses of other thinkers (Burawoy 1990; Chesnais and Serfati 2003, Feenberg 2002, Hobsbawn 1996, Mészáros 2002, Noble 1979, 2001), the author argues that such a "stage-ist" understanding (due to its defense of the need to firstly develop the PF in order to then alter the SRP) of the construction process of socialism makes a fundamental error in outlining, for technological development, understood as autonomous and neutral, a certain linear inexorability. This position ends up ignoring the instrumental and ideological content of the PF, based upon their organic links to the SRP that, remaining intact, prevent the self-organization and the self-management of social production by the workers; thus, perpetuating the domination of the socio-metabolic system (Mészáros 2001) of capital, even after the collapse of capitalist property relations.

Trigueiro (2008, p. 23) summarizes this debate thus:

> The non-autonomy of science in society is focused, in literature, above all by the Marxist current (Bukharin 1971, Braverman 1977, Cohen 1978, Burawoy 1978, Aronowitz 1978, Therborn 1980, and Goonatilake 1984). Within this tradition, the dominant trend is that which considers science to be a productive force; the controversy, however, revolves around the emphasis given to the productive forces or to the relations of production in historical-social development. Also highlighted, in these discussions, are authors such as Jurgen Habermas and Hebert Marcuse, who, despite developing approaches that are not strictly Marxist, in that they combine elements from the Weberian discussion on the process of rationalization of contemporary societies, provide important contributions for a critique of science and technology, diagnosing the politicization and establishment of the ideology of these two human activities within the current context of capitalist development; these discussions being very close to the Marxist analysis of the "commodity fetishism" and the increasingly alienating tendency in the form of capitalist production.

With the posing of this question as a starting point, Andrew Feenberg, in his publications *Critical theory of technology* (1991) and *Questioning technology*

(1999), presents a promising theory for technology, based upon the social critique of technics, present in Marx, Marcuse, Habermas and Ellul. It concerns an essentially political interpretation of technology in which it is seen as "an ambivalent process of social development suspended between various possibilities" (Feenberg 1991, p. 22), even if it is, as he admits, ultimately a force modeled by capital and which, as such, "favors the tight objectives of production with a view to profit" (Feenberg 1999, p. 22).

Behind this Marxist-inspired critical reading of the role of technology, is the notion of commodity fetichism, here extended to technology (Feenberg 2002). Thus, if, for Marx, the commodity itself hides a set of social relations (and, therefore, has a particular socio-historical content, masked by fetichism that serves class domination), the same scheme can be used to understand the production and use of technology in our society that, through the ideology of technology, hides its "social content".

If it is true that the process of technological development is not inexorably determined by an economic structure that is neutral and completely autonomous, but permeated by cultural and political disputes experienced at the heart of society, being guided, as Feenburg defends, by the class struggle itself, the notion of social content of technology, for us, cannot be assumed in a way that outlines an open field of infinite possibilities either, as in a deliberative game, without structural restraints or dominant forces. In so far as it is subject to the conditionings of the class struggle, and is, therefore, asymmetric in terms of the dispute for power between capital and labor, exploiters and exploited, the process of technological development is part of a war in which "only one of the sides is armed" (Noble 2000, p. 6).

In relation to this particular point, the formulations of Louis Althusser (1979a) are of special interest for the theoretical consideration of this phenomenon. Employing a powerful critique of the deterministic readings of Marxist theory, that includes the economic factor as being solely responsible for historical development, Althusser finds in Marx and Engels the recognition of a relative autonomy to the superstructures and their particular effectiveness or practices.

As the author argues, the use of the dialectic method in Marx fundamentally differs from the use of the dialect in Hegel, and not only in its structural inversion, that turns it on its head. It operates, above all, by adopting a concept of contradiction that does not exist only amongst simple principles and ideas, as in Hegel, but rather as an overdetermined contradiction, that incorporates different factors (the physical means, human productive organization, the existing ideological superstructure and culture, amongst others), in constant interaction, reciprocally influencing and altering each other. To the different configurations and arrangements between these overdetermined aspects, there correspond different social realities and modes of organization of production in each given society. Such practices, in their specificities, and with mutual and contradictory ties one to another, are, however, arranged in a hierarchy between each other in terms of the economic aspect, that ultimately conditions them.

As such, the mode of production of a given society does not mechanically determine, its superstructure, in such a way that both, structure and superstructure, each affecting the other reciprocally (as a retroactive effect on the cause), and in a non-deterministic manner, will, in its infinite number of factors, over-determine the contradictions and movements of social change over history, allowing us to understand and evaluate the social and political processes, in this way, based upon multiple causes. Thus, a "structured (or overdetermined) whole" is presented, in which other, relatively autonomous, instances or practices can be decisive or dominant in a given context without necessarily being determinant.

In accordance with this formulation, supported by a reading attentive to the theoretical contributions of Karl Marx, in their myriad of possibilities, we deny, in an attempt to investigate those societies ruled by the capitalist mode of production, the separation of economy and politics as distinct or "pure" dimensions of reality – even as an analytical resource. This vision, permeated by a conceptual dimension of the whole, is therefore trying to understand the general movements of the Political Economy as determinants, ultimately, of the "social". The interweaving of the different practices or spheres that converge in the composition of the so-called "social content of technology" is part, as a metonymy of such, of the very interweaving that ontologically characterizes, in this approach, the social as a systemic complex. The restraints or barriers to production of an emancipatory technology are, therefore, analogous to the structural restraints imposed on the intentions of a broad emancipatory construction of the organization of social life.

As such, with certain technical idiosyncrasies being maintained, and the due exceptions that are often quickly integrated into the existing order, the technological production of societies moves in the direction of its dominant power, even though it is not completely closed within it, since it is also a product of the social contradictions engendered by the class struggle itself. The neutrality of technology, so present in the popular understanding, is no more, therefore, than ideology (Marcuse 1979).

As such, with this brief summary as a basis, we are establishing our position in favor of a materialist, rather than deterministic, approach to technology, in so far as it is understood as being non-neutral and partially autonomous, ontologically anchored in its "social content", and overdetermined, ultimately, by economic practice.

3.2 Technological Development and Financialization of the Economy: Theoretical Starting Points

This approach (which, as we intend to demonstrate, will be especially fitting to understand this discussion) having been assumed, the relationship between technological development and the structural operation of the capitalist economy should be more directly demonstrated, in an effort to highlight the theoretical starting points that anchor our hypotheses.

As we mentioned earlier, we believe that by strengthening and consolidating the process of financialization of the economy, and, more specifically, by help forming the finance-dominated accumulation regime, the development of the Information and Communication Technologies (ICT) operates in three dimensions that, together, form what we have called the cycle of operation of digitalized finance, that is: (i) the displacements (shortenings) of the space-time flows, that by pressuring the increase in the number and volume of trade operations and transactions, point toward; (ii) additional difficulties in the technical and political spheres for the supervision and regulation of these markets and their agents, a situation that reinforces the; (iii) concentration and centralization of capitals within and between the markets.

Based upon Marx's formulations, especially those found in *Capital*, but also in *Grundrisse*, some of which have been touched upon earlier, and with the help of readings of the work of David Harvey on this matter, in *Seventeen Contradictions and the End of Capitalism* (2014) and in *The Condition of Post-Modernity* (2013a), we will look at some of the aspects of technological development, within the capitalist mode of production, that we deem to be especially important in support of these working hypotheses.

It is understood that it is in order to expand the obtaining of relative surplus value within the sphere of competition between capitalists, that technological development, within the manufacturing process, tends to promote and coordinate the division of labor, in order to maximize efficiency/productivity, profitability and valorization.

This is because, as Marx suggested, in addition to the absolute surplus value, obtained by means of the exploitation of overwork based upon increased workloads and intensive labor (elements that take workers to their physical limits), capitalists further rely upon an additional means of increasing their profits in the manufacturing process (beyond simple market eventualities and forces): by means of exploitation of the relative surplus value that establishes an increase in the productivity of the workforce due to technological progress (an increase in the so-called organic composition of capital). This increase in productivity provides the capitalist with additional competitive strength in his struggle with the others, in so far as it allows him to lower production costs, thus increasing profits. Initially explored without other capitalists having access to them, these innovations produce super-profits for these, shall we say "pioneers", since they guarantee that products sold at market prices (or less) – and which, as such, are anchored in another relationship with the labor time that is socially necessary for their production – guarantee even more return. Therefore, after having been consumed, in part, these super-profits are reinvested in capital and the labor force for corresponding expansions in production.

As such, as a direct extension of this aspect, we find a tendency toward the constant evolution in the production of technologies for the control of labor and workers, and the establishment of various organizational arrangements that combine machinery and operations systems (the three, therefore, understood as being orgwares, softwares and hardwares, seen here, in the wider sense, as technologies), amongst which we can cite as examples Taylorism, Fordism and Toyotism.

Here, we can recognize that technological development as a dimension of the expanded reproduction of capital, addressed by Marx in Chapter 18 of *Capital*, is closely connected to the processes of centralization and concentration of capital, as mentioned earlier. Due to investments in innovations being uncertain, expensive and risky in terms of the possibility of them providing returns, only a few capitalists – and it is no accident that these are the biggest or richest – obtain these innovations. As for the others, they continue achieving "average" profits in their markets, in so far as they are able to obtain these advances later on, only after the pioneers have already exploited the mentioned advantages.

Based upon the competitive advantage they offer, these technological advances allow their owners to exploit and concentrate super-profits that allow for growth in their capacity for productive investment and expansion, be it in the form of new factories, or by the absorbing of the competitors that cannot handle the competition. The centralization of capitals, motivated, in this way, by competition between capitalists, has, in technological development, a determining factor. If, within the contexts of expansion, there exists centralization, in situations of crisis, equally within which only the biggest and richest survive, there is a concentration[2] of capitals through mergers, acquisitions

---

2 Despite being pertinent and opportune the differentiation between the concepts of centralization and concentration in the work of Marx which, despite outlining distinct processes, both demonstrate the focusing of capitals in the hands of a shrinking number of capitalists; for the effects of simplification within the limits of this book, in relation to the financial market and the capitals market, we will use, to interpret trends which can be generalized as such, just the term "concentration".

and bankruptcies of competitors, thus opening up space for the exploitation of other slices of the market. As such, we find here, in the general trend of technological advances to reinforce the centralization and concentration of capitals, an important theoretical support for the issues we will address next, which relate to the financial markets found in the scenario we can call *digitalized finance*.

Into the sphere of this discussion, there should be included the fact that, as Marx pointed out, the financial market, through the exponential expansion of credit, contributes to this process of concentration and centralization, in so far as it allows for it to be performed in advance and expanded, through the increase in productive scales and the number of workers brought together under the command of a single capitalist. As we have explained, globalization, in the form of the expansion of capital worldwide, has, as one of its characteristics, the removal or reduction of the barriers to circulation and the valorization of capitals and, therefore, the drastic increase of competition between capitalists worldwide. Within the financial market, but not only here, in accordance with the general tendency described by Marx, competition is a determining factor for the concentration and centralization of capitals. This means supporting the diagnosis made by Chesnais (2005) in relation to the brutal increase of the centralization of capitals due to financial globalization and, equally, our formulation concerning financial technology as a factor in the increased concentration and centralization of capitals in the hands of a few financial agents and marketplaces.

Harvey (2013a) holds that the contradictions always existent in capitalism, including monopolization and competition, centralization and decentralization, have presented themselves in a way that is essentially new. One of the crucial developments for this, according to Harvey, is also a central element in flexible accumulation together with the abovementioned elements discussed in the works of Marx and Chesnais (2005, p. 152): "the complete reorganization of the global financial system and the emergence of much bigger powers of financial coordination".

Along the same lines, as part of the unquestionable needs of the production process, it is possible to highlight the development of technologies of knowledge, information and communication and, tightly bound to these, those technologies focused on the management and circulation of money and finances. With practically inseparable frontiers between themselves, both allow for the organization of the pricing system and offer information that guides deals, decisions and investments in market activities, as well as making it possible to hoard, allocate, circulate and calculate money, by means of which profits and losses are measured and economic decisions are made in the capitalist economy.

Over the past few years, these technologies have been seen to make unprecedented advances. The trend toward exponential growth in computer capacity and speed, that has practically doubled every two years[3] over the past few decades, has enabled incredible advances in monetary and banking technologies, opening up a vast complexity of new forms of business and investments. The introduction of new technologies for the processing of information, such as computerized negotiations in the financial markets, carries important implications for the way in which capitals operate today.

> The trend to create fictitious capitals that circulate freely has accelerated remarkably alongside all manner of predatory practices within the credit system that have contributed to a wave of accumulation by dispossession and speculation in asset values. Nowhere else do we see so dramatically the acute interaction between new hardware possibilities, the creation of new organizational forms (private equity firms and hedge funds and a host of complicated state regulatory agencies) and, of course, an astonishing rate of software development. The technologies of the world's monetary and financial system are an acute source of stress at the same time as they are a field of capitalist endeavor unsurpassed in these times in terms of importance and in 'messy vitality'.
> HARVEY 2014, p. 235

These technologies, however, not only demonstrate the necessary types of information that guide investment and the operationalization of market activities, but also stimulate the concepts and ways of thinking that facilitate manufacturing activity, guide decisions on consumption, and provide an incentive for the creation of new technologies.

This is because, if technological development can be understood as a constitutive factor in the dynamic of expanded reproduction of capital activated by the increased extraction of relative surplus value in the race for growing productivity gains in the competition between capitalists, it is a fact that, by

---

3   In 1965, Gordon E. Moore, the co-founder of the Intel Corporation, drew attention to the trend for the number of transistors in integrated circuits to double every two years throughout the history of hardware computation. His prediction proved to be correct and came to be known as the Moore Law, used in the semiconductor industry to guide long-term planning and establish targets for research and development. The increase in the capacities of many electronic digital devices started to behave in the same way – the prices of microprocessors being fixed in terms of their quality, memory capacity, sensors, and the number and size of pixels in digital cameras, all of which have seen exponential rates of advance. For more on this, see: Brock, David (Ed.) (2006), *Understanding Moore's Law*: Four Decades of Innovation. Philadelphia: Chemical Heritage Press.

occupying such a position, it ends up being transformed into a lucrative business and, naturally, as if it could be any different, into commodity. The market of technical artifacts therefore exceeds its function as a factor of production, to produce and explore other use values, creating markets providing different technological products, focused on different needs (be they productive or not), many of which come into being through ideological mechanisms for the construction of desires, such as advertising, shows, entertainment, etc.; and even through their planned obsolescence, that points to the need for the ever growing production and consumption of these goods.

As part of this same chain, we can highlight military technologies (that today represent the planet's biggest research and development budget and either directly or indirectly stimulate technical developments that are later absorbed into various other sectors) and others designed for the management of the state and our social life: such as health care, education and social welfare. These forms of technology act in a secondary manner or function as industries that have their own dynamics and forms of production, reproduction, circulation and accumulation, in line with other needs, in dialog with different cultural, ethical and normative contexts.

To the state is relegated an additional role in another two dimensions: to protect the capitalists who develop these innovations (amongst whom, above all, are those capitalists operating in the technology market) through the creation and compliance with patent and intellectual property laws; and to guarantee, in the wider sense, the continuity of investments in research and development (R&D), a field that is extremely risky and involves high costs for the individual investors. If investment in R&D is difficult for small capitalists due to the high costs (and scale), for the large ones, many of whom hold monopolies or oligopolies, as well as due to protection, by the state, of these investments from segregated exploration, this becomes less necessary as a weapon in the competition wars. From this there arises a certain encouragement from the public sector for technological development in both productive and non-productive activities, above all in those related to social needs.

Due to all that has been outlined, one aspect which appears to us to be absolutely central to capitalist technological development, and which goes to the heart of the situation of financial globalization, is its tendency to act in the displacement, or better still, in the compression of the space-time flows, in the spheres of production and circulation, and, in the wider sense, in the dynamics of sociability as a whole. As the abovementioned[4] passage from Marx pointed out, the more developed the capital, the greater the tendency toward

---

4   Epigraph (Marx 2013b, pp. 538–539).

the "annulment of space across time" in an attempt to extend its "special trajectories of circulation" (markets). This process cannot be performed in any way other than by means of the development of innovations and technical artifacts that allow these physical and cognitive barriers to valorization to be brought down. It is this central point, therefore, seen on a large scale in different sectors, areas and aspects of technological development, some of which were mentioned earlier, that we find one of the most important keys for interpretation of the relationship between technical innovations and their material, technical and capital base, in the form of capitalist production.

The supposed cumulative nature of capitalist technological progress, in which adopted innovations delineate contexts that allow for the appearance of others, and so on, occurs precisely in the direction of the increasing acceleration of the productive or destructive movements and processes. This acceleration as the overcoming of space across time (and equally of time across space, as also occurs, as we will see, in the capitals markets) can be observed since the end of feudalism and the start of the colonial period, especially since the advent of industrialization and the "modernization" of societies. And, as such, an increasingly sophisticated constitutive phenomenon of operational cognition of the dynamic of reproduction of capital itself, is always being pushed to accelerate in each of its phases.

This interpretation can also be drawn, to a certain extent, from the ideas presented by Marx and Engels in *The Communist Manifesto*. In their analysis of the transition from feudalism to capitalism, the authors describe three of the fundamental expansion tendencies of capitalism (Musse 2010): the immanent expansion, defined by the constant revolution of the means of production and the technologies of work; an intensive expansion, that encompasses other spheres of society, going beyond the sphere of production; and, finally, a third extensive tendency, that is responsible for expanding the reach of capitalism, and crushing the internal and external pre-capitalist sectors. The unfolding of all these tendencies, in line with the consolidation of the processes of accumulation of capital, is an acceleration of both the perceptions of time, and the "integration" of areas and regions of the world that had remained previously unexplored.

In its battle against physical and temporal distances, the increasing speed of transportation and communications systems transforms the spatial and temporal condition of capital into a dynamic that goes far beyond a fixed resource of the social order. Capital therefore, in its own way, creates its own time and space, in such a way that the mobility of its different forms (production, commodities, money), just like the workforce, is always submitting itself to revolutionary transformations. It should be remembered, in relation to this, that, in

Chapter 4 of his book *Capital*, Marx offers us two complementary definitions of the concept of capital: (i) as a social relationship of purchase and sale of the labor force, and (ii) as a dynamic or movement of the valorization of value.

It is based upon these theories that Harvey (2013a) presents a more focused reading of the centrality of this element in the current configuration of capitalism, in dialog with what, as mentioned earlier, he calls a flexible regime of accumulation. If it is true that this acceleration is a constitutive tendency of the "movement of valorization of value",[5] it is possible to observe its unprecedented intensification in the dimension of the centrality given to financial valorization in today's world.

There is, therefore, as has been argued, a constitutive connection between the set of transformations that articulate the implementation of new organizational forms and of new technologies that accelerate the times of production, exchange and consumption; the growth of the services sector, the predominance of the short-term as a hegemonic time period in decision making in different productive, political and social spheres; the increasing mergers and acquisitions (concentration and centralization of capitals); and the striving for the relative advantages of industrial location and relocation; the rapid advance of Information and Communication Technologies; and, naturally, the growth and advance in prominence of the financial markets.

This constitutive connection is found in the "extraordinary flowering and transformation of the financial markets" (Harvey 2013a, p. 181), something "that appears to be truly special" in the period starting in the 1970s. In defense of this argument, the author notes that during other phases of capitalism (1890 and 1929) financial capital was capable of acquiring an important position but ended up losing it in speculation crises. Currently, the financial system, with its financial innovations that are indispensable to the mentioned "flexibilization", shows itself, in his vision, to have even more importance in comparison to other factors responsible for overcoming the stated "rigidity" characteristic of the previous period.

> I am, therefore, tempted to see the flexibility achieved in production, in the labor markets and in consumption rather as a result of the search for financial solutions to capitalism's tendencies toward crisis, than the other way around. This would imply that the financial system achieved a degree of autonomy in relation to real production unprecedented in the

---

5 "…in the monetary economies in general and in capitalist society in particular, [at] the intersection of the domain over money, time and space form a substantial nexus of social power that we cannot give ourselves the luxury of ignoring" (Harvey 2013a, p. 119).

history of capitalism, taking this latter to an era of equally theretofore unseen financial risks.

HARVEY 2013a, p. 181

The flexible accumulation has been established, in this way, following successive phases of devaluation of financial assets, within the scenario of a crisis of over-accumulation, that has led to the seeking of another means of obtaining profit in two ways: absolute and relative surplus value, or in other words, an extension of the working day with a reduction in salaries, a technological development and organizational changes. Additionally, as Chesnais (2004) has pointed out, the financial markets have, through speculation with assets, become their own sources in the search for new gains capable of placating the difficulties or complimenting the gains of the productive sector.

In this sense, of special interest in relation to the basis of our line of argument in this work, is the interpretation provided by Harvey (2013a, p. 161) that the increase of speculative negotiations with commercial papers (especially the proliferation of futures markets and derivatives in general) "discounted future time in the present time". Technological innovations, especially Information and Communication Technologies (ICT), that reduce physical distances and enable the performance of operations in real time (or better, in "low latency") in different parts of the world, allow for the rise of a complex maze of activities and deals that are difficult to understand and operate safely. The growing formation of fictitious capital for which this process provides a groundwork, reveals, in a certain way, how the future is really being expressed in the present, without the corresponding guarantees that it has any real possibility of being made concrete. As a result, there arise various technical resources and organizational forms (such as, for example, outsourcing, flexibility of hiring, futures markets and securitization) of avoiding "future shocks" (Harvey 2013a, p. 263). By means of this approach, the transactions on the financial markets can be read as a dangerous form of temporal displacement. At the same time as they anticipate obtainable or non-obtainable future profits (above all speculative ones, that are illusory from the productive point of view), allowing individual gains to be made in certain sectors, they are not capable of resolving the restraints that are essential in over-accumulation, whilst, on the contrary, there is a chance of them intensifying.

Without outlining unidirectional casualties that would otherwise attempt to go against materialist dialectics, Harvey further suggests that these compressions of time-space, by configuring "processes that revolutionize the objective qualities of space and time to the point that they force us to alter, sometimes radically, the way in which we represent the world to ourselves" (Harvey 2013a,

p. 219), are related to the changes observed in different fields of sociability, due to the disorienting and disruptive impact that this acceleration has produced on "political-economic practices, on the balance of class power, and on social and cultural life" (Harvey 2013a, p. 257).

Within other profiles, the diagnosis of this same affinity can also be found in Santos (1992), Ianni (1994) and many others.

> The notions of time and space, fundamental to our Social Sciences, are being revolutionized by social and technological developments incorporated and streamlined by movements of the global society. The realities and imagined situations launch themselves on other horizons that are broader than a province or nation, an island or an archipelago, region or continent, sea or ocean. The realities of these articulations and strategic alliances of companies, corporations, conglomerates, foundations, research centers and institutes, universities, churches, parties, unions, governments, and printed and electronic means of communication, all of which constitute and develop a fabric that stimulates relations, processes and structures, spaces and times, geographies and histories. The local and the global are both distant and close, diverse and similar. The identities are mixed up and multiplied. The articulations and speeds are deterritorialized and territorialized in other spaces with meanings.
>
> IANNI 1994, pp. 155–156

Harvey's suspicion (2013a, p. 256), rooted in his methodological materialist contribution, in dialog with the formulations of Marx and Engels discussed here, is that "post-modernism is a kind of response to a new set of experiences of space and time, a new round of 'compression of time-space'" in the history of the development of the capitalist mode of production (that annihilates space by time and shoots down the future in the present). As such, the new ways into which we are being induced to "live" time and space, that are somehow tied to the myriad of cultural, political and social transformations, experienced in the sphere of the "post-modern", are somehow based upon the new form of economic organization that has been installed since the advent of the crisis of over-accumulation of capital, noted in the twilight of Fordism-Keynesianism.

That said, we should suggest that, despite being clearly directed toward the strengthening of the accumulation of wealth, particularly financial wealth, the development of Information and Communication Technologies, and even the compression of space-time, parts of the contradictory complex that is capitalist society, can also act in the sense of promoting greater transparency, democracy, visualization of tensions and social needs that were previously hidden, and even the articulation of subjects for anti-systemic struggles. There are countless cases that demonstrate this eminently political dimension of technology, suspended as it is between hegemonic and counter-hegemonic possibilities of appropriation, such as, for example, the leaking of secret documents by Wikileaks and Edward Snowden, as well as the "Arab Spring" and the "Occupy" movements around the world. In this way, turning away from the supposed neutrality that would be the equivalent of the diagnosis of an "equality of conditions" in the field of technology, we need to reinforce the evaluation presented in the previous session that points to a materialist rather than deterministic understanding of technology, in so far as it is understood as non-neutral and partially autonomous, ontologically anchored in its "social content", and overdetermined, ultimately, by economic practice.

CHAPTER 4

Digitalized Finance: Informatization at the Service of Financial Dominance

4.1   The State of the Art of Digitalized Finance at the Beginning of the 21st Century

> Remember that time is money [...]
> BENJAMIN FRANKLIN[1]

When we think of the stock exchange, the first thing that generally springs to mind is a mass of people carrying mobile telephones and incessantly shouting at each other about share purchases and sales, whilst they look anxiously, with expressions of euphoria or panic, at screens that quickly relay price information and quotes. In fact, this image, practically a metonymy of financial capitalism established in photo, television and cinema coverage, hardly exists anymore. Now silent, the physical space at the stock exchange, just like the people who previously shouted on their floors, have little or no practical function. Trades now take place on powerful computers and in data centers that are operated 24 hours a day throughout the world. Instead of the old criers, buyers and sellers of stocks, there are physicists, astrophysicists, mathematicians and economists trained at the world's most prestigious universities who design algorithms and automated business strategies that are to be implemented in speeds of milliseconds. The "animal spirit" of the markets, free from many of its material bonds, today runs along incredibly high-speed fiber optic transmission lines. This important change occurred thanks to the advance of the Information and Communication Technologies that have taken place, mostly, over the last two decades.

Since the beginning of the 1980s, a moment that, as we have discussed, marks the acceleration of the process of structural economic transformation defined as financial globalization, this advance in technological development, in relation to the capitals markets, has basically followed two main tendencies: (i) large-scale investment in the construction of systems for the production and circulation of information in real time; and (ii) the production of means

---

1   Franklin 1736 *Apud* Weber 2004, p. 42.

capable of allowing trades to be made simultaneously in different markets as fast as possible.

To cite two examples of business models that became paradigms for these two respective tendencies: it was in 1981 that Michael Bloomberg, at the time a fired Wall Street broker, founded the company Innovative Market Systems, later renamed with his surname, to compile and present financial information on terminals (systems visualized on monitors) for companies, banks and brokers, and to use this technology to make electronic trading on fixed income commercial papers. These days, the communications conglomerate Bloomberg is one of the biggest in the world, a leader in its field of commercialization of information and data for the financial market.[2] One year later, in 1982, having worked from various universities and for the US intelligence service, the renowned mathematician James Simmons opened Renaissance Technologies, a financial resources administration firm that believed in the use of complex mathematical models processed on computers to locate inefficiencies in high-liquidity securities. By means of this strategy, the company now administrates the biggest and most profitable hedge fund[3] in the world.

These days, the radicalization of this process points to the joining of these two dimensions into a single unit, or in other words, the complete integration of production and circulation of information at different levels with automatic high-speed trading on the markets, by means of the highly intensive processing of data in increasing volumes, varieties and complexities, structured in chains of significance, with the assistance of high-performance computation within what is generally referred to as Big Data.

---

2 Defining itself as news agency and compiler of financial and economic data for monitoring the market, Bloomberg now has more than 12,000 employees around the world (including mathematicians, physicists and astrophysicists) and has been operating in Brazil since 1998. This international giant's system for the financial market synthesizes more than 500,000 news items per day and offers its own reports, studies and analyses. As well as allowing trades to be performed in seconds, directly from its information platform (in a manner that is automated and high-frequency, depending upon the needs of the clients), it offers a chat system in which all those subscribing to the platform around the world (around 350,000, amongst which are Ministers of state and directors of large banks, and state and private companies) can be contacted directly. Each of these systems, called "Terminals", can be leased for US$2,000 per month, this being a business model used other companies such as Reuters and Agência Estado in Brazil. In 2013, a Bloomberg publicly accepted the accusation that it had improperly used its clients' business information. For more on this visit <http://www.nytimes.com/2013/05/13/business/media/bloomberg-admits-terminal-snooping.html>. Accessed on: Nov 28, 2017.
3 Highly-speculative high-risk investment fund, with few restrictions, that simultaneously combines currency transactions, shares, commodities and securities.

If this scenario starts to materialize, bringing with it new developments and consequences that need to be investigated, the current state of integrated, fast and complex globalized finance, as well as its economic and social consequences, will also need more organized explanations. It is this objective that we now wish to address.

Since times long past, the access to privileged information has been a fundamental element in the management of business and trade. This continual attempt to predict future events, be they natural, social or political events, or even information on products, resources or raw-materials in the markets, existed long before the rise of modern capitalism as it exists today. A telescope made available to a grain trader in one port, for example, could serve as an important technical instrument in gaining a competitive advantage over his competitors, in so far as it would allow him to know in advance which ship would be bringing a certain product and, as such, make trade deals based upon the advance information. Here, just as (or more) important than the information itself – since after docking, the vessel and type of cargo would be common knowledge – is the time difference between it being obtained by one player and another, making it a key element for the exploration of the potential gain that this difference entails. In some way, the same analogy can be applied to an understanding of the reasons that engage the movement of technical development for the operation of modern financial markets: anticipate, compile and organize information in advance and/or before your competitors, in order to use them for economic gains. Hence, these dimensions, information and time are the basic center points of the rapid advance in the use of Information and Communication Technologies in the financial markets. "We deal with the most perishable product that exists: information", commented Interviewee A,[4] an executive at a company that produces technology products for the Brazilian financial market.

In his book *The Protestant Ethic and the Spirit of Capitalism*, Max Weber cites the sermon given by Benjamin Franklin "Necessary Hints To Those That Would Be Rich", written in 1736, providing a voice to what he defined as the "spirit" of capitalism, the utilitarian ethos of the modern bourgeois businessperson. The phrase "time is money" originally comes from this text, and it has become one that would be forever recognized as one of the best-known phrases of the philosophy of practical life under the modern capitalist world. Almost three

---

4   Information obtained during an interview given by Interviewee A, an executive at a capitals markets technology company, to the researcher on 10-Jun-2014, in the city of São Paulo. 1 file .mpeg4 (90min 32sec).

centuries later, few phrases could be more didactic in the attempt to explain the logic and dynamics of the operational functioning of the financial market in times of the information revolution: time, today divided into units that would have been unimaginable to both Franklin and Weber, means a great deal of money in the markets.

Exploring the increasing flexibilization and liberalization of the financial markets at the global level, the technological advance has ended up imposing itself as one of the principal frontiers of competition between investors, jealous of ever greater gains in the smallest period of time possible. The trajectory of this advance, that we are looking to identify in this book, ended up creating a scenario in which automated "High Frequency Trading" is used as a tool for speculation and arbitration between different assets in the markets, in margins of micro-seconds or even nanoseconds, increasing the gains of those investors who take best advantage of these technologies.

This tendency for the compression of time, however, has its origins, as we are seeking to demonstrate, in the very process of configuration of the financial dominance in the globalized capitalist economy, in so far as this search finds new forms of valorization for the capital that has over-accumulated in other areas of the economy. Institutional and regulatory changes, explicitly designed to increase competitiveness, have opened the way for a market structure that is favorable to automated negotiation. This is because the increase in volume and speed of the – now liberalized – transactions in the markets, have, in turn, forced a reconfiguration of the structures of negotiation. In a matter of just a few years, the time spent on the processing of offers and closure of trades on the stock exchanges has moved on from being measured in minutes and seconds to being counted in "milli-", "micro-", and even "nano-" seconds, as is now required. This is an important competitive advantage when in the hands of those players who have these resources, and who thus find, through increasing gains, conditions and incentives to continue investing in these advances. As such, each piece of technology is quickly overtaken by another, as the level of ability and sophistication continues to rise, forcing new challenges and difficulties for all categories of investor.

Even though the old rationale of obtaining the most gain in the shortest amount of time possible continues as the comprehensive pivot of the *modus operandi* of digitalized finance, the new reality is capable of producing instabilities and problems that have never been seen before. Thus there arises the importance of being well understood; there is no way of properly explaining the financial markets at the beginning of the 21st century, or the role they occupy in the globalized economy, without moving further into a discussion of the logic and dynamics of its operational functioning. Be it due to the increasing reduction of the human factor in all stages of the negotiating process in the markets, or be it because of the new possibilities that the – literally – virtual gains open up (through assets, financial innovations and trading models that had previously been inviable without the support of these technological resources), a reading directed toward an understanding of the state of the art of the current technology of the financial markets could sustain and provide new elements to the important discussion concerning the sophistication of the commodity fetishism in the capitalist economy (in its various dimensions), as well as of the continued expansion of the gap between the markets and the most pressing material needs of social life.

As we discussed in Chapter 2, if it is ultimately subject to economic determination, it is true that this process of development of the Information and Communication Technologies, in relation to the financial markets, still has a series of other influences, consisting of factors and logical-cognitive antecedents as an expression of the various social practices that materialize in the content of these technical artifacts. Outlining some of these is, therefore, of central importance to the context of this book.

One of the most important logical-cognitive antecedents that make possible the automation of the operations in the markets is the sophistication of the mathematical models used for pricing and prediction of the ways financial assets will perform, and in the establishment of strategies for its negotiation. It is known that such advances have had a great impact on the evolution of computerization as a whole. In the financial markets, particularly, the algorithms of negotiation (logic sequences of parameters that, once executed, lead one to a certain activity/goal) have become the basis for the cognitive support of the "robots" designed to automatically execute orders.

In the 1980s and 1990s, mathematicians, economists and investors started to use Chaos Theory and Stochastic Calculus to find patterns in the financial markets. Combining mathematics, statistics, knowledge of patterns, Game Theory and large stocks of commercial data, they developed complex models supported by powerful algorithms to predict the behavior of the markets and thereby obtain advantages in trades. Since then, even after the 2008 financial crisis, when many were put to the test, agents have placed their fervent confidence in these models. With the passing of time, these mathematical models have become more sophisticated in so far as they have advanced the capacity for the processing of the data and information used to define their parameters. Out of this was born Algorithmic Trading or "AlgoTrading" (AT), the automated negotiations performed by computers, that execute mathematically-guided strategies for purchase and/or sale to obtain financial gains in the markets.

High Frequency Trading (HFT), a direct outcome of this technical advance, is no more than a form of Algorithmic Trading that executes orders based upon its strategy at ultra-high speed, thanks to the support of cutting-edge information technologies in various dimensions (software, hardware and network infrastructures). The most sophisticated High Frequency Traders (HFTs) use automated learning and artificial intelligence to make gains from knowledge of the negotiating structure of the markets and information about the flow of orders from investors. The general principles for the adoption of this model of negotiation are, basically: i) economy of work and reduction of risks from the "human factor"[5] (emotions, subjectivity) via automation; ii) an increase in the speeds and volumes of negotiation for the obtaining of large-scale gains through small arbitrations performed thousands of times in minute periods of time and, simultaneously; iii) the obtaining of a certain "omnipresence" in the operationalization of trades through the processing of a high volume of data and information on assets, prices, offers, etc., made in the markets. Based upon the exploration of these possibilities, the market players design their short, medium and long-term strategies, with or without high-speed support, depending upon the gain objectives and the investment profiles. Even in relation to the HFTs, there are various distinct strategies for their application and use in the markets. Beyond these specifications, we are here most interested in the construction of a general overview of how they function and what they do from the point of view of technological advancement in the markets.

Innovations in hardware and software to meet the needs of the globalized capitals markets, that have seen enormous growth in their volumes, and volatilities in relation to various types of assets in different locations, have required the development of sophisticated electronic negotiation strategies. As part of this increasingly complex context, investors have been relying principally on solutions of connectivity to access opportunities for gain in different parts of the world in the shortest amounts of time possible. The almost simultaneous analysis and exploration of these differences of liquidity are some of the various challenges facing every type of investor. Amongst these participants in the market, the ability to accelerate processes, analyze and react to this absolute avalanche of data is a fundamental component in the composition of their competitive advantage. Regardless of the interests, objectives or nature of the investors, speed becomes an overriding factor in their activities. This ends up

---

5   The human factor, however, is always present in all the systems, since these are conceived and produced, originally, by other human beings who are equally likely to make "errors". On the other hand, systems fail, neither only or centrally, as a result of their human "content", but because of the very imperceptible unpredictability of the complex reality.

being the determining factor in the advance of the discussed technologies: the search for a low level of latency.

Latency is a technical term widely used in the day-to-day operations of digitalized finance. Despite being defined in different ways in different contexts by agents of the market, it can be generally understood as being the period of time that a package of information takes to travel the distance between its origin and its destination, or in other words, the amount of time that a system waits to receive the information traveling from one party to another. Therefore, to further reduce the latency means reducing times and/or distances in the circulation of data and information, an objective that is absolutely determinant in the implementation of operation and negotiation technologies in the financial markets.

But there are limits to the increase in speed in the world of electronic negotiations. By definition, the maximum theoretical limit on the speed of the transit of information in a network is the speed of light, something that is a very long way from being a reality in any current network, even the fastest ones. This is because there exists an inherent latency, amongst other reasons, in the makeup of the materials of the hardware used, as well as a period of time necessary for the processing of the software. And it is on overcoming this frontier that the big players are hard at work. As soon as one of the participants in the market surpasses a certain speed limit, the competition for the gains obtained from this advantage mean that the others have to achieve it as well. As such, the cycle of competition in the digitalized markets, anchored, especially, in technological advancement, is never ending, and the constant changes that we see in the capitals markets demand ever more technological advances. Furthermore, the increase in the volumes and numbers of trades performed increase the production of more data. Indeed, the technical advances in this field themselves further lead to the collection of other, previously unexplored information, that pushes the capacity of the systems even further. This, in turn, further increases the need for greater performance, at an increasing level of evolution, which, on average, doubles every two years, as Interviewee B,[6] a high-level executive in the technology area of BM&FBovespa, who has been monitoring the evolution of this market for years, explained to us.[7]

---

6 Information obtained during an interview given by Interviewee B, an executive in the technology area of BM&FBovespa, on 09-Jun-2014, in the city of São Paulo. 1 file .mpeg4 (64min 25seg).

7 This observation fits in well with the statement from the Moore Law, which was explained in the previous chapter.

The much commented upon (and dreaded) latency – that, despite usually being measured in milliseconds, is relative according to different types of operators and their negotiation strategies, and which require more or less speed for their execution – has various origins. As such, the search for the reduction in time of the trajectory of data occurs in different ways. The three principal areas highlighted by numerous specialists and members of the market as providing the fundamental origins of latency, or the technological dimensions in which the innovations seek to reduce it, are: i) the network through which the messages pass; ii) the programs and the applications that operate them; iii) or the hardware that processes such information. Without having any real ability to measure these failings, which in themselves only demand other technological resources, it becomes difficult to discern whether the "slow" speed is caused by a network which does not have sufficient band width, by a badly programmed application, or by a lack of power in the servers that process the information. Therefore, from the technological point of view – that is continually extending into deals as a whole on the markets – negotiation has reached a level at which the entire infrastructure needs to be monitored so that any traces of slowness can be identified and eliminated. Depending upon how an investor explores his gains and relies upon high speed execution, he should be aware of these three dimensions as integral parts of the same whole.

Aware of this reality, one Brazilian company, a leader in the domestic market of provision of technological solutions for investors' operations, ended up extending its activities, with greater intensity beginning in 2007, into the three areas mentioned. With clients in 34 countries, the company has five data centers located outside Brazil, as well as two within the country, and even its own power generation plant, which, in cases of emergency, can supply its needs for up to four and a half days. With its own infrastructure network, which has its own system of fiber optic cables, the company provides a niche telecommunications service for investors who cannot consider being at the mercy of the slow connectivity provided to other Brazilian consumers by the large telecommunications companies. As Interviewee C,[8] a representative of this company, told us:

> [...] we basically divide our technological solution services into three factors: quality information, or in other words, data that is correct, reliable and intelligently packaged; software containing top-quality features; and

---

8 Information obtained during an interview given by Interviewee C, a representative of a capitals markets technology company, on 04-Jun-2014, in the city of São Paulo. Field notes.

a solid infrastructure, capable of protecting them and ensuring they continue functioning well. This triumvirate, this mix of data, software and infrastructure, is our daily mantra, and we always create new products by using it. By working this way, we obtain the aggregated value of our solutions (verbal information).

As such, it can be seen that the discussion over low latency loses its substance when it is not accompanied by other dimensions such as processing capacity, stability, reliability and quality in the execution of the trading systems, since the speed will have little value if the execution of the orders is not intelligent and precise in terms of the best trades. Even so, the advances in the area basically continue with a focus upon the reduction of time, always accompanied by the greatest possible efficiency in the executions.

This situation led a number of technology consultants to the financial market, including Larry Tabb, one of the most well-known in the US market, to discuss the viability of pricing of time itself in the operation of the markets. Even though the exercise he performs in the 2008 report *The Value of a Millisecond*, is, in itself, not well supported from a theoretical point of view, the report is eye-opening in that it presents a didactic perspective on the technical meanderings of the race we are discussing here, to the extent that it could, in general terms, but with some differences in intensity and dimension – above all due to the institutional factors and economic scenarios – be seen in the reality of the Brazilian capitals market, where we will venture in search of some of the information and conclusions discussed in this book. Based upon our observations, the author is correct when he points out, for example that, due to the high level of competitiveness, investors in the financial market are generally found in the first sectors to adopt new, cutting edge computer technologies.

> But as with any technology, one thing is clear: the innovation in financial data acceleration is arriving from all areas of software and hardware research. Financial services institutions are always willing first adopters, as competitiveness affects profitability.
> TABB 2008, p. 13

Interviewee D,[9] a representative of an important Brazilian stockbroking firm, when discussing the transformation that the new business model has brought

---

9 Information obtained during an interview given by Interviewee D, a representative of a stock brokerage firm, on 09-Jun-2014, in the city of São Paulo. 1 file .mpeg4 (47min 07seg).

about at his company, confirmed that: "we are no longer simply a brokerage. More than an investment manager that invests in technological modernization, we now define ourselves as a technology company that negotiates investments". In line with this statement, we can see, for example, that all the most successful Brazilian brokerage firms have entire departments, sometimes as big if not bigger than the others, focused on programming and the production of niche technological solutions, developed especially to meet the needs of their clients.

In fact, as we will discuss later on, the new scenario is especially challenging for stockbroking companies and their employees. Many have had to close their doors, and those that have survived are fighting against the same fate. The inexorable trend toward concentration of the markets, clearly seen amongst stockbrokers, is pushing them to completely reconfigure their functions.

The business models of the stock exchanges (as well as the alternative markets, since there are countries, such as the United States, where financial assets/instruments are also traded outside the exchanges) depends, above all, on their ability to receive, aggregate and meet purchase and sale orders of assets. The traditional model for stock exchanges, that still co-exists, in a certain form, with the new emerging one, entrusts to human beings, specialists, the mission of attracting buyers and sellers to the same trading space. The specialized professionals and companies, the stockbrokers, basically take their gains from the commission or brokering that they charge for this work. They are also, based upon their specialist knowledge, still responsible for advising and supporting their clients on the best investment options.

However, anchored in the greater use of high-speed automated trading, the new model is increasingly abandoning qualitative evaluations of market behavior and combining purchase and sale orders by basically using two variables: time and price. If this is increasingly becoming the reality, as the picture of financial dominance in the global economy becomes ever more entrenched, the intensive use of technology makes such logic that much more pressing, above all for the large investors. As such, brokers and the stock exchanges themselves are led to reconfigure their business models, as we will discuss later on, in relation to the reality of the Brazilian capitals market.

Within this scenario, in which the increasing reduction in operating times benefits and attracts investors, above all those who trade in large volumes, the ability to quickly receive and send information on what is in their portfolios has become essential for the competitive standing of the stock exchanges themselves, which charge high prices for some of this data. In response, they embrace the electronic trading model even more, adopting the technological advances and solutions that support it. This means that short-term trades with single day effects (intraday), focusing on speculation and the arbitrage of assets by means of the high-intensity processing of market data, which is more susceptible to competition working with a low level of latency, have additional incentives to become dominant. Thus, just as the increasing desire for fast and safe short-term gains activates the development of new technological strategies, tools and solutions in order to perform automated trades at high-speed, such advances, in turn, enable and further expand these opportunities for gain, encouraging more resources to be directed into the advancement of this trading model.

In the modern version of Cronus' children's battle against his merciless, all-devouring power, there still remains one more frontier: space. After increasing the band-width, simplifying the program codes and increasing the processing ability of the machines, there is another way used to reduce latency: reduce the physical distance or the length of the journey along which the data and information must travel. This is what IT specialists usually term the exploration of "network topology" or proximity in financial market jargon.

The best-known method by which investors attempt to reduce the route between their production servers and the stock exchanges and markets, is by ensuring that both are located in the same place. This resource, known as Co-location, allows investors to place their server units (hosts) inside the stock exchange building itself (which naturally charges for this facility), thus reducing the distance between the trade order and its execution in the market.

This segment therefore demands and encourages a whole series of additional investments in the low latency market: servers, connectivity providers, and means capable of technically enabling these partnerships between stock exchanges and markets and their new class of privileged clients, or in other words, high-intensity operators who accept that they will pay high sums to be physically closer to the center of the operations, thus reducing latency in terms of external communication, and therefore profiting through the competitive advantage that this difference offers over investors who do not possess this resource. The competition, however, does not end here. Even within this "special class" of investors, the race to reduce latency continues in the other aspects that we described earlier.

This proximity of the centers of execution and processing of trades on the stock exchanges and markets is not explored, however, only through the co-location service. The race for low latency gets further extended by the installation of operations infrastructures in buildings and external locations that are physically close to the stock exchanges, which, causes the value of real estate and rents in the surrounding neighborhoods to rise. The same applies

DIGITALIZED FINANCE

to the materials used and the routes taken by fiber optic cables that form these networks.

The co-location resource is already widely used in Brazil.[10] Starting with a minimum of 0.2 percent of the total daily volume traded in the Bovespa segment (share market) in September 2010, the use of co-location – the category that brings together Algorithmic Trading and High-Frequency Trading operations – was 15.6 percent of the total average daily volume traded in December 2016. In relation to the percentage of the total average number of daily transactions, it starts at 1.4 percent and reaches 43.5 percent of the total in the same time period, as can be seen in Figure 2. Since November 2013, when it was responsible for 15.6 percent of the total volume traded, Bovespa has stopped publishing the sums corresponding to the trading share of HFTs. However, its growing importance can be estimated based upon the number for the use of the co-location service that, despite also taking into account algorithmic strategies/trading that are not just those performed at high-speed, it is mostly used, as we know, by HFTs, for which, keeping their servers within the physical

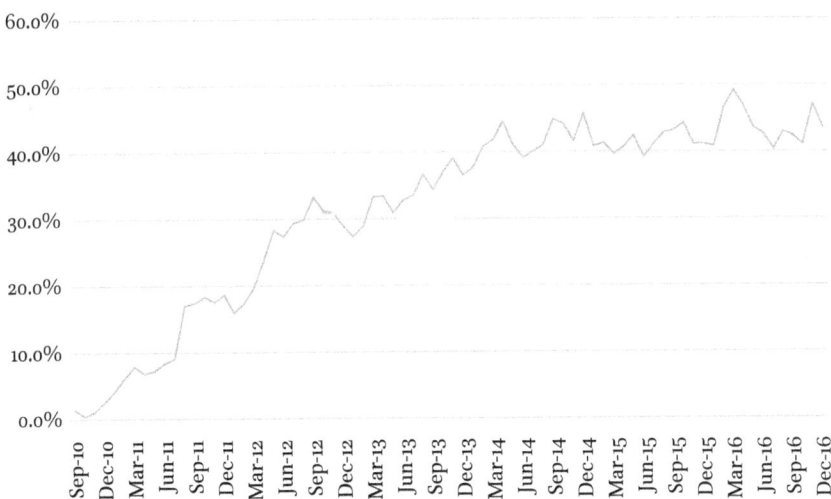

FIGURE 2   Co-location (number of trades) – Bovespa segment.
SOURCE: BM&FBOVESPA; OWN ELABORATION

---

10   The stock exchange does not make public the amount charged for an investor to operate in this way. According to the information of a financial market technology businessperson, provided during one of the interviews performed for this publication, the price in 2014 was US$10,000 per month per machine (host) hosted under co-location together with the stock exchange's servers.

trading spaces is essential in the formation of their latency arbitrage strategies. To get an idea of this, also in November 2013, while the HFTs alone, as we have seen, accounted for 15.6 percent of the total volume traded on Bovespa, the financial volume of the trades made via the co-location service (that includes the HFTs) amounted to 14.1 percent of the total, a differential of just 1.5 percent. Using this margin of approximation, it is possible to confirm that more than 40 percent of all the transactions made on Bovespa were performed by automated negotiation mechanisms/strategies (Figure 2). In every case, the growth in the period was astonishing.

Something not so different takes place in the BM&F segment (the futures and commodities market), a space where financial derivatives and commodities are traded. From the insignificant level of 0.15 percent in January 2009, the HFTs reached 22.5 percent of the average daily volume traded (Figure 3).

And the trend for growth continues. According to information from Interviewee E,[11] an executive at BM&F Bovespa, the space reserved for the co-location service at the Brazilian stock exchange was completely occupied in 2014.[12]

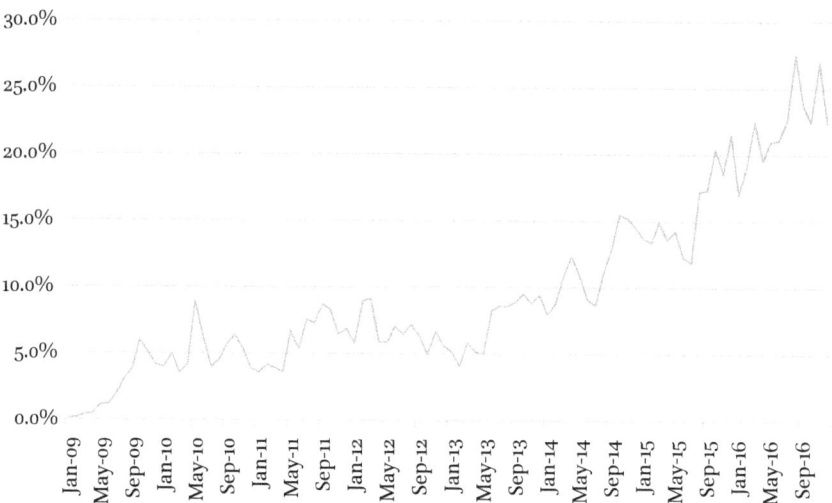

FIGURE 3 HFT (daily number of trades) – BM&F segment.
SOURCE: BM&FBOVESPA; OWN ELABORATION

---

11 Information obtained during an interview given by Interviewee E, an executive at BM&FBovespa, on 06-Jun-2014, in the city of São Paulo. 2 files .mpeg4 (122min19seg).
12 According to Interviewee F, the owner of an important technology company serving the financial market: "UBS [Swiss investment bank and brokerage], that bought Link [in 2010], that was one of the most important Brazilian brokerages, is now the one with the most robots operating in co-location. If I'm not mistaken, they have about 80 robots

Also, according to the executive, meeting the growing demand for this service was one of the reasons that led stock exchange to build a new and bigger[13] Data Center in São Paulo.

Put simply, if, during the era in which the trading floor was physical, the traders elbowed their way into space on the stock exchanges and markets as they tried to make the best deals, this elbowing is now done between computers, in the geography and topology of the trading systems networks. Basically, the human operator has been replaced by a software (robot),[14] and the time difference necessary to make an offer has been cut to milliseconds – precisely the time that a robot takes to make a decision based upon the technical standards available.

To cite one example that demonstrates the point to which the race for high-speed has reached, in 2010, the company Spread Networks (that became famous after its story was told in the book *Flash Boys*[15]) completed the construction of its own high-speed connection between the New York and Chicago financial markets. Whilst the old fiber-optic connection between these two financial centers zig-zagged between train lines, mountains and other geographical obstacles, the company's cable followed a route – thanks to great effort and extremely high costs, estimated at US$300 million – that was practically dead-straight. So, what was the result of this investment? It reduced the communication time of the round-trip journey between New York and Chicago from 16 to 13 milliseconds, a difference considered to be enormous for big investors and HFT companies, for whom arriving three milliseconds after their competitors could be quite simply fatal for their businesses. To have an idea of what this means, the blink of an eye by a human being generally takes about 400 milliseconds. At the time, this could certainly be an awful lot, but by the end of 2013, the Spread Networks cable had already become obsolete. This is

---

      operating inside the stock exchange. The majority of these robots that are currently in the stock exchange belong to large foreign investors: Credit Suisse, JP Morgan, Morgan Stanley etc.". (verbal information). Interview given on 14-May-2014, in Uberlândia (MG). 1 arquivo .mpeg4 (208min54seg).

13   For more information on the new Data Center see: <http://datacenterdabolsa.com.br/en/>. Accessed on: Dec 03, 2017.

14   The meaning of the word "robot", connected with the dimension of software, covers the automation of operations that involve the sweeping of a large search area, and which, as such, requires heuristics to take advantage of an intelligent search, that in any other way would take much longer to obtain the same results. What classifies an algorithm as a robot, therefore, is the possession of heuristics, or in other words, empirical rules for navigation and the taking of decisions in a certain space of data searches.

15   Lewis, Michael (2014), Flash Boys: A Wall Street Revolt. New York: WW Norton &Company.

because another company, Microwave Technology, reduced this period of time first to 10, then to 9, and finally to 8.5 milliseconds.[16]

But if the race is anchored, principally, in the reduction of time, it is important to note that, despite all the other factors fulfilling a specific role, as we have shown, the software[17] plays an absolutely central role in the configuration of the strategies of the most competitive HFTs. As such, taken as starting points, the other factors come to support the most sophisticated trading softwares in their daily operations.[18]

This is because information technology follows an evolutionary pattern that, in a certain way, has structured its levels (hardware, middleware, software), and the Internet is the crowning peak of the stratification process. This is a modular form of architecture, with independent layers, in which one can be developed and can operate without directly interfering in the use or potential significance that could occur in another, even though they may, naturally, complement each other's operations. It is necessary, therefore, to understand the function which each one of these elements occupies within this complex. Without a good operations software, a powerful computer or a privileged position in the geography of the network function relatively ineffectively. As Pedro Rezende,[19] a Professor at the Department of Computer Science at the University of Brasília,[20] with vast experience in programming languages, the

---

16   Investment has also been made in ultra-high-speed connections via microwaves. Renaissance Technologies, one of the world's biggest hedge funds, is developing an ultra-fast trading system based upon atomic clocks to keep itself ahead in the Wall Street race for speed.

17   In line with the formulations created by Andy Clark (2003), we believe software to be a prosthesis of thinking, that enables communicative capacity and the reasoning, deduction, treatment and filtering of data for the production of information in the mind of a specific receptor.

18   It is worth noting that the growth of HFTs on a global scale is not only about speed. Especially in the United States, where this trading model has reached its most advanced level, banks, which have had to face more rigid regulation and more pronounced capital demands in the aftermath of the 2008 financial crisis, have been abandoning the old business model of selling to buyers and buying from sellers so that they themselves perform the transactions, something that is called market-making. In some cases, High-Frequency Trading firms have closed impressive deals with these financial giants. Such is the case of JP Morgan Chase, which, in August 2016, agreed to the use of the Virtu Financial technology to trade on the United States' Public Securities Market. The banks have also returned to the High-Frequency Traders, including Global Trading Systems (GTS), to complete their clients' currency purchase and sale orders.

19   Interview given on 26-May-2014, in Brasília (DF). 2 files .mpeg4 (137min38seg).

20   He also occupied the position of Professor in the Mathematics Department at UnB (1976 to 78) and at the National Hispanic University (USA, 1986). In Silicon Valley, he worked

organization of hardware and software, cryptography and data security, explained to us in an interview:

> [...] hardware has become a commodity, is replaceable, and in this case, the stock exchanges are always on the vanguard. Furthermore, there is a part of the software that is equally commoditized, and this is the software called middleware – an operating system, web support, and database. It is only at the application level that the bulk of the specialization will exist. In the financial market, this is done extremely securely and with ruthless competition. They are automation softwares, developed in house, to automate the investors' business models. The logic is simple. An office automation software automates the activities performed in an office – writing, classifying, printing, etc. – and a factory automation software automates the manufacturing process, and so on. The same thing takes place in the financial market, where software automates trading processes (verbal information).

In summary, information does not show itself to have any value, *per se*, in the markets. In line with Stiglitz (2001), we agree that information can only be exploited, as such, based upon its asymmetries, which exist in all economies. These informational asymmetries or imperfections, as the author explained when receiving the Nobel Prize for Economics, are fundamental to understanding not only the market economy,[21] but also the political economy, with consequences for the whole political process of every society.

Furthermore, anchored in a reading that seeks to draw points between semiotics and cybernetics, in the understanding of socio-technical systems, as the financial markets currently are, and together with the questions posed by Rezende (2009), we are led to conclude that the information does not exist, in itself, nor as an abstract entity, be it in cyberspace, or be it in the physical world, but only in a communication context that involves, at least, a pole with

---

with quality control for the Macintosh operational system at Apple Computer, with consultation systems for digitalized voice databases at DataDial, and with the first hypertext applications, the precursors of the web, developing HyperCard stacks for Macintoshes (1986 to 88). For his full curriculum, visit <http://cic.unb.br/~pedro/curriculum_curto.htm>. Accessed on: Jul 20, 2017.

21 In the words of Interviewee G, a representative of a large, international technology company serving the financial market: "The most valuable thing in the market is information. The capitals market is essentially made up of information" (verbal information). Interview given on 09-Jun-2014, in the city of São Paulo. 1 file .mpeg4 (74min42seg).

cognitive abilities. The information can be understood, therefore, as the capacity that a flow of data has to transform the state of knowledge of whoever receives or transmits it. In the case of the one who transmits it, this change is indirect, secondary, connected with the shift in knowledge of whoever receives the information.[22]

As such, the data, which should not be taken as a synonym of information, is simply a group of symbols in any cognitive context, in which these symbols may or may not represent information to someone. For this representation to occur, however, it is necessary for there to be a cognitive screen that is capable of organizing it, or in other words, a language. It is this language that allows the information to produce the referred change in the state of knowledge. What allows the economic exploitation of this process, therefore, is not necessarily the change of the state of knowledge, but the change in a secondary context – "who else knows what I know". Put simply, data is the raw material of information (economically exploited in the markets).

Therein resides the HFTs' gains in the exploitation of time as a competitive advantage, as an instrument for obtaining privileged information. Once again, as Stiglitz (2001) points out, it is the asymmetry of information that is conditioning the exploration of this gain (revenue). This reality is expanded in a context of a high and increasing flow of information, such as that of the capitals markets, that thus makes it possible for new exploitable asymmetries of information. Those who have the best channels for obtaining privileged information in the shortest period of time and the best strategies for exploring such asymmetries therefore make the greatest gains.

Within this context, if it is obtained quickly, for automated operation in the markets, or if it is in its organized, intelligent and practical assimilation to allow investment decisions to be made, including automated decisions – a niche explored by communications giants such as Bloomberg, Reuters and others –, the information obtained and operated quickly and intelligently by softwares and their respective infrastructures is, certainly, the Gordian knot of competition in the markets. As Interviewee C, a representative of one of the biggest companies providing technological solutions for the financial market in Brazil, very well summarized it:

> From then until now [from the 1980s to today] the Internet has changed practically everything. The dispute is concentrated on the software, on the intelligence of the systems, and our biggest challenges today basically involve minimizing latencies in the means of communication, and in the

---

22 For a discussion of information from a semiotic angle, see Coelho Netto (1983, pp. 119–195).

software, and presenting information in a way that is organized, intelligent and flexible, and that can be customized (verbal information).

4.2 The Consequences of Digitalization in the Capitals Markets

Tell me what the rules are and I'll figure out how we can make money around them.
JEFFREY C. SPRECHER, CEO, Intercontinental Exchange – ICE

The interminable race to obtain more speed, in terms of the markets becoming digitalized, is far from showing signs of abating. Over recent years, the adoption of HFTs has grown considerably throughout the world.

In Brazil, data from BM&FBovespa shows that, in 2013,[23] HFTs were already responsible for 15.6 percent of the entire financial volume involving shares (Figure 4). In 2010, this percentage was no more than 5 percent. If the other AlgoTradings (ATs), are taken into account, deduced from the data presented

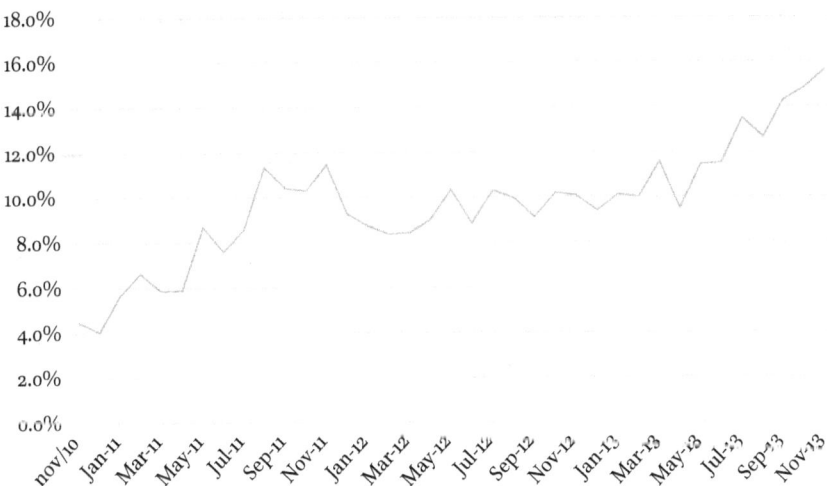

FIGURE 4 HFT (daily financial volume) – Bovespa segment.
SOURCE: BM&FBOVESPA; OWN ELABORATION

---

23   As we have seen, since November 2013, when it was responsible for 15.6 percent of the total volume traded, Bovespa has stopped publishing the sums corresponding to the trading share of HFTS.

above concerning the transactions performed through use of the co-location system, more than 40 percent of the total stock exchange transactions are now made by robots, through automated strategies.

In the US markets, it is estimated that this percentage surpasses the 50 percent mark, having reached its peak of around 60–70 percent between 2009[24] and 2014. In the European markets, including the United Kingdom,[25] the estimated average use is currently around 40 percent of the total number of transactions.

Due to difficulties in making estimates, the projections are not consensual and generally tend to vary. A report by Shorter and Miller (2014), based upon data from the Tabb Group, an American capitals markets technology consultancy company, points out that, in 2012, HFTs were responsible for more than 60 percent of the volume of contracts in future markets in the United States. A 2013 study carried out by the Commodity Futures Trading Commission (CFTC) concerning automated trading reported that, in 2012, around 92 percent of the volume of contracts in exchange traded futures in the United States was performed electronically. Also, according to the CFTC, in 2010, trades made using automated trading systems represented 50 percent of the total volume traded in a significant series of exchange futures products. A report from the Deutsche Bank (Kaya 2016), also based upon data from the Tabb group, divides into two phases the evolution of the participation of HFTs in the total number of trades: i) the pre-crisis period, notable for its increase on both sides of the Atlantic; and ii) the post-crisis period when they supposedly drop off. In Europe, the participation of HFTs in the total number of share transactions rose from practically zero in 2005 to around 40 percent in 2010. In the United States, from 20 percent of trades in 2005, HFTs were responsible for more than 60 percent of the market in 2009. However, with the financial crisis, this ascension would have been interrupted and its share of the market would have started to fall. The figures in the report show that, as of 2014, the participation of HFTs in the shares markets fell to 35 percent and 50 percent of the total market in Europe and the United States, respectively. According to the author, a series of factors explains this drop in market participation of HFTs in the total number of shares traded, amongst which are: a) a drop in the revenue and profit due to

---

24 Tabb, Larry.; Iati, Robert; Sussman, Adam (2009), *US Equity High Frequency Trading: Strategies, Sizing and Market Structure*. Tabb Group, 2009.

25 Foresight: The Future of Computer Trading in Financial Markets. Final Project Report. The Government Office for Science, London, 2012. Available at <http://www.cftc.gov/idc/groups/public/@aboutcftc/documents/file/tacfuturecomputertrading1012.pdf>. Accessed on: Jul 04, 2017.

the rising cost of HFT infrastructure and the unrelenting competition within the segment; and b) the rise of alternative trading platforms. He also mentions that the projections concerning greater regulatory rigidity have affected investments in the sector. In Brazil, however, as we will see, these tendencies to decline were not noted during this period; rather, the contrary occurred.

The advance of this process has led to great changes in the reality of the markets. As this concerns a relatively recent matter, there is little published work available. The majority of the work that addresses this issue is restricted to reports by consultancies, financial institutions and regulatory organs, as well as papers which take technical angles of an econometric nature, evaluating the financial impact of its adoption on the return on investments, without the slightest look at the broader electronification of the markets and, as such, providing little in the way of a conclusive look at the focus of this book.

Taking a different approach, however, the non-fiction book *Flash Boys*, by Michael Lewis, published in the United States in 2014, takes an approach which clarifies the issue, by breaking down the situation behind the scenes of this new business model for banks, large investors and technology companies. Lewis' central claim is that the financial markets are being rigged by means of the use of predatory HFTs, in such a way that the few who make this ultra-fast technology available for the completion of trades, especially the large Wall Street banks, make sizable gains to the detriment of the other investors, by simply exploiting periods of time obtained thanks to the use of supercomputers and special lines of transmission dedicated to the stock exchanges and markets. The author describes one of these predatory algorithm strategies,[26] in which the advantage of milliseconds in relation to the other investors allows programs to identify their orders, place the same order before those investors' orders, in order, a few milliseconds later, without them realizing, to be able to

---

26   The owner of one of the biggest Brazilian stock brokerages told us that his company had suffered attacks and attempted hacks on his system, which have, so far, been blocked. The owner of another Brazilian company providing technology to the financial market, told us of a case of economic exploitation of technical failings in one of their systems: "Once we found a defect in our order planning system. It wasn't [exploited by a robot], it was a human, and he started operating on this defect. This is what people look for. This was the case of our client, who identified a defect in the risk system and started operating on that defect. He started building himself up, until the day he suffered a loss. When this occurred, he wanted to charge us for it, but, as we keep a record, we discovered that he had acted in bad faith. He had discovered a defect and had exploited it for 40 days. The client engaged the broker, who alerted us, and we realized that he had been acting in this way. I have no doubt that similar defects can be exploited by robots, but I don't know of any such cases" (verbal information).

offer them back to the same investors, but this time at a new price. By doing so, whenever the investor sends in an order, in step with the market price, it will not be executed, evaporating as a consequence of the new price that is updated in fractions of a second, imperceptible to the human eye.[27]

The book, that outlines the scenario of an unfair and fraudulent financial market, generated intense debate amongst the American public, forcing regulators and large investors to make statements and even take measures in relation to their activities. The day after publication of the book, the Federal Bureau of Investigation (FBI) announced an investigation into high-speed trading, and in particular into manipulation of the market and abuse of privileged information through the use of technological resources.

The problems arising from this operating logic, however, have not become evident only now. Defects, errors and different sorts of problems on the markets have been tied to the electronic trading model, especially AlgoTraders (ATs) and HFTs, for some years now. Since at least 2010, but with even more distant antecedents, the US market has experienced a number of adverse events as a result of its complex, fragmented and anarchically free institutional model, in direct interaction with failings involving technological resources – trading algorithms with unexpected behavior,[28] bugs in softwares or congested hardware. On top of a general and widespread rise in the volatility of the market, these mechanisms have also been related to the risk of large-scale breakdowns, upheavals and disruptive breaks that, by the looks of them, have reached alarming levels of recurrence. This is the case of the so-called flash crashes.

The most infamous of these breakdowns took place on May 6, 2010, at the New York Stock Exchange, one of the world's most important exchanges, when the Dow Jones Industrial Average (DJI) index dropped around 1,000 points (9 percent) in less than 20 minutes due to operating errors involving automatically performed algorithms, that influenced the other trades, thereby bringing the entire market down frighteningly quickly (see the article below, published

---

27   Operators, investors, programmers and even a mathematician specializing in calculations for the financial market, with whom we spoke, told us that there are many different predatory algorithm strategies in addition to this that we have outlined; from the exploitation of lapses in time by high-speed mechanisms, to plugins that force a delay in competitors' orders, etc. "The majority pay to catch and lose, whilst a few others pay to hit and win. That is how the game works in the markets with automated strategies", the abovementioned mathematician told us.

28   In the words of Professor Pedro Rezende: "a great deal of heuristics is misleading because it can simply tilt. No heuristic is 100 percent guaranteed and they can have an unexpected feedback effect that makes a robot behave completely unexpectedly" (verbal information).

in the New York Times[29]). As though it could have been any different in a reality in which financial markets are connected, the problem had immediate consequences throughout the world, and the leading share indexes started plummeting one after the other. In Brazil, the São Paulo Stock Exchange Index (Ibovespa), that gauges the performance of trading on our stock exchange, dropped 6.38 percent in the same period.[30]

In Table 1, below, we briefly outline some of these events. They concern events that highlight a growing systemic risk to which the markets have been subjected as they strive for more and more profit in shorter and shorter periods of time. There is also a series of other smaller but similar events, also known as mini flash crashes (Golub et al. 2012), that recur at a very high rate of frequency and, despite generally not becoming public knowledge, produce serious instabilities and risks for the markets.[31]

If they could be seen more clearly, above all those since 2005, when the use of automated trading by computers intensified, and also due to flexibilization in the regulation of the US markets, that opened up the way for expansion, there are those who claim that these problems have origins that stretch much further back. In a discussion of the changes caused in the markets due to the adoption of automated trading systems, Smith (2010) recalls a series of events that have taken place over a number of decades that, according to him, have allowed and consolidated the penetration of High Frequency Traders on the US market to the extent we see today. Listing important changes in the institutional and technological dimensions in the trading environment, its time line starts in the 1960s (see Figure 5), with the founding of Nasdaq, the first stock exchange to use computers to process data, through to 2010, when the first Flash Crash occurred on the New York Stock Exchange.

Going back in time with the help of this systematization, it is possible to find evidence of the way in which the growth and strengthening of the supremacy of the financial markets, as a configuring element of their financial dominance in the world economy, is closely tied to the implementation of technological

---

29 Available at: <http.//www.nytimes.com/2010/10/02/business/02flash.html?_r=1&s- cp=1& sq=flash+crash&st=nyt>. Accessed on: Dec 04, 2017.

30 In Brazil, as Interviewee C, a representative one of the country's leading technology companies providing services to the financial market, explained to us, there are cases of robots having led brokers to bankruptcy due to trades that could not be covered. Other errors and structural bottlenecks related to automated operations could have led to problems at the exchange itself. According to Interviewee F, another executive in the technology sector, in 2009, a robot belonging to the Swiss investment bank UBS caused problems throughout the exchange trading system with the bank having to deactivate it.

31 To read more about some of these cases, visit: <http://money.cnn.com/2013/03/20/investing/mini-flash-crash/>. Accessed on Dec 04, 2017.

TABLE 1   Sudden events relating to the operation of HFTs and/or incorrect functioning of automated trading mechanisms and systems

Agent/date	What happened
New York Stock Exchange (NYSE) May, 2010	Drop of the Dow Jones Industrial Average (DJI) index by around 1,000 points (9 percent) in less than 20 minutes due to operating errors involving automatically performed algorithms. Estimated losses: more than US$800 billion.
Bats Global Markets Mar., 2012	Cancellation of its IPO. Problem with the stock exchange's technological structure.
Facebook May, 2012	IPO on Nasdaq. More than 30,000 orders did not reach the stock exchange due to being "trapped" in the system. Indemnification paid to the most protected clients: US$62 million.
Knight Capital Aug., 2012	*Software* malfunction. Estimated loss: US$450 million.
Chicago Board Options Exchange Aug., 2013	The world's biggest options market was paralyzed for three and a half hours due to software problems.
Shanghai Stock Exchange Aug., 2013	Purchase orders mistakenly placed, such amounting to 23.4 billion yuan. The stock exchange that was losing 1 percent recovered to rise 5.6 percent in two minutes.
Goldman Sachs Aug., 2013	Updating of internal systems resulted in a trading crash. Estimated loss: US$10 million.
Nasdaq Aug, 2013	A connection problem caused by a bug in the software, caused a suspension of the trading system for more than three hours.
Nasdaq Nov., 2013	Error during the transfer of data. Freezing of the Nasdaq Composite Index for around one hour.

DIGITALIZED FINANCE 83

Agent/date	What happened
New York Stock Exchange (NYSE) July, 2015	The Stock Exchange stopped operating for three and a half hours due to a computer malfunction, forcing investors to send their orders through other trading routes.
Foreign Exchange Market (FX) Oct., 2016	A sudden drop of 6.1 percent in the pound sterling against the dollar, pushing it to its lowest level since 1985 in just two minutes. The recovery took almost 30 minutes.

SOURCE: OWN COMPILATION

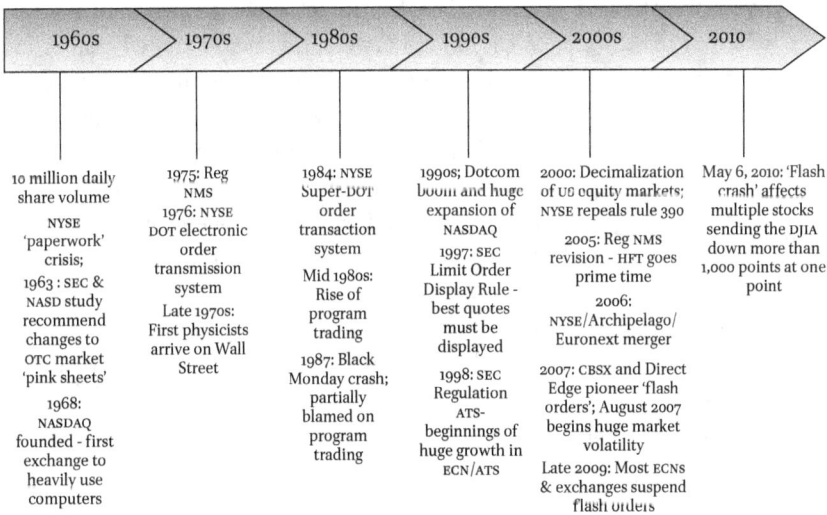

FIGURE 5 The rough timeline of the events spanning decades that led to the current market penetration of high-frequency trading.
SOURCE: SMITH, R. 2010, P. 7. IS HIGH-FREQUENCY TRADING INDUCING CHANGES IN MARKET MICROSTRUCTURE AND DYNAMICS? CORNELL UNIVERSITY LIBRARY. AVAILABLE AT: <HTTP://ARXIV.ORG/ABS/1006.5490>. ACCESSED ON: JUL 20, 2017

advances that allow for the exploitation of new ways of profiting in the markets, and by doing so increasing the systemic instabilities and risks.

A sharp fall in the world's stock markets had occurred in a way that was very similar to the Flash Crash of 2010, around 23 years earlier. On October 19, 1987, that has gone down in financial market history as *Black Monday*, the Dow Jones Industrial Average (DJI) index of the New York Stock Exchange dropped more than 22 percent, creating international panic. Amongst other factors, an automatic trading system that was already in use at the time for handling certain assets was considered to be one of the factors most responsible for the fast spread and intensification of the fall. In an interview given for this book, the economist and University of Campinas professor and researcher Maryse Fahri,[32] who was working in the financial market at the time, described the way in which this relationship worked.

> Let's say we forget about HFTs for a moment. In the 1980s, when the signal still came along a telephone line specifically for the purpose, there was already something called Program Trading, that was used to perform arbitrage in the share market between the spot market and the derivatives market exchange index. For this though, the operators had to know whether the difference exploited between the basket traded shares and the future traded index was higher or lower than the interest rate for the period. This is a relatively time-consuming calculation, so the machines not only made the calculations, but also automatically sent the trade orders in place of the operators. Then came the crisis of 1987 and with it an enormous problem with these systems. This was because the stock exchanges dropped much more than had been expected and the computers simply went crazy. They went so crazy that they brought down the stock exchange lines worldwide. This was a warning that this was serious. After this episode, the stock exchanges had to change a few things and they decided that the computers would work within an established limit of price swings and that on days with a lot of volatility the lines of these computers would be cut (verbal information).

As we have pointed out, the accelerated process of digitalization of the markets, over the last few decades, of which the growing use of ATs and HFTs in trading is, now, the greatest expression, highlights situations of commercial fraud (in which technological supremacy draws a picture in which a few gain

---

32   Interview given to the researcher on 04-Jun-2014, in São Paulo. 1 file .mpeg4 (57min06seg).

to the detriment of many who predictably lose) and additional instabilities in the operation of the capitals markets that, absorbed by arbitrage at the level of milliseconds, in a scenario of global connectivity, expand its risks even more. Encouraged by the belief in neutrality and technical infallibility in the overcoming of errors arising from the "human factor",[33] operators and investors are placing their belief in even more daring and risky trading strategies.

Additionally, the increase of this systemic risk is closely tied to the rapid growth in the technical[34] and institutional complexity of the markets, which motivates the appearance of financial innovations and the trading of instruments that would not be possible if not through the mechanisms that already exist in this conjuncture of technological advancement. This is because, in response to the technical development, new mechanisms, forms of trading, operating regulations and even the existence of parallel markets are growing in number and complexity, always activated by the fierce competition for ever greater gains. Added to this is the exponential growth in the volume of new information compiled and processed by these high-performance systems.

This complexity causes the systems to operate in a conveniently confused manner, that few experts or operators can completely control. This means a growth in the opacity of the markets as an element of control and management of strategic information in the hands of elites of investors that are increasingly closed, making access difficult not only to governments, regulators and the understanding of society, but also for the operation of small investors who, on the edges, are increasingly dependent on large funds, brokers and financial institutions to manage their investments, which is usually done with

---

[33] The fast reduction in the use of human beings in the operation of the capitals markets, something that is a global trend, demonstrates important institutional and operational changes in the dynamic by which the markets work. As we were informed by Interviewee H, an economist, just one large international bank that operates on the Brazilian capitals market performed around 100,000 operations per day, with these being controlled by just three human operators. In addition to the criers (those traders who shout the commercial paper purchase and sale options at the stock exchanges), a profession that is practically extinct, the case of the small and medium-sized brokerage firms and their employees is especially interesting. These companies fight for survival, seeking to reinvent themselves within a context of accelerated technological transformation, in which the role of the broker as mediator between buyers and sellers is losing importance within the model of automated trading. We intend to deal with this issue within the context of the Brazilian capitals market, where we can observe it in its most arrested state. Interview given to the researcher on 06-May-2014, in Brasília (DF). 1 file .mpeg4 (91min02seg).

[34] As Professor Pedro Rezende explained to us: "The number of potential defects and errors increases exponentially in accordance with the number of lines of code that the software has. As such, the more complex the software, the more probable that it will present errors and defects" (verbal information).

very little transparency. As such, in addition to being an extra resource for strengthening the march toward concentration of gains in the markets, this opacity emerging from the growing complexity increases risks of management and governance, in so far as few people truly understand how the digitalized financial markets really work.

Furthermore, the very growth of this operating complexity opens new trading opportunities, since it demands even more investments in technologies that allow the efficient management of financial operations in an environment of this type. The very management of the complexity therefore becomes an attractive business, especially for large cutting-edge companies in the technology sector. This was admitted by Interviewee G, a representative of a large international technology company operating in the Brazilian capitals market. "If the market gets more complex, you need more IT to decomplexify [sic] it, to make it easier, and that's where I come into the game. For my niche in the market, for example, it's good if the market gets more complicated and is consolidated into ever smaller groups" (verbal information).

This trend for increased complexity, that has different expressions in different markets, countries and regions, based upon different historical, sociotechnical and regulatory contexts, has ended up, in the United States, where the majority of the largest and most lucrative markets on the planet are concentrated, creating an anarchically decentralized and opaque operating structure. Here, different markets and stock exchanges resort to multiple and risky expedients in their attempts to attract investors to their trading spaces, thus increasing the incentives for the intensive use of technology in the arbitrage of assets between these trading environments, such as the previously mentioned ATs and HFTs, that in the US have the greatest rate of penetration in the world.[35]

As we will demonstrate later on, the operating structure of the Brazilian capitals market is considerably different from this, above all in relation to decentralization and regulation. Based upon studies performed for this book, however, we have identified the recurrence of a certain pattern in the different markets, even in their particular contexts, in relation to what we are here calling the *spiral of complexity of digitalized finance*.

---

35 In relation to this, an enlightening look of the panorama of the workings of the US capitals market is provided in Bector, Raj, Marrato, Anthony and Sparrow, Chris (2013), *The Hidden Alpha in Equity Trading: steps to increasing returns with the advanced use of information*. Oliver Wyman report. Available at: <http://www.oliverwyman.com/our-expertise/insights/2014/mar/the-hidden-alpha-in-equity-trading.html>. Accessed on Dec 05, 2017.

By using these findings, we believe that this increase of systemic risks in the financial markets is not only or simply because of the adoption of technological advances, even though these are essential to the establishment of this scenario. We believe that it is in the nature of the socio-technical systems, amongst which we include stock exchanges and financial markets, to be structured in a number of different dimensions. In line with this point of view, that points to a complex dynamic in the relationship between financial gains and increasing technological advances, we can explain a spiral of increasing complexity in the markets as follows: (i) the search for unexploited financial gains requires technical means that allow for the material and technical obstacles currently standing in its way to be overcome; (ii) the adoption of these technologies leads to the need for new institutional configurations, modes and socio-technical operating dynamics in the markets, that are reconfigured using the present socioeconomic conditions and the political and social conflicts surrounding its consequences; and, finally, iii) the possibilities open for more gains arising from the new institutional and technological environment, encourage the development and implementation of new technical solutions, through competition between the investors and the investment in research and development, that return to feed this cycle of growing complexity (as shown in the illustration below).

More objectively, this scenario, as well as in its broader sense, suggests a trend toward the subdivision of trades that, as an element of the same process that shortens time and distances, forces arbitrage and speculation to a level of the smallest cents. As a complement to this, as times, distances and fractions of traded assets are reduced, the volumes traded grow, thus increasing the aggregate financial gains on the markets.

However, defenders of the electronic trading models argue that, while turbulence and instabilities can be mitigated and opposed by means of other technical resources relating to governance and risk management (and it is indeed a fact that there exists a lucrative technological-solutions market for investors in this specific area), the high-intensity operations benefit the markets, in so far as they provide liquidity, reducing the margins between the traded spreads, which is considered healthy for the markets. It is also argued that the employment of technology allows transaction costs to be brought down, whilst also offering more efficiency and transparency to the pricing systems.

If this is true in part, there are, however, as we have seen, numerous cases indicating that, instead of becoming more transparent, above all when anchored in complex algorithms, they become more opaque because they are more unpredictable in their complexity (see Figure 6). It should be remembered, furthermore, that any technological artifact and/or mathematical model is

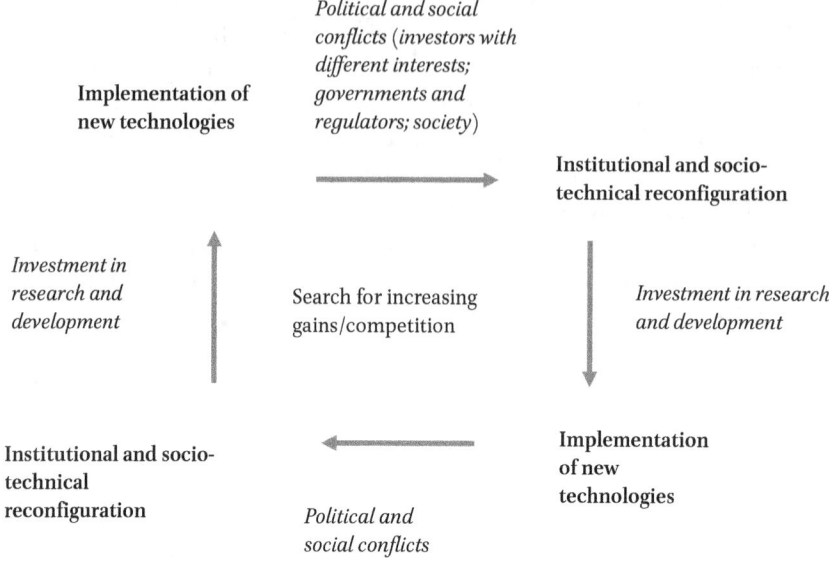

FIGURE 6 The spiral of complexity of digitalized finance.
SOURCE: OWN ELABORATION

susceptible to defects in unforeseeable situations,[36] as in the so-called Black Swans Theory (Taleb 2010). The number of potential errors and defects in a system rises, as we know, in line with its complexity.

If ATs and, above all, HFTs provide additional liquidity for markets in times of acceleration or stability, they can aggressively increase their losses during the low periods (Farhi and Prates 2015). In relation to risk control, if it is true that there have been sophisticated technical advances in use, it is obvious that these systems, such as the very logic of regulation per se, always tend to follow on behind the innovations that, in contrast, increase the risks, making for a very dangerous game.

As has been seen, defenders of the practice – and there is a growing number of studies and research that supports this belief (Hagstromer and Norden 2013,

---

36   One ironically enlightening example of this was the bankruptcy of the Long-Term Capital Management investment fund, at the time directed by Robert Merton and Myron Scholes, who had shared the 1997 Economics Nobel Prize for the development of one of the most important mathematical tools used in the calculation of derivatives – the Black-Scholes-Merton formula. In 1998, one year after its directors had been awarded their laureates, the fund recorded a loss of US$4.6 billion and had to close. The fact was that their complex mathematical model did not take into account the possibility of two extreme events, the Asian Bubble of 1997, and the moratorium of the Russian Government in 1998.

Hasbrouck and Saar 2013, Weems and Tabb 2014) – argue that it provides more liquidity for the markets, and reduces the trading costs for all classes of investors. But if it is true that they produce extraordinary gains, especially for the administrators of trading venues and the suppliers of market data, as well as other categories of investors, the algorithmic trading and, above all, the HFTs are far from being unamity. One independent study involving consumers, partners and others operating in the market, carried out in 2014 by Convergex, an American market trading services supplier, revealed that for 70 percent of the respondents – professional investors and brokers on Wall Street – the market is not fair for all its participants. The survey[37] also revealed that for 51 percent of them, the HFTs were either damaging or very damaging for the market as a whole.

The critics, including large investors such as Warren Buffett[38] and others, argue that the markets become overly dependent on advanced technology, and that high-frequency traders, with their focus on extremely short-term returns, have damaged the other investors who are concerned with the economic foundations and long-term success of the companies. It also highlights the increase in the number of cases of abuse and illegal manipulation of the market,[39] with practices such as spoofing[40] and layering.[41]

---

37 For a summary of the most important points in the study, visit: <https://pt.scribd.com/document/220054793/ConvergEX-NEW-Market-Structure-Survey>. Accessed on Dec 05, 2017.

38 For more information on this, see: <http://www.cnbc.com/2014/05/05/buffett-gates-and-munger-criticize-high-frequency-trading.html>. Accessed on: Dec 05, 2017.

39 Such as, for example, the payment of US$154 million by Barclays and Credit Suisse in January 2016, as compensation in the face of accusations that they had misled their clients over the manner in which they worked with high-frequency trading. For more information on this, see: <https://www.theguardian.com/business/2016/jan/31/barclays-and-credit-suisse-to-pay-biggest-ever-fines-for-dark-pool-trading>. Accessed on: Dec 05, 2017.

40 An abusive practice in which trading algorithms ("robots") create offers to create an impression of false liquidity in the market and force asset prices to levels that benefit the investors behind this strategy. For a case of spoofing detected by BM&FBovespa, see: <http://www.bsm-autorregulacao.com.br/supervisao-de-mercado/casos/4>. Accessed on: Dec 05, 2017. In 2015, Navinder Singh Sarao a market trader working in the high-frequency area, was arrested in London for having practiced spoofing on a large number of commercial papers on the American markets, which had, according to the authorities, worsened the flash crash of May 2010. For more information on this, see: <http://br.reuters.com/article/businessNews/idBRKBN0NC2P820150421>. Accessed on: Dec 05, 2017.

41 Name given to the practice of inserting layered offers in the list of offers to influence other investors to insert or modify their offers, thus providing conditions for trades to be made on the side opposing that on which the layers were inserted. For a case of layering

Recent studies have highlighted the negative impacts of the predatory practices of automatic trading systems in the markets. Kirilenko and Lo (2013) maintain that the HFTs contributed to the sharp drop in the market that abruptly wiped out almost US$1 trillion from the US stock exchanges in May 2010. Gai, Yao and Ye (2013) show that faster trades do not necessarily translate into direct gains in the reduction of spreads or into higher volumes, but rather they increase volatility in the markets.

In so far as the HFTs have been held responsible for causing or worsening disruptive events such as flash crashes and mini flash crashes, in particular, and/or for accentuating the volatility of the markets, in general, regulatory authorities throughout the world have investigated whether high-speed trading damage the stability of the markets and give some investors an unfair advantage. In the midst of these growing concerns, high-frequency trading have come to be directly regulated by the European Securities and Markets Authority (ESMA) and many European countries have, amongst other regulatory measures, started to evaluate the need to tax the volume of trades to ensure that these mechanisms and strategies are not so predatory.[42]

Regulators in other countries have brought similar concerns to the public's attention. Japan announced that it too plans to intensify the regulation of high frequency trading,[43] the growing presence of which on the Tokyo Stock Exchange raised concerns that such trades could destabilize the market and place retail investors at a disadvantage. In August 2016, the capitals market regulator in India affirmed that it was considering installing various potential limits on AlgoTraders, including the imposition of random speed bumps, that would randomly delay the execution of some orders.

Taken out of context in relation to the wider economy (including its manufacturing dimension) and ignoring, as such, the financialization process that, as we have sought to highlight, has consequences in various social areas, some of these arguments do, in fact, correspond (despite being the focus of intense

---

detected by BM&FBovespa, see: <http://www.bsm-autorregulacao.com.br/supervisao-de-mercado/casos/5>. Accessed on Dec 05, 2017.

42   One of the efforts designed to maintain the supposed benefits provided by HFTs, whilst at the same time seeking to avoid market manipulations, received the support of the US Securities and Exchange Commission (SEC) in June 2016, which approved the registration of the Dark Pool IEX (Investors Exchange) as a fully-fledged stock exchange. The IEX, directed by Brad Katsuyama (known to the general public as one of the characters in the book Flash Boys (Lewys 2014), who tells his story of fighting the market manipulations perpetrated by the Wall Street HFTs) claims that his operating model weakens the advantages of some of the predatory high-speed operators.

43   For more information on this, see: <http://www.reuters.com/article/japan-regulations-hft-idUSL4N1CP1Y1>. Accessed on: Dec 05, 2017.

and inconclusive debate) to the earnings outlook in important sectors of the market. Whether they are correct or not, as a backdrop to these defenses, however, is the fact that, be it for exchanges and markets, that have been increasing their earnings possibilities with rates and fees based upon the increase in the number and volume of high-speed trades performed in their venues, or be it for large investors and the big players providing technology for market operations, who have been attracting increasing percentages of the markets, the model is extremely lucrative.

As we have highlighted, in so far as it has social origins and consequences, the substantial increase of the earnings in the financial sphere cannot be read in isolation, simply as a piece of accounting data. Inter-related with the functioning of the financial markets are, in addition to industrial and agricultural production, different countries' sovereign debt, welfare and pensions systems, personal investments, and even the food supply in the world economy.

A study performed by the United Nations Conference on Trade and Development (UNCTAD),[44] and published in 2012, demonstrates how the large-scale involvement of financial investors and their growing investments in commodities, traded as financial assets, has altered the functioning of the global foodstuffs market. Also, according to this study, the advance in the use of HFTs outlines a new direction in the financialization of the commodities market, especially affecting the poorer countries, that end up finding the security of their food supplies conditional upon the volatility of the price movements in digitalized finance.

In addition to other aspects, it should be noted that the colonization of the business world by the financial dominance fundamentally affects the production of knowledge and information. This is the case with the large domestic and international news agencies, which are increasingly focused on meeting the requirements of producing information in large volume and at high speed for use by the markets, even financing, as such, their own journalistic coverage.[45] To get an idea of what this means, in 2014, of the 150 journalists who worked at a large Brazilian news agency, 120 of them were dedicated solely to the production of information in real time for the capitals market. There can be only one reason for this; Interviewee I,[46] representing the agency we spoke

---

44   Bicchetti, D., Maystre, N. "The Synchronized and Long-Lasting Structural Change on Commodity Markets: Evidence From High Frequency Data". UNCTAD *Discussion Papers 208*, United Nations Conference on Trade and Development, 2012. Available at <http://vi.unctad.org/devblog/506-high-frequency-trading-contributes-to-deviate-commodity-prices-from-fundamentals>. Accessed on: Dec 05, 2017.

45   For more on this subject, see Puliti (2013).

46   Interview given to the researcher on 03-Jun-2014, in São Paulo (SP). 1 file .mpeg4 (99min54sec).

to about this subject, told us that the sector concerning real time information for investors is extremely lucrative, with a margin of return of more than 30 percent profit, and is responsible for 4/5 of the agency's entire revenue.

Thus, if the increase of the profits in the financial markets over recent years finds support in reality, we can argue that such a reality is, in fact, a product of a wider process of restructuring of the global capitalist economy, in line with the so-called finance dominated accumulation regime, which increases autonomy for the accumulation of fictitious capital.

The advances in Information and Communication Technologies, particularly in relation to their adoption in the capitals markets, as part of this wider process, is not the element upon which it is founded, but concerns a crucial dimension to making the logic of financial dominance more urgent and essential. If it is true that the international financial system would not exist as it does at the moment without making use of the technological resources that it does, it is not correct to say that the technological advance is the fundamental cause of such economic transformations; which continue to have as a shaping axis the quest for the accumulation and valorization of capital, to which such technical advances serve in last instance. Whatever the case, this dialectic does not necessarily point toward a simple submission of the technological aspect to the economic one, but to a mutual dynamic of influence – pervaded by various social and political dimensions, capable of providing multiple and varied profiles to this process – even though it is ultimately governed, directly or indirectly, by the striving for economic gain as an instrumental goal.

Based upon the conclusions obtained from the research we have performed here, we argue that, in the way presented, such dynamic is pervaded by three dimensions in which technology acts to consolidate financial dominance in our time, outlining what we call the *cycle of operation of digitalized finance* (see Figure 7): i) whilst they work for the shortening of the space-time flows, the advance and use of ITC allow for an increase in the number and volume of trades on the financial markets, increasing the accumulation capacity of fictitious capital, and as such, increasing the gains arising from its valorization; ii) due to the intense speed and adaptive ability of these intelligent systems, the work of controlling and regulating the markets becomes increasingly thankless and costly, whilst the markets are always at the forefront of technology to overcome the technical, material and institutional boundaries, in their attempts to access still unexploited sources of revenue; and finally, iii) in times of a hegemony of fictitious capital, this scenario reinforces the centralization and concentration of capitals and their gains in the hands of a few investors, in a few global financial marketplaces, where the gains tend to be kept in

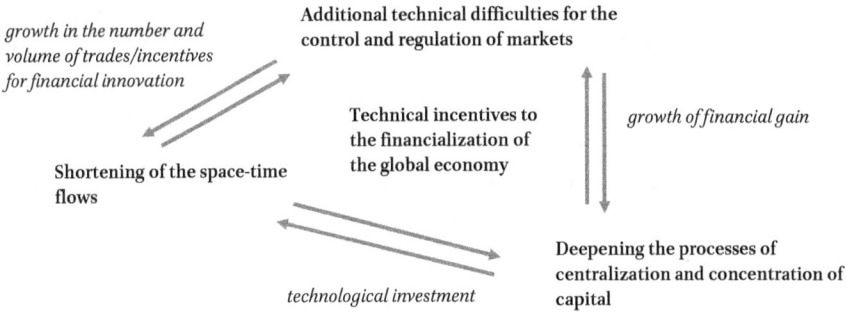

FIGURE 7 Cycle of operation of digitalized finance.
SOURCE: OWN ELABORATION

applications focused on auto-appreciation, without satisfying other important social and economic needs.[47]

As such, the theoretical function conferred on the financial markets as the allocators of economic needs, making it possible for them to bring together buyers and sellers, and users and suppliers of resources to enable business and economic production as a whole, loses more and more relevance in detriment to a growingly speculative logic that leads to the draining and concentration of the surplus of corporate production in the financial sphere, that start to be exploited retroactively through arbitrage at a scale of microseconds, made possible by cutting edge technological advances. We can, therefore, see that the incentives for the contamination of the short-term logic, reinforced by these other dimensions, have increased in distinct areas of the capitalist economy in our time, thereby broadly strengthening its own process of financialization.

It would be no exaggeration to state that such a scenario points toward the collapse of the modern faith in the stock markets by common investors, who are now able to see it for what it truly is: a casino in which the "house" always wins, right in front of the eyes of the agents of the state, who are incapable of correctly intervening in these processes, or are equally committed to the game.

It is no accident that this reality has attracted the attention of governments, regulators and civil society organizations. Is there a way of reversing this

---

47 As we have attempted to demonstrate, these tendencies do not include simple or unidirectional relations, which would be an attack on the complexity of their operation, but are activated in various directions, influenced as they are by various conforming factors. The mutual influences between these factors are, therefore, multi-directional.

process and reconfiguring the role of the financial markets in the capitalist system, submitting it to the socio-economic needs? How should risks in the markets be predicted and contained? How can the growing inequalities and instabilities within digitalized finance be avoided? Is it possible to regulate the financial markets within this scenario?

This is a complex set of questions that, as well as serious theoretical discussion, demands studies and new research. Without trying to answer them or even discuss them more closely, we intend now to briefly present a few of the elements surrounding this debate.

Mindful of maintaining the gains obtained through the markets' new way of functioning, and at the same time avoiding its recognized and accepted risks and instabilities, market agents, regulators, specialists, and even the stock exchanges and markets themselves, drew up a series of technical and/or institutional control mechanisms to be applied in their various environments. These measures, as we show in the table below, which is based upon information available in a report produced by a British Government Research Organization,[48] provides a menu of options that are rarely adopted on a large scale by the markets, which are more used to opting for a few of them, based upon their contexts, conditions and objectives. The Brazilian capitals market, globally speaking being widely recognized as more regulated than average (see Table 2), has adopted a number of these mechanisms.

As we have insisted in this book, in addition to the measures outlined above, the debate over regulation of the markets requires a structural approach, focused on an understanding of the broader process of financial globalization. More than mechanisms operating within the microstructures of the markets and stock exchanges (which is an important and necessary issue too), the tendencies that create the operating dynamic of digitalized finance at a global level are dependent upon wider dimensions in the Political Economy sphere, and involve an understanding of the general operating structure of the capitalist mode of production in our present situation. Based upon this approach, in line with the reality seen in the field, and in conversations with regulators and market agents, the following issues are raised:

(i) Above all in the current scenario of financial, manufacturing and informational globalization, in order to be able to produce substantial effects,

---

48 Foresight: The Future of Computer Trading in Financial Markets. Final Project Report. The Government Office for Science, London, 2012. Available at <https://www.gov.uk/government/uploads/system/uploads/attachment_data/file/289431/12-1086-future-of-computer-trading-in-financial-markets-report.pdf >. Accessed on: Dec 05, 2017.

TABLE 2 Measures for regulation and risk control in the financial markets

Measure	What it is	Adopted in the Brazilian capitals market
Circuit breakers	Interruption of the trading systems for certain periods of time, from a given percentage drop, when there occur sharp and/or untypical movements in the market, producing excessive volatility.	Yes
Minimum Tick[a] size policies	The price movements of the different financial instruments, or their minimum possible fraction of negotiation, vary in the markets. This policy is defined by the establishment of minimum scales for the trading of instruments in an attempt to avoid their hyper-fractioning during trading.	No
Notification of algorithms	The requirement that investors who use ATs and/or HFTs provide the regulators (inside and outside the stock exchanges) with a description of their strategies, with details of their trading parameters and limits, their principal risk control mechanisms, and details of how these systems work and how they are tested.	Yes
Obligations imposed on market makers	Obligations imposed on market makers are requirements that investors (operated manually or by computer), acting as market makers, should always set the purchase and sale prices of instruments at competitive levels, regardless of the market conditions, as a means of improving the provision of continual liquidity and ensuring that such market makers provide competitive prices during periods of market stress.	Yes (for some markets)
Establishment of a minimum waiting period on order times	Establishment of a minimum time period that a purchase and sale limit should remain in effect. The objective order	No

TABLE 2 Measures for regulation and risk control in the financial markets (*cont.*)

Measure	What it is	Adopted in the Brazilian capitals market
	of the imposition of this minimum is to avoid thousands of orders being sent that are then canceled soon after having been sent simply as a diversion tactic in the markets, this being a trick that is commonly used these days by ATs and HFTs.	
Maker- taker[b] taxation	The taxation structure in electronic markets by means of which those providing liquidity, by means of the submission of orders at the trading price limits at a given moment (the "makers"), receive a discount or rebate on the rates paid on their executed orders, whilst the liquidity buyers or users (the "takers") pay additional sums to execute trades against these orders at the price limits. Different stock exchanges and markets organize the manner in which this taxation structure works in different ways. The objective is to increase the liquidity of the markets.	No
Orders to execution ratios	This involves the imposition of restrictions on the cancellation of orders through the establishment of a maximum ratio between the number of purchase and/or sale orders in relation to the number of related trades executed. The objective of this measure is to encourage, by means of incentives, or oblige, by means of regulations, investors to cancel fewer offers and, consequently, contribute to the creation of more transparent and predictable order books in the markets.	No
Virtual central limit order book – CLOB	The "CLOB" – Central Limit Order Book is designed to consolidate all the purchase	No

Measure	What it is	Adopted in the Brazilian capitals market
	or sale orders at the price limit in a single line for trading on the market. By doing so, the objective is to reduce the incidence of blocked markets (when the best purchase price is equal to the best sale price) or crossed markets (when the best purchase price is lower than the best sale price). A central line of orders also aims to guarantee that the providers of limit orders are treated fairly in terms of price or time priority.	
Call auctions	Limited orders are collected at determined moments over a fixed period of time to correct potential imbalances in prices (enormous purchase or sale offers, opening or closure of prices at the beginning or end of daily trading sessions, etc.). At the end of this period of time, they are processed at an auction in which all the investors can participate. The price that allows the highest number of orders to be executed is the winner.	Yes
Internalization (Dark Trading)	This is not exactly a means of protecting the markets, but of constructing environments that are more advantageous for investors who do not wish to submit themselves to the transparency regulations of public markets. As such, it is defined by a practice by means of which some investors, above all the bigger ones, who are accustomed to operating in large volumes, execute their trades in parallel spaces, created internally by specific brokers or intermediaries, and which operate, therefore, outside the public markets.	No

TABLE 2 Measures for regulation and risk control in the financial markets (*cont.*)

Measure	What it is	Adopted in the Brazilian capitals market
Trading bands and limits	The idea, in addition to economizing on the fees paid to the exchanges and public markets, is that, within their own spaces, these large investors are less susceptible to the arbitrages of other speculators based upon their purchase and/or sale options, which can condition the movement of prices thereby reducing the revenue earned. This is also known as darktrading. The range of variation of prices defined by the stock exchange for each asset. The range can be configured symmetrically or asymmetrically and can be applied to offers or trades when their closure is imminent. Once violated, the band decides on the automatic distribution of specific shares in the trading system, depending upon the type of asset, aimed at reducing the operational risk.	Yes

a A Tick is the minimum price movement of a trading instrument. For example, if the movement of the minimum price of a certain stock of instruments is 0.01, then the stock has a scale value of one cent (each tick is worth one cent per stock).
b A market-maker is an investor who is always ready to purchase and sell a certain share on a regular and continuous base for a publicly quoted price, hoping to profit off the difference (spread) between these operations. See the definition provided by the SEC (U.S Securities and Exchange Commission). Available at: <http://www.sec.gov/answers/mktmaker.htm>. Accessed on: Jul 19, 2017.
SOURCE: BM&FBOVESPA; OWN ELABORATION

regulation of the capitals markets needs to be international. It is therefore necessary for basic, global regulations to be adopted, but this is extremely difficult in a scenario in which the operation of these markets occupies a strategic position in geo-political conflicts, to oppose different interests, that end up placing countries and international agents in different, and often opposite, positions in the balance of world power. The Basel agreements, in relation to banks and financial institutions, have aimed, without much success, to fulfill this role. To some extent, the statement by Ary Oswaldo Filho (Barcellos 2010, p. 170), president of the Brazilian Securities and Exchange Commission ("CVM") and a member of the Conselho Monetário Nacional ("National Monetary Council" – "CMN") from 1990 to 1992, a period notable for the opening of the Brazilian market to foreign investors, reinforces this understanding:

> There was a whole learning process. At the beginning, there was a lot of confusion, but there were agreements for the exchange of information, documents and knowledge involving the CVM and the Securities and Exchange Commission (SEC) and the Commodity Futures Trading Commission (CFTC), that controls the futures on the US market. In so far as the market starts to go international, the regulatory institutions also, obviously, have to organize themselves and work together.

(ii) In relation to this facet of the situation, is the need for the institutional framework itself to overcome neoliberalism, the main weapon of attack of which lies in the movements of expansion of the autonomy of finance. It is this scenario that, by guaranteeing full and unrestricted freedom for the accumulation and valorization of capitals, with the consequent reduction in the power of the governments to use expedients and instruments of economic, monetary and fiscal policy, allows abuse and even the anarchic race for speed within digitalized finance. As part of this picture, the belief in the economy as an exact science and the consequent blind belief in the mathematical models reinforce this way of understanding the role of the markets in the economy that, once maintained, will continue serving as fertile ground for the rise of new problems tied to the riddle of increasing financial valorization.

(iii) As part of this process, it is essential that the regulatory organs are up-to-date and technologically equipped to perform their work, being able to follow the rapid advances in the sector, and with the ability to be proactive, something that, at least in the context of the Brazilian market, is not the case. As Interviewee B, an important executive at the stock exchange, pointed out:

> [...] the technological evolution of the systems designed to monitor the market that are used by the regulators are much slower than the technological evolution that is taking place throughout the market. To quote one example, while today we speak of the use of Big Data, the

regulators will probably only start to implement this in their work once everyone has stopped using it (verbal information).

In 2000 and 2001, when the bubble burst on the "dot com" companies, a series of cases of accounting fraud, performed with the intention of avoiding the depreciation of the companies on the stock markets, came to the surface, making the crisis that appeared at the time even worse, and starting a heated discussion concerning the relationship between companies, regulators and independent auditors in the markets.[49] In an interview conducted for this book, Professor Pedro Rezende explained how some of these cases of fraud are performed using advanced techniques made possible by Information Technologies.

> Inspection is usually performed by checking a sample band of data or information, due to the difficulty of examining such a large number of accounting records belonging to any given company or business. Using IT, certain companies and members of the market, very often in collusion with the consultant companies that know the twists and turns of the forms of detection of abuse and illegal practices by these systems, develop automated techniques to reduce the risk of detection of problems. This is generally done by producing a bump in the sample spaces. The cost of doing this, however, is only worthwhile if automation of the process is possible, and this is done, in some cases, by performing merely fictitious automated operations designed to dilute the risk of the cheating being detected (verbal information).

(iv) Finally, we should highlight the connection of the state to the financial elite through the lobby and other protective relations, which produce additional difficulties from the political point of view for the very serious work of regulation and social control of the capitals markets. The following figures, both published in The New York Times,[50] with data from the Center for

---

49 For a more in-depth discussion on this issue, see Dembinski, Paul H. et al. (2006) (ed.), *Enron and world finance*: a case study in ethics. Observatoire de la Finance and Palgrave Macmillan. New York: Palgrave Macmillan.

50 The following figure, published in The New York Times with data from the Center for Responsive Politics, provide a panorama of the investments made by High Frequency Trading companies and large banks in recent US elections from 2006 to 2010. See: <http://www.nytimes.com/imagepages/2011/07/18/business/18fasttrade_g.html>. Accessed on: Dec 05, 2017. Some related data are available at: <https://www.opensecrets.org/lobby/indusclient.php?id=F03&-year=>. Accessed on: Dec 05, 2017.

Responsive Politics, provide a panorama of the investments made by High Frequency Trading companies and large banks in recent US elections.

4.3 Recent Trends: The Next Steps for Digitalized Finance

As we have seen, countless transformations over the last few decades have contributed to making the socio-technological systems of the financial markets that combine direct and indirect human and non-human actions, as part of a complex that has come to be known as digitalized finance. Within this, we can see a growth in volumes and, especially, the number of trades performed on the markets, tied as they are to the shortening of time-space flows, in search of growing speculative gains and the consequent increase in the difficulties for regulatory activities. And out of this, finally, we see vast sums of capital in the financial sphere that is increasingly concentrated in the hands of large investors which, as a result, face additional difficulties in connecting with the most pressing economic and productive needs of social life. Given that the process of technological development of the markets in this direction does not tend to turn around but rather the contrary, then understanding what this complex system and its components consists of and how it works becomes essential due to the necessary task of foreseeing and regulating the behavior and the undesirable consequences of the actions of these robots and human beings that are in a process of integration.

A great deal points toward the ICT continuing to modify the nature of work, the structure of manufacturing and even other social relations. According to the projections and evidence that appeared at the beginning of the century (Marcial 2015, pp. 99–115), the forthcoming decades should see the appearance, within a scenario of increased investment in automation and robotics, of nanotechnology and biotechnology, and the acceleration of multidisciplinary technological development, with applications that are ever more integrated.

Both following and demonstrating this trend, a central theme of the 2016 World Economic Forum was the "Fourth Industrial Revolution" (Schwab 2016), that foresees a great "fusion of technologies, erasing the dividing lines between the physical, digital and biological spheres". Together with the processes listed above, the Fourth Industrial Revolution points toward the development of new materials, the Internet of things, 3D printing, drones, new ways of processing and stocking data and energy, autonomous vehicles, cognitive computing and artificial intelligence. There is talk, in relation to our definition of digitalized finance, of the "extreme automation in business, government and private life" connected with "extreme connectivity, [that] wipes out distance and time as obstacles to communication in a way that is increasingly broader and faster". (UBS 2016, p. 3)

> This means that the production chains will tend to be shorter, unleashing another period of verticalization of the production of cutting-edge technology and of distribution of the simpler technologies. (...) It is also expected that this new economic scenario could strengthen the dollar, as the currency of payments and international reserve, due to the competitive advantages held by the United States in relation to the technologies – and intellectual property – of the Fourth Industrial Revolution.
> CINTRA 2016

Within this context, there is an advance in the reliance on financial technologies as a means of avoiding the uncertainties of the global economy, and more broadly reconfiguring the systemic relationship between banks, governments and society. We should highlight the enthusiasm that exists around so-called Fintechs (the financial technology and banking startups), Blockchain technology and digital currencies such as Bitcoin. The idea is that they will allow for management that is more predictable and transparent and, above all, requires less intervention from the state and central banks in relation to monetary and financial flows.

In the most restricted area of the capitals market, which this book has been addressing, a general increase in transactions has been taking place, as we know, along with more data, greater speed, and greater specialization of services and products. Concerning Brazil, the period following the 2008 crisis brought with it an explosion of financial technology in the country, which was also an effect of the growing financial openness and the optimism surrounding the country's macroeconomic situation. However, the technological dissemination, understanding, adaptation, and assimilation by new entrants suggested a gradual reduction in the profit differentials (or technological revenue) seen in the past, in a scenario of constraint for the global economy, in general, and for the financial sector in particular. Within this technological race, and to the extent that the tools are disseminated, the players have seen a fall in the cost-benefit relationship of large investments in the area.

As such, processing speed and capacity, as we have seen, still represent an important differential, but it is certainly no longer the only one. In order to avoid these restraints, the recent trends point toward the introduction of artificial intelligence and machine learning[51] together with trading algorithms, and Big Data processing, as new ways of handling, organizing, mining and using data in trading. To do so, investments in infrastructure (even though some of these hardwares are considered to be commodities in many sectors) should rise. Together with this, movements toward greater mobility of the financial centers, and employment of the workforce should advance in the sector.

Whatever the case, and along the lines of the *spiral of complexity of digitalized finance* that has already been discussed, the growing use of computers and information technology in financial systems over the coming decades will probably become more (rather than less) opaque and complex than has ever been seen before. This complexity should reinforce the asymmetries of information and cause even more problems, which may in turn damage confidence and make the financial systems less "efficient" and riskier. Currently, amongst the concerns that deserve more attention, are the volatility and sudden instabilities that occur in certain circumstances, the so-called electronic front-running and periodic illiquidity. Restricting and reducing this complexity will be a fundamental challenge for policy makers and regulators who, furthermore, will need to be properly equipped and updated in terms of technology.[52]

As far as this is concerned, it is possible to note that, little by little, and perhaps still in its incipient stages, the regulatory powers are starting to appear as a response to these developments, in the form of regulations that, as we have seen, address the area involving the technical functioning of these mechanisms. This also happens due to the pressure applied by certain classes of investors who have been negatively affected, or who are not benefiting directly or relatively from these high-speed advances in trading. This is enlightening not only in terms of the contradictions and internal conflicts that permeate the digitalized finance complex, but also in that it attacks the often-diffuse idea of the inevitability or uncontrollability of these mechanisms. A tension is

---

51 Certain evolutionary stages still need to be processed to produce the necessary digital transformation that increased artificial intelligence can provide for the markets as a whole, although some companies have already adopted some of these mechanisms in their operations. XTX Markets, for example, one of the world's fastest growing operators in the market, announced that it uses no human operators in its trading. Self-learning machines help to place XTX amongst the world's leading currency traders, overtaking the big banks and financial institutions. For more information on this, see: <https://www.bloomberg.com/news/articles/2016-10-13/this-bank-beating-trading-powerhouse-doesnt-use-human-traders>. Accessed on Dec 05, 2017.

52 In line with other mechanisms and measures, the development of softwares for the automated forensic analysis of adverse/extreme market events, for example, could provide valuable assistance for regulators involved in supervising the markets.

therefore being drawn between the supposed systemic control and lack of control, and regulation and deregulation, in which each player or interest group is attempting to shift the optimal point of this socio-technical and institutional disjunctive in their own favor.

Summing everything up, and despite the resistance from some of those involved, the local, regional and international coordination of policies for the monitoring and regulation of the markets, designed to address their growing systemic risks, seems to be slowly returning to the fore.

CHAPTER 5

Digitalized Finance in the Brazilian Context

As demonstrated by Paulani (2009), Brazil has figured in the history of the financialization of capitalism since its beginnings.

> Initially, the country formed a large part of the demand for credit that caused the first global asset bubble of finance-led capitalism, united in the crisis of Latin-American debts in the first half of the 1980s. From the second half of the 1990s on, it became an emerging financial power, having implemented the necessary structural reforms, from monetary stability to unconditional financial openness, and from social welfare reform to changes in the bankruptcy law. It thus positioned itself as an international platform for financial valorization, or in other words, as an emerging economy in which it was possible to make extremely high gains in a strong currency, with these gains sometimes being the highest in the world. At the time of the fixed exchange rate, this was possible thanks to the very high interest rates and, following the crisis of 1999, and more particularly after 2003, thanks also to the recurrent and self-referenced appreciation of the Brazilian currency, boosted, as it only could have been, by a reliance on derivatives. [...] This way of inserting the Brazilian economy into the world economy strengthened the domestic rent seeking sectors and imposed financial logic on the domestic process of accumulation.
>
> PAULANI 2009, p. 34

Citing Bruno et al. (2009), the researcher highlights various points which indicate this situation. The rate of accumulation of productive fixed capital, for example, fell by around 40 percent at the beginning of the 1980s and stayed at this low level for almost 25 years. Furthermore, the relationship between the stock of financial assets and the stock of productive assets grew enormously, rising from 15 percent in 1992 to around 75 percent in 2008. This has been evaluated thus (Paulani 2009, p. 33):

> Over the last 30 years, the means responsible for financial wealth have been changing, but it has grown in all situations. During the years of high inflation, the existence of two currencies (one functioning as an account unit and means of exchange, and another as a store of value) formed the

basis for rent seeking accumulation and the financialization of wealth. After the stabilization of currency, inflation is replaced by extremely high effective rates of interest, by even greater differences between the interest paid and that received by the financial and banking sectors, and by the unshakeable growth of the public debt as a proportion of the GDP.[1]

Data also drawn from Bruno et al. (2009, pp. 16–21) further demonstrates that an investor who acquired a government title indexed at the Selic[2] rate in January 1991, would, in January 2009, have seven times that amount of capital – the result of an average annual appreciation rate of around 28.4 percent over the period; this, according to Paulani (2009, p. 37), is a performance that is "virtually unobtainable by any project tied to the real economy anywhere in the world (except through contravention)".

As such, it is by means of the flow of dollars, or in other words, by absorbing the scarcity of US savings, that Brazil has inserted itself as a peripheral platform of valorization in finance-led capitalism, contributing to a system whereby the direction of finance is not so shaken at its center, whilst staying strong here in Brazil. Such logic – that anchors its fragile sustainability on financed consumption through extensive credit (that also strengthens financial dominance in the Brazilian economy) without the corresponding investments in infrastructure and manufacturing capacity – imposes a high cost on development in the country in so far as it pressures the exchange rates (almost entirely defined in the derivatives market), upsets the trade balance, prevents investments in manufacturing, and increases the remunerated public debt to one of the highest interest rates in the world, a valuable asset traded on the markets. Therefore, the current economic policy, centered on a three-point base consisting of inflation targets, primary surplus and a floating exchange rate, with ample freedom of mobility for the capitals, strengthens the privilege for interest-bearing capital, by providing high remuneration for the fictitious forms of capital. With the country playing this role in the scenario of international financial valorization, its capitals market gains additional importance.

As far as its operating and management model is concerned, however, the Brazilian capitals market differs in various aspects from that of the United States, where the scenario that we refer to as *digitalized finance* is especially representative. The first, and perhaps most important of these, in this case, is

---

1 Data drawn from Bruno et al. 2009 pp. 16–21.
2 The Sistema Especial de Liquidação e Custodia (SELIC) (Special System for Settlement and Custody) is the Brazilian Central Bank's system for performing open market operations in execution of monetary policy. The SELIC rate is the Bank's overnight rate.

the fact that here we have a single stock exchange, or what is called the "central market".

This condition, achieved thanks to a process of concentration, in which the stock exchanges of São Paulo absorbed the regional exchanges (especially important being the Rio de Janeiro stock exchange, with greater volumes) to then come together as one,[3] is the result, especially, of the difficulties and opportunities arising from the economic contexts and occurrences in Brazil, from the late 1980s through until today. If, in the US, the abundance of currency and over-accumulated capital, together with the deregulation that the financial market experienced, allowed trading to be performed on stock exchanges and in markets spread throughout the country, then concentration could perhaps have been the only course possible for an unconsolidated market with low financial volumes[4] such as that found in Brazil, to insert itself in the international scenario so soon after the country had passed through such a difficult economic period.

Besides being one less factor forcing the Brazilian stock exchange to loosen up its pre-requisites and self-regulation norms as an element of competition for new investors in relation to the other exchanges in the same country (even though this incentive continues to exist, in a certain way, and in another

---

3 The comments on this situation made by Gilberto Mifano, General Superintendent of Bovespa at the time (found in Barcellos 2010, p. 187), are particularly enlightening: "Bovespa already represented 93 percent of the Brazilian market, whilst the Rio Stock Exchange handled 5 percent and the others handled the rest. We thought that, to be able to compete in a world that was becoming increasingly globalized, we should not be wasting our efforts by competing internally. It was unproductive. Our attentions should have been focused on the international competition. We needed to expand the São Paulo Stock Exchange to the rest of the country and, to achieve this unification of the Brazilian market, the São Paulo brokers would have to concede a little. Convincing them was a complicated process. This was because, as well as convincing the brokers here, we had to find an honorable way out for the other exchanges. The solution was for them not to cease to exist, but to be integrated into a single market, within Bovespa, that started to be called the 'Bolsa do Brasil' ('Brazilian Stock Exchange'). To do so, the title of 'Bovespa' was divided into 12 parts, and we allowed the brokers from the other exchanges to enter Bovespa by buying these parts. However, those who would be selling these titles were the São Paulo brokers. Or in other words, we were pleasing both sides: we allowed those on the outside to enter Bovespa at the same time as the brokers here made a profit from selling the titles. They sold half of their titles, since they were required to retain at least 6 of the 12 titles. The brokers from outside São Paulo started to operate on Bovespa whilst we still maintained the possibility of the other stock exchanges subsisting under franchising from Bovespa, sharing part of our revenues with them".
4 For a comparison of the different sizes of the stock exchanges around the world, see: <http://www.visualcapitalist.com/all-of-the-worlds-stock-exchanges-by-size/>. Accessed on Dec 06, 2017.

dimension, in relation to the international markets), the central Brazilian market offers fewer incentives for the HFTs to exploit the arbitrage of milliseconds, through the exchange of financial assetes between different stock exchanges in the same country, which, as we explained earlier, is the case in the US, where the same assets can be traded simultaneously on various markets, exchanges and dark pools[5] around the country.

This situation allowed the Brazilian stock exchange to be able to count upon a set of self-regulatory measures in the institutional and technical-operative spheres, some of which are included in Table 2, in the previous chapter. The Brazilian system of electronic trading, developed in partnership with the CME Group (the Chicago Stock Exchange), operates by means of full and close technical monitoring, from the moment an order is sent until the liquidation and payment of the completed transaction, with individual monitoring, at the level of Registered Individuals (CPF), of the user, and the machine the order was made from, here being performed without intermediaries, using the DMA (Direct Market Access) system. Through this form of operating, the trade order sent by the user, even though guaranteed by a broker who authorizes its operation and joint responsibility is assumed in case of any loss,[6] is processed and completed directly in the exchange's system. In the US however, there is a so-called "internalization", by which the sent order is first received by a broker who, only afterwards, forwards it (either in a block with others or not) to the stock exchange's system. At this point, under the Brazilian scenario, there arises the need and possibility of outlining each market movement in an individual level.

It is by means of this system, for example, that the Brazilian stock exchange is able to monitor and track the behavior of robots handling automated orders (ATs and HFTs) and, in some cases, when more serious situations affect the pricing system as a whole, block the system and even fine those investors responsible for the problem. "This happened once, when there was a package of orders and a robot sent them all at one. When a large investor has a problem of this kind, it ends up creating a pricing problem on the entire exchange", explained Interviewee E, one of the directors of BM&FBovespa.

---

5 Parallel markets created by large investors (banks, hedge funds, etc.) to negotiate amongst themselves, without public participation or transparency of information. The objective is to facilitate the trading of large blocks of shares outside the central markets, under conditions that are, therefore, more favorable for these buyers and/or sellers.

6 The brokers operate as guarantors, being required to cover their clients' losses, including, in part, by means of a compulsory stock exchange guarantee. The BM&FBovespa, in turn, operates as a central trading counterpart, guaranteeing that these trades are actually paid.

As such, the technical control of the HFTs is performed using a risk control system and "locks" for classified clients, like the heavy users – the ones that impose high stresses on the systems. This is stablished following the criteria defined by a technical committee. In addition to this, according to what a number of players in the market told us, BM&FBovespa's information technology sector is in daily contact with brokers and other operators in order to avoid or resolve technical problems. In summary, therefore, Brazil is seen as an international benchmark in relation to its model of risk control, post-trading and monitoring of its trading ecosystem.

These advances, however, are not capable of reversing the general trends outlined in the previous chapter. As Interviewee F, the owner of a Brazilian company providing technology to the capitals market, explained to us, "(in Brazil) the technology battle is a battle for time. How much time I spend getting to the exchange, how many orders I manage to send per second, and the time of my market data. It is based upon this that investments are made in proximity, in co-location, etc."

As we will demonstrate next, the history of the technical-operational evolution of the Brazilian capitals markets to the level at which it stands today – a completely electronic market that is integrated into the international context – is a process that started in the 1990s and has been evolving over time with the opening up of the Brazilian market. "The truth is that the foreign investor has put everyone to move around", explained Interviewee E. "These days there are no barriers. Investors have every possibility of searching for and finding the best opportunities in the world", he said.

Within this scenario, the stock exchanges themselves are acting as corporations, fighting to attract investors from all over the world. The guiding light for this competition, naturally, is the particular set of economic contexts within which it is inserted and, especially, the opportunities for gain that it offers, but the technology is recognized, practically unanimously by those operating in the market with whom we spoke, as a strategic factor in the configuration of this competition. The most advanced stock exchanges within this issue are, therefore, the most attractive for global investors, whose use of technology is equally as intensive.

The increase in the competition, in which technology plays a fundamental role, pressures the markets by the production of more financial innovations. Eager to attract new investors and believing in the supposed security guaranteed by their robust and sophisticated systems, the exchanges and the markets as a whole, are led into taking more risks. This technological race, permeated by greater exposure to risk, marginalizes those players who do not have access to innovation on a large scale.

Seen by the market as being little prepared or equipped for this scenario (demanding in the processing of growing volumes of data and information), the regulation from the official organs ends up creating a scenario that is more favorable for the exploitation of regulatory "vacuums" by the players with the help of their advanced technologies. Within this context, the Brazilian market, recognized amongst trading environments as a "conservative" market at its various levels, drafts a certain self-regulation through the definition of the operating techniques' requirements and standards. This is not enough, however, to reduce the appetite of investors, above all the larger ones, for additional gains through the intensive use of technology.

As we pointed out earlier, the use of HFTs in trading has systematically advanced in Brazil over the last few years. The same can be said of co-location, the growing demand for which has had to be met by the construction of another Data Center by the stock exchange. The most demanding clients are the banks,[7] financial institutions and large investment funds, above all the international ones, for whom cutting-edge technology is a central factor in the competition.[8]

In order to serve this new class of clients, the stock exchange has been constantly updating its systems. The current operating system, the Puma Trading System, installed in the BM&F segment[9] in 2011, and in the Bovespa segment

---

[7] In the words of a former IT manager for a number of large international banks, who was interviewed for this book: "Banks use a lot of HFTs, and have their own robots, but they end up operating in different sectors, meaning that the business strategy, the financial engineering used to achieve the result, is a little broader than just the capitals market and the derivatives market listed on the stock exchange. So, they have a strategy behind this that involves the exchange rate, the over-the-counter market, and own issues themselves, whilst the great challenge for the bank is to manage its risk, its exposure, be it in assets, in currency, in indexes" (verbal information).

[8] It is no accident that we had enormous difficulty interviewing and talking with representatives of large banks who, when they didn't ignore our requests, were evasive and unclear in the reasons for the negations. When speaking with other researchers and players in the financial market during this research, all of them confirmed that this was a typical form of behavior by the large banks and funds, for whom the strategies for gain are produced and maintained by a rigid policy of preservation of corporate information. According to the reports of some of those interviewed, amongst them one from the Brazilian Central Bank, this pattern of behavior became more intensive following the serious crises of image that the banks suffered due to their involvement in the financial crisis of 2008. In some cases, we got around the lack of interviews with bankers by talking to former managers/professionals from large banks.

[9] The current BM&FBovespa was formed in 2008 by a merger of the São Paulo Stock Exchange (Bovespa) and the Commodities and Futures Exchange (BM&F). The company, that has open capital listed in its own trading venues, currently operates in two segments: shares (Bovespa) and commodities and futures (BM&F).

in 2013, was created to handle the large volume and speed of the data. Interviewee J,[10] one of the Information Technology directors at BM&FBovespa, explained to us that the exchange's current trading system is able to process an offer in an average of one to 1.5 milliseconds. As such, the system is scaled to accept around 100,000 orders per second. The peak sum seen so far has been between 12,000 and 13,000 orders per second.

This evolutionary process is part of an important amount of spending devoted to IT in Brazil. According to data from the Brazilian Federation of Banks (Febraban),[11] adding up the spending on bank technology (including those of commercial, retail, banks), 18 percent of all the spending on IT in the country is made by the financial sector (if we include the insurance sector in this, the figure rises to 25 percent). The concentration seen at various levels in the capitals market as a whole is a reality that is also observed, according to the majority of those interviewed in the sector, in the technology market itself.

In a scenario of growing global competition, in which the requirements of the financial sector are ever more sophisticated and demanding, there are fewer and fewer, and bigger, hardware factories, due to the concentration in large scale gains, the lowering of prices, and the limited number of big companies developing software. In accordance with the idea that the technology market for the financial system is undergoing a process of concentration, Interviewee C, a representative of one of the largest companies providing technology to the financial market in the country, explained that his company alone has bought ten other smaller companies since it was founded in the 1980s. "Globalization speeds everything up. The IT sector is pressured by the financial market and provides its responses to the needs. The financial market is in a process of consolidation and downsizing, and the result is that this becomes a trend for the IT market as well", he explained.

As can be seen, except for some important exceptions, the large investors (banks, funds and financial institutions, above all the foreign ones) are generally served by international technology companies. The medium and small clients (amongst which are the majority of Brazilian stock brokers) are usually served by Brazilian companies providing technology to the financial market. Of these, we can highlight the only three that develop Home Broker systems in Brazil, and the only two companies that develop robots or automated trading systems. These companies tend to offer programmed solutions customized for

---

10   Interview given on 05-Jun-2014, in São Paulo (SP). 1 file. mpeg4 (77min56sec).
11   Febraban Banking Technology Study 2017. Base Year 2016. Available at <https://portal.febraban.org.br/pagina/3106/48/pt-br/pesquisa>. Accessed on: Dec 06, 2017.

different Brazilian investors and brokers. There are also five Brazilian brokers who are amongst the biggest in the "individual investors" sector, who develop their own systems and solutions in partnership with other players in the technology industry.

As we will present next, the technological advance of the Brazilian capitals market has contributed, in addition to the great increase in the volume and number of trades, to concentration at virtually every level of the market. Many of the players who invested in technology, principally the small and medium-sized ones, have not experienced the expected returns, due to reasons involving the market, that has also become more and more concentrated. Others, under pressure from the scenario of rapid evolution, cannot afford the high investments in IT required in the context of the Brazilian capitals market.

As we will argue in the next few chapters, everything suggests that the operating logic of digitalized finance creates a situation that is unfavorable for the small direct investor who, as such, has additional reasons to leave the capitals market or seek other ways of investing, including outsourcing his economic decisions to large banks, financial institutions and their investment funds – meaning that, in this case, his decision-making power as a shareholder becomes merely formal (and even weaker than it would be in other contexts). Within this scenario, in which the access to technology provides better opportunities for some more than others, including access to, and the privileged compiling of data and information, there is discussion around the now relatively inactive role of the market jurisdictions and regulatory organs in the protection of small and medium investors and in the guarantee of equal access by all to the same information, allowing the markets to fulfill their hypothetical functions as promoters of the meeting of those offering and assuming credit, to stimulate the growth of companies and economic production. But is this possible in these times of digitalized finance?

5.1   A Brief Overview of the Technical-Operational Development of the Capitals Market in Brazil

The technological advance in the Brazilian capitals market has intensified, above all, since the 1990s, most specifically between 1992 and 1994, when the country underwent a process of liberalization and was opened up to foreign investment, anchored, essentially, in macroeconomic and monetary stabilization and, a few years later, in a program of privatizations. This technical modernization followed a global trend for the integration of the markets, which advanced worldwide during this period. In the words of Interviewee E, a top executive at BM&FBovespa:

> [...] all this coincided with the opening of the market for the arrival of the foreign investor. From one moment to the next, we were welcoming foreign investors here every day, and the trends for trading are global. Brazil wouldn't be able to be open to foreign investors, to be a new economy, with all this promise of stability, etc., whilst playing the game with a market that was lagging behind. Everyone, even the local investors involved in the new competitive structure, started to press for faster and more transparent trading. So to be a part of this game, you had to change the standards of that which is the minimum acceptable (verbal information).

To get an idea of what this change meant, in 1994, with the unfolding of the adoption of the Real Plan and the election of Fernando Henrique Cardoso as President of the country, there was a massive entry of foreign capital into Brazil, and Bovespa closed the year with record levels of trading: a growth of 129 percent in its volumes in relation to the previous year, even considering an adverse scenario due to the Mexican crisis that had international repercussions. It was obvious that, from then on, the Brazilian market started to become truly globalized, with all that was good – the entry of capitals – and all that was bad – increased vulnerability in the international scenario – that was involved, and it was necessary to be prepared for this new scenario. As the attorney Ary Oswaldo Matos Filho (Barcellos 2010, p. 170), President of the Brazilian Securities Commission (CVM) and a member of the National Monetary Council (CMN) from 1990 to 1992, pointed out when interviewed:

> At this time, two important events took place. On the one hand, foreign institutional investors arrived; on the other, the Brazilian institutional investors started to be extremely active because they started to grow. That stock exchange, that until 1989 had basically been maintained by transactions made by individuals – perhaps half a dozen large investors – changed radically. Everything was crushed, destroyed, taken off the map. Then the market started to be much more professional, getting to where it is today.

As such, and following an intensified global trend, especially from this moment on, the Brazilian capitals market started to introduce important technological advances into its operations. In 1990, trading started to be performed by means of the Computer Assisted Trading System (CATS). CATS is an automatic trading system that was developed by the Toronto Stock Exchange in 1977. It was one of the first forms of technology that allowed complete automation of the price establishment process in stock exchanges. Implemented in numerous stock exchanges around the world in the 1980s, this technology was adopted in Brazil at the beginning of the 1990s. By means of this system, operators could buy or sell stocks anywhere around the world in markets that, from the 1980s on, were becoming increasingly liberalized.

These changes were important, but not necessarily substantial. It is possible to say that the trajectory toward a completely automated capitals market, as the Brazilian market now is, truly started in 1996, with the purchase of the automatic trading system called the "NSC" ("Mega Bolsa"). Acquired by the Paris Stock Exchange in 1996, the Mega Bolsa was implemented into the Bovespa segment on July 14, 1997, and underwent successive and important updates as it sought to meet the growing demand for speed, integration and processing capacity. These updates took place in 1998 (Mega Bolsa Plus), 2001 (Mega Bolsa 3), 2003 (Mega Bolsa 380), 2007 (Mega Bolsa 836), 2008 (Mega Bolsa 837) and 2009 (Mega Bolsa V900), until it was finally replaced in 2011/2013 by the PUMA system, produced locally in partnership with the CME Group (Chicago Stock Exchange). Alfredo Rizkallah (Barcellos 2010, p. 86), who headed Bovespa at the time explained how and why the change was made:

> A group of technicians from Bovespa investigated the most modern stock exchanges around the world, such as Frankfurt, London, New York, Chicago and Tokyo, to look at the trading systems in place at the time, and to think about what would be most adaptable to our reality. Four systems were chosen. I personally went to Madrid, Paris, London, New York and Chicago. We decided to transform our trading system, which at the time was tied to a single large IBM computer that processed all the operations, the liquidation of these operations, controlled the security, the bookkeeping and all the administrative side of things. Every time our volume increased, we had to change the computer. We decided to separate the operation and the administration of the stock exchange and we switched over to a new operating system, the 'Mega Bolsa'. We chose a system that had first been employed on the Paris Stock Exchange, and we included some American equipment. These machines that managed the exchange transactions were modular.

The importance of this change lay, essentially, in the fact that this system, as well as operating at a speed that was much faster than the previous one, could transmit information straight to the brokers. Directly out of this evolution started the electronic trading system itself, that would become more and more sophisticated until it reached the current levels. Despite being a relatively efficient electronic system considering the standards at the time, the truth is that the CATS system was complex and difficult to operate and, as a result, it didn't substantially modify the old way of trading stocks on the open outcry trading floor. When the Mega Bolsa was implemented, with the graphic interface of Windows and all the facilities that this entailed, the incentives for substantial changes in the way trading was conducted grew enormously.

But if the switch to electronic systems was, at the time, a global trend, the Brazilian exchange was cautious in its adoption of the new solution. This is because the end of the open outcry trading floor, with human operators, something that still did not appear to be very likely at the time, was seen with great trepidation by the brokerages and their operators. We should remember that the stock exchange at this time was still mutualized, or in other words, operated as an association of "non-profit" brokers. Between the need to adapt to the trends of the globalized market and the desire to maintain the old, satisfactory, business model, the brokerages, formally and politically responsible for any decisions concerning the direction of the stock exchange, went with conciliation in the form of a subtle integration between the two manners of trading – in-person and electronic. "We joined the electronic system with the trading floor. We could see that the whole world was moving toward electronic trading, so we created a system that allowed the coexistence of the trading floor and the electronic system, without either one having an advantage over the other", explained Rizkallah (Barcellos 2010, p. 86). In the words of another former President of Bovespa, Gilberto Mifano (Ibid., p. 185):

> When I took control in December 1994, Álvaro Vidigal, Alfredo Rizkallah (presidents of Bovespa in the 1990s) and I decided that the CATS system needed to be modernized. We started to look around for solutions. The first decision was that we shouldn't develop our own system. The foreign market was a few years ahead of us. Next, we visited the chosen stock exchanges. We started a round of bidding and ended up contracting the French trading system called NSC. In one year, we had adapted it to our needs, taking into consideration our unique characteristic of having the open outcry trading floor and the electronic system at the same time. And so we had created the 'Mega Bolsa'. This adaptation was performed with the help of the French, and it was there that they discovered this parallel system and decided to adopt it. Using the same system, we traded the spot market and the options market. In France, the open outcry

traders went on strike against the electronic system. It was the end of their open outcry: they decided to go solely with the electronic system, and the French open outcry operators watched their ship sail away.

As a result of this model, that integrated the electronic trading system and the open outcry trading system, an important change was necessary: the implementation of the exchange's auctioning system. Due to the fact that two parallel systems existed, there was a risk that the price of a stock would go up in one, but at the same time, drop in the other. Because of this, Bovespa developed a system that guaranteed the convergence of prices by means of auctions. Thus, whenever there was a divergence of prices, an immediate auction would be held to equalize them. By means of this system the stock exchange had found a way of preventing operators arbitrating or creating better or worse trades simply in order to be able to trade in the other space. The auction system still operates today, as mentioned earlier, even after the end of the open outcry trading system. It now operates with another objective, however; to avoid potential market imbalances caused by purchases and sales of stocks in blocks by large investors. Thus, whenever a player activates the purchase or sale of a group of stocks that is disproportionately large in relation to the exchange's trading patterns, this volume automatically goes to auction so that other investors can take part in the trading.

As discussed previously, it is part of the process involved in expanding the frontiers of financial valorization, and an important element in the establishment of financial dominance in the global economy, that the stocks and financial assets markets should be able, by different means, to attract sums accumulated in savings, personal investments and even pensions throughout the world. In 1999, with the advance of personal computing and use of the Internet in Brazil – noted since 1995, with the creation of the Internet Management Committee – a new transformation was set to further accelerate the move toward the complete electronification of the markets and the end of the open outcry trading systems: the implementation of an interface for the use of Home Broker via Direct Market Access (DMA) which, in the way in which it worked in Brazil, was a world pioneer.

The Home Broker is a platform that allows for remote participation in the financial market from personal computers connected to the Internet. By means of the DMA system, the individual user/investor can send in their purchase and sale orders directly to the stock exchange's trading system, that automatically executes and updates the operations, volumes of shares and their market trading prices. In the United States, where Internet trading already existed, it worked differently, under a system that, in a certain way, accepting changes and updates, still exists today. In general, a client in the US sends their purchase or sale order to the broker, who, as the mediator in the process, receives it and then decides what to do with it. In the system employed by the Brazilian stock exchange, the order leaves the client and arrives directly in the stock exchange's system, along with all the other orders in the market. Here, even though he has direct access to the exchange's system, however, a broker has to filter the orders, recognize the user as his client and check that he has sufficient credit to execute them.

The reasons pointed out by Gilberto Mifano (Barcellos 2010, p. 186), Superintendent General of Bovespa, for the implementation of the system, reinforce the aims of attracting new investors, reducing operational costs and reducing or eliminating human interference in the trading process.

> We believe that that was a means of reaching the individual, who did not have a way of being attended to at the brokers' tables due to the operational costs. He would make a telephone call and ask to speak to the same operator who might have been speaking to a fund or a foreign client, investors who operate with a thousand or a hundred thousand times more. Our new idea was to use this new instrument to replace the telephone. In a pioneering move, two brokerages had already replaced the telephone with the Internet – Souza Barros and Socopa. The client sent in his order by Internet, it would appear on a screen and the operator typed it into the Mega Bolsa, but even so there was human interference. We therefore developed this concept of Home Broker, but we decided to limit ourselves to creating a technological base, an infrastructure that we called Gateway that could be used by brokers to develop their own way of communicating with the client. This Gateway would allow a client's order to be introduced directly into the Mega Bolsa. The Home Broker moved away from the concept of having a single Bovespa system available for all the brokers and their clients. Each broker had to create their own portal and, on top of this, the direct link with the client would differentiate the brokerages.

But if this was a technological resource that increased the possibilities for the entry of more resources and new investors, above all individuals, into the capitals market, due to the operational facilities and the reduction of its costs, there was, at the same time, resistance from the brokerages and their operators, as explained by Raymundo Magliano Filho (Ibid., p. 48), President of Bovespa from 2001 to 2007, and himself a broker:

> [There was resistance to the implementation] at the beginning because there was a fear that the functiono of the broker would come to an end. We were gradually overcoming these difficulties, and demonstrating the

other aspects of this modern way of operating. It was the broker's responsibility to provide a service to their clients – support, counseling, management – rather than buy and sell stocks.

The brokers' fears, however, were not necessarily unfounded. This "redefinition" of the role of the brokers mentioned by Magliano is still being performed. This, however, requires enormous investments in modernization and new technologies for which many brokerage firms were not properly prepared. Since then, the number of brokers has not only fallen, but the market has become concentrated in the hands of a few of them, and this within a scenario of growth in the number of investors, trades and financial volumes. From 2003 to 2016, the number of brokerage firms operating in the Brazilian stock market fell by around 16 percent (from 94 to 79). Whilst this number fell, the percentage of purchases and sales of stocks concentrated in the hands of the few rose. Of the five biggest brokerages operating in the Brazilian stock market at the end of 2014, four were foreign and together they handled almost half the total volume traded (around 45 percent); at the beginning of 2017, the five biggest brokerages accounted for more than 51 percent of the total daily volume of trades. Despite the obvious affinity between these processes, this movement of concentration is, however, strengthened by various other factors and cannot be explained by the simple implementation of technologies, as we will now explain. The very consolidation of the Home Broker took a long time in coming.

In addition to the brokers, the adoption of the Home Broker encountered various other difficulties. As Gilberto Mifano (Barcellos 2010, p. 186), points out, "the implementation [of Home Broker] was very slow, because distrust remained over dealing with money on the Internet". Summing everything up, the march of technological advance in the Brazilian capitals market toward its full updating and international integration did not occur without bumps; it ended up requiring the ability to mediate and conciliate the interests of the different players involved in the changes, so that they could be implemented.

The following years, however, would further the process of modernization of the Brazilian capitals market, in line with the global trends for development of the regime of accumulation with the dominance of financial valorization. The objective of this process, as we can see, is, not uncommonly, established precisely by means of a set of technical advances and institutional changes that, as we have outlined, are mutually reinforced within the sphere of operation and the functioning of the markets.

In 2000, inspired by the French, Italian and, principally German models, Bovespa launched the "Novo Mercado" ("New Market"), a forum that established standards and created different levels of corporate governance[12] for the companies listed on the exchange. This standard adjusted the Brazilian market, in line with the need to attract individuals – who increased their participation from 15 percent to 20 percent in the Brazilian stock market from 1999 to 2000 –, and the need and global trend, as systematized by Chesnais, for reconfiguration in the sphere of administration and management of companies to conform to the needs of stock markets throughout the world.

As such, it is the role performed by these "assets markets", in addition to the "expansion of the number of salaried shareholders by means of the importance of the institutional investors in finances and in the governance of companies as a primary instance of regulation" that establishes the expression "patrimonial regime".
CHESNAIS 2002, p. 18

Jealous of their participation in the international market, Bovespa hired researchers and specialists to contribute to the process of identifying and proposing changes with this objective. This was the peak of the "New Economy", of the "dot com" companies, of media and biotechnology. As Gilberto Mifano (Barcellos 2010, p.189) noted, the investigations noted that there was a great deal of mistrust in relation to the products that were traded in Brazil. This was an important period for the Brazilian capitals market that, between 1999 and 2000, saw a series of important transformations: the adoption of the Home Broker in the Bovespa segment; the implementation of the Global Trading System (GTS)[13] electronic platform in the BM&F segment; the creation of the

---

12 According to Rosa Marques and Paulo Nakatani, translators of the book "La finance mondialisée" by François Chesnais (2005), in relation to the concept of corporate governance: "The government of companies (or corporations) was systematized by the OECD in the form of a set of principles that should be followed by companies, to provide greater stability to the financial system, the central point of which arises from the separation of ownership and control and the relationship between shareholders and the administrators of companies" (Ibid. p. 42, translator's note). More details can be obtained in the document OECD, *Principles of the OECD about the government of companies*.

13 B&MF Circular "106/2001 – DG", dated August 23, 2001, concerning the launch of financial products to be traded exclusively on the new system, explained the way it worked and provided notes that were especially interesting in relation to the theme of this book, and we quote: "Since September 2000, the Brazilian derivatives market has worked with electronic operations by means of the BM&F's Global Trading System (GTS). This period is noted for the learning, both by the Stock Exchange and its members and clients, of the new peculiarities of the trading in the electronic space for derivatives, in comparison with the traditional and efficient open outcry trading system. But this was a learning

"New Market" and, in the macroeconomic sphere, the liberation of the currency, that started operating on a floating exchange rate. In comparison with the growth of 4.3 percent of the country's GDP between 1999 and 2000, the number of trades closed on the stock exchange rose more than 42 percent, and the total financial volume from them increased by something like 20 percent during the same period.[14]

Here, once again, the measures were not implemented without disputes and the need for new agreements and intercessions due to the Brazilian reality. The objective of the stock exchange and its directors, at the time, was to consolidate the changes of the new standard of corporate governance in Brazilian legislation, something that was considered to be very costly, since it required great effort on the part of the government and the companies themselves. Inspired by the German model, that encountered similar resistance in relation to changes to the country's legislation for the application of the new rules, the Brazilian stock exchange opted for a self-regulatory model, in which adhesion to the new standard was performed by means of a contract signed between the stock exchange and the companies, as Gilberto Mifano (Ibid., p. 189) explains:

> The reaction of the companies, represented by the Brazilian Association of Publicly Traded Companies (ABRASCA), was strong and understandable. The solution was to create a form of progression. Contrary to what our consultants wanted, we created different levels and separated the rules of the New Market into packages. At Level 1, there are all the rules relating to transparency. These were the easiest for the companies already listed to comply with. At Level 2, we brought together some asset rights for the defense of the minority investor, but we still maintained preferred shares. At the New Market level, all the rules and more were in

---

period not only for Brazil. Our partners in the Globex Alliance have also been through it, which explains the constant improvement of the electronic trading system, through the new versions made available to the stock exchanges. During this process, the BM&F sought to introduce trading only outside the open outcry trading system operating hours, with all possible assets, leaving it to the market to show its interest in the electronic trading. During this period, the electronic system attracted an impressive share of 7 percent of the trading, even though it was operating during hours when there had not previously been any trading, meaning, clearly, that there was a growth in volume. In the version first put into operation, it was not possible to record direct trades, which are used very much in our market. Operating strategies such as spreads, straddles etc., also proved difficult to implement. Now, with this new version, these operations will be possible". Available at <http://www.bmf.com.br/bmfbovespa/pages/Clearing1/Derivativos/agropecuarios/internacionalizacao/oficios/InformesOficio10601.asp>. Accessed on: Jul 20, 2017.

14 Data from BM&FBovespa.

place, with requirements for the maintenance of solely common shares. This was an entirely private initiative, without any influence from the government. We received assistance from Armínio Fraga, President of the Central Bank at the time, and from José Luiz Osório de Almeida Filho, President of the CVM at the time.

In so far as these big steps were being taken, the electronification of the Brazilian markets as a direct consequence of the technological advances either imported or produced locally using international technical standards, the important institutional changes outlined by the "New Market" initiative would demand corresponding standardization in the technical-operational procedures of the capitals market. If, since the beginning of the 1990s, as the fruit of the economic openings, as we have explained, the Brazilian market has continually advanced in its process of modernization until today, then 2005 marked a fundamental point in the configuration of this trajectory: the establishment of the Operational Qualification Program (PQO).

The PQO[15] is a certification system that was created with the aim of certifying the quality of the services offered by the brokerage firms acting in the market as members of the so-called intermediation industry. The criteria are measured in terms of quality of service, operational efficiency and the financial capacity of the brokerage to assume risks. As such, upon meeting the criteria defined by BM&FBovespa, the certified brokers can, by means of their qualification stamps, prove the standard of their services to the market and their clients.

The impact of the measure, that required substantial changes in the form adopted for the administration of its business and, especially, large investments in operating technology, was enormous amongst the brokerages; many of whom, facing difficulties in working within the new scenario, ended up closing their doors. "The PQO raised the bar for everyone. We had to show the world that this was no longer a 'banana republic', in which a foreign investor sends their money and doesn't know what's going to happen to it", explained Interviewee E, an executive with BM&FBovespa. The adoption of the program, which coincided with the end of the open outcry trading system at Bovespa, led to important changes. Since then, the number of brokers operating in the market started to fall; a process that has continued up until today, with increasingly large slices of the market being concentrated in the hands of just a

---

15 A basic outline of the modus operandi of the PQO, dated 2010, can be found at: <http://www.bsm-autorregulacao.com.br/assets/file/leis-normas-regras/roteiro-basico-pqo-bvmf-2010-10-07.pdf>. Accessed on: Jul 20, 2017.

few brokers, above all international ones. As Interviewee C, a representative of a large Brazilian company supplying technology to the financial market, told us, "the PQO required a lot of investment because it presses and changes the standard of the market to keep in line with the international context. This is expensive and the small companies simply can't afford it".

Along the way, important transformations took place in the market. In 2002, a program aimed at making Bovespa more accessible was started. An audacious move, in line with the context and objectives discussed earlier, it aimed to drastically increase the number of small investors, such as individuals, through marketing and advertising campaigns, as well as through other mediums, that would attract them to invest in the capitals market. Through the program called "Bovespa vai até você" ("Bovespa comes to you"), for example, the exchange set up stands on beaches and at large public events to meet people and explain what it was, how it worked and why it was profitable to invest in the capitals market. Although it provided important gains in terms of the domestic and international image of the institution, the program had little practical effect.[16]

In 2003, according to information provided by Interviewee E, the stock exchange started welcoming its first investors using a number of Algorithmic Trading (AT) strategies that were still non-too advanced, but which became more sophisticated, due to the demands of large foreign investors, and in 2004 the Web Trading (WTr)[17] system was implemented in the BM&F segment.

Also in 2004, the so-called "boom" of Initial Public Offerings at Bovespa started, when companies opened up their capital and started trading shares on the stock exchange. During this period, between 2004 and 2008, 109 companies

---

16 For a balance of the results of the program, and a discussion of the current participation of small investors in the stock exchange, see the article "Não fuja da Bolsa, diz ex-presidente da Bovespa" in the Exame magazine issue dated June 6, 2014. Available at <http://exame.abril.com.br/seu-dinheiro/noticias/nao-fuja-da-bolsa-diz-ex-presidente-da-bovespa>. Accessed on: Jul 25, 2014.

17 "The WTr is a system developed by the BM&F for the trading of derivatives contracts by means of the worldwide computer network – the Internet. This type of system, in which the clients themselves place their offers using a work station connected to the Internet, is very popular in a number of international derivatives markets. Its most important characteristic is its ability to offer services to a large participant base with relatively low operating costs. The first objective of the WTr was then to enable a substantial increase in the number of clients served by the brokers associated with the BM&F. The users of the WTr were identified as being small investors, especially individuals and non-financial companies" (Appendix B of the BM&F Circular 086/2005-DG, p. ii). Available at <http://www.cmcapitalmarkets.com.br/brasil/archives/Webtrading_BM&F.pdf>. Last accessed on: Jul 20, 2017.

opened up their capital. Through their IPOs, together they brought in the sum of R$86.4 billion (an average of R$823 million per IPO).[18] Adrighi (2010) points out that amongst the factors responsible for this boom are: the macroeconomic foundations of the Brazilian economy, considered to be solid by investors at the time; microeconomic reforms, with an emphasis on the reform of the so-called "Companies Law", in 2001, and the approval of the law that regulates the attributes and responsibilities of the CVM, in 2002; high international liquidity; and the implementation of Bovespa's "New Market", in 2000, with different levels of corporate governance requirements.

In 2005, the fatal blow was dealt to the old form of trading on the Brazilian stock market: the end of the open outcry trading system at Bovespa, that would be followed by the same move at BM&F in 2009. This was a very important event, above all symbolically, with enormous repercussions. In 2005, being almost up to date in all its operational aspects, that later on would evolve toward integration with global standards, the Brazilian market was on the verge of reaching a level equal to that of the world's other principal capitals markets: it was completely electronic; it used advanced trading technologies; its operational standards were guided by a qualification program that pressed for updating throughout the sectors linked to the financial market; it had a fully operative corporate governance policy for those publicly traded companies listed on the exchange; and it had favorable economic and regulatory scenarios that would contribute to enabling companies to open their capital on the stock exchange during the period.

But this result did not happen overnight. The change was planned, matured and put into practice, step-by-step, over a number of years, and not without arguments and the need to accommodate different interests, as the former President of Bovespa Alfredo Rizkallah (Barcellos 2010, p. 86) remembers:

> We had to overcome very strong resistance from those people who thought that the trading floor could never cease to exist, because it was the symbol of the stock exchange. It was a process that involved a lot of hard work to make them see the advantages and advances. We had to

---

18   For more information on this, see: Aldrighi et al. (2010). The article provides a broad panorama of the period, with a discussion on the profile of the companies and what led them to open their capitals at this time. Amongst the results of the study, summarized by the author, are: (a) larger, more profitable, companies, with higher investment spending, which are growing more than others, show a greater likelihood of going public; (b) financial restructuring and diversification of the wealth of the business owners do not seem to be motives for the IPOs; and (c) the favorable conditions of the international capitals market contributed to the wave of IPOs during the period.

manage the interests at stake. The negotiations for the gradual phasing out of the trading floor was not pleasant for us.

Another former president of Bovespa, Raymundo Magliano Filho (Ibid. p. 48), expressed his feeling in a similar way, with emphasis on the problem of the trading floor operators or "traders", many of whom had to retire earlier than expected or lose their jobs.

> The decision to put an end to the open outcry trading system was extremely difficult. We realized the trend for the trading floor to evolve to the electronic system, and we thought about what to do with the operators, the people who knew the market. I spoke with Paulo Pereira da Silva, 'Paulinho' of 'Força Sindical', the trades union organization, and he advised me to retrain these people.

The Superintendent General of Bovespa, Gilberto Mifano (Barcellos 2010, pp. 185–186), explains that the stock exchange developed encouragement programs and provided financial incentives, to overcome the resistance to the process of gradual migration to the complete automation of the trading.

> You have to see it and do it. At that time, the trading was done by open outcry and we had more than a thousand people working on the trading floor at any one time. I miss that time, because the human energy was something so wonderful to see, but at the same time, that process was very inefficient. [...] We needed to move all the operators over to this new world of technology and to a more transparent way of trading, without shouting. We even provided incentives for the brokerage firms to take the first steps toward the electronic system – they would pay less fees. They all started to use it, principally the investors. The less liquid assets started to be traded electronically. This system also allowed strategies such as, for example, making an offer appear only when the market price reached a certain level. This could also be arranged with the trading floor operator, but as it depended upon a physical person, it did not work so well. Under the electronic system, it was mathematical and exact. People started to understand how to make trades with baskets. Between 20 and 30 commercial papers were being traded at the same time. And the process grew.

This transformation expanded between the years 2007 and 2008, due to important institutional changes. As we have discussed, the Brazilian stock exchanges worked in a mutualized form, as an association of non-profit brokerage firms that had quotas and titles that gave them the right to take part in this company. Within a context of growing international competition between stock exchanges and markets to attract capitals, getting past this model was important in moving toward better global insertion.

In 2007, occurs the processes of demutualization of Bovespa, and later BM&F, with their subsequent IPOs, that were real successes from the financial point of view. In practice, the stock exchanges stopped being non-profit entities and started to be publicly held companies; the previous holders of membership shares were now shareholders, with the advantage that these brokers were now more capitalized to compete with the growing competition. In some way confirming our hypotheses concerning the increasing concentration of the operations into a limited number of markets and a reduced number of global financial marketplaces, in 2006, prior, therefore, to the demutualization of the stock exchanges, Nelson Bizzacchi Spinelli (Ibid., p. 54), owner of a large brokerage firm and member of a traditional São Paulo-based family of brokers, stated that:

> I have been talking about demutualization for many years, but I should stress that, in order to go public, it is necessary to have money in your purse. We need to insert ourselves in the global market that will shortly be concentrated in three or four trading centers: the Asian, European, American and South-American, with these last two possibly transforming into just one.

The process was very successful and guaranteed the entry of enormous volumes. The next year, in 2008, Bovespa and BM&F, now public companies, merged as one company, forming BM&FBovespa, and so became the third largest stock exchange in the world, and the largest in South America in terms of market value.[19] That same year,[20] Brazil received the title of "Investment Grade" from the US (ratings) agency Standard and Poors (S&P). By contributing to the development of the market in Brazil, the demutualization, IPO and merger of the exchanges had a number of direct effects on the technology market, which saw enormous growth during the period, as we learned from Interviewee F, the owner of an important company supplying technology to

---

19 Source: <http://ri.bmfbovespa.com.br/ptb/889/Pressrelease20080326.pdf>. Accessed on: Jul 27, 2014.
20 In 2008, the Lehmann Brothers bank also went under, one of the notable moments at the beginning of the great global financial crisis, which would still take a while to have more serious effects on the Brazilian capitals market.

the financial market, and one of just three companies developing Home Broker software on demand in Brazil. His observations are particularly enlightening, since he refers to the focus of this book, as he discusses the relationship between market movements and the demand for new technological solutions.

> The IPO was crazy. The volumes were extraordinarily high, and a lot of money was made. By means of this, the brokerage firms, that up until then had been owners of the exchange, made an enormous amount of money. Being more capitalized, many started to make large investments in technology and infrastructure. And for us, this is directly proportional. It is easy to see. You only need to start growing and you start receiving emails, contacts and orders for products. When the market starts to drop, it's the other way around. People start calling and asking to finalize projects and cancel orders (verbal information).

In parallel with these important institutional changes that took place in the market, the stock exchanges were also preparing for full integration with the international technical-operational scenario. First, at the BM&F, in 2007, and then at Bovespa, in 2008, the FIX[21] (Financial Information eXchange Protocol), protocol was adopted. This is an international interface for the exchange of data used by the world's largest and most important stock exchanges. This was an absolutely fundamental step toward the complete technological updating and interaction of the Brazilian stock exchange with the global trading modus operandi. With this new way of working, everything became easier, above all for operations by foreign investors, who have adapted their systems to operate in various markets throughout the world at the same time.

The following years, from 2009 to 2010, would be notable for the complete implementation of the co-location trading modality in BM&F and Bovespa, which increased the capacity, especially of large domestic and foreign investors, to operate using ATs and HFTs in the Brazilian markets. As Interviewee F, the owner of a company supplying technology to the capitals market, told us, these years saw a great deal of movement in the sector.

---

21   In the definition provided by the stock exchange itself on its website: "The FIX (Financial Information eXchange Protocol) involves a series of specifications of messages for the electronic communication of trading, that allows secure and standardized communication with BM&FBOVESPA. The FIX interface can be used within one's own trading solutions, that is, those developed by the participants, as well as by means of solutions offered by specialist companies, such as independent suppliers of software (ISVs – Independent Software Vendor), suppliers of back office integration systems etc.". Available at <http://www.bmfbovespa.com.br/pt-br/servicos/solucoes-para-negociacao/sessao-fix/sessao-fix.aspx?Idioma=pt-br>. Accessed on: Jul 27, 2014.

[...] with this in place, it was even easier for foreigners to come to the country. This coincided with the period when Brazil received the Investment Grade, meaning that 2008 was a year in which the technological scenario for the capitals market in Brazil changed a great deal. The stock exchange was modernized, and foreigners started to find it easier to come here, but we did not have our own solutions, programs or systems in the country that were suitable for the new protocol. This meant that an enormous technology race started. Banks and brokers started to invest more and race after solutions that were adapted to the new protocol. And it was during this time, between 2008 and 2010, that we saw our greatest period of growth.

In August 2010, the stock exchange started to make use of the "LiNe" ("Limite de Negociação") platform (at the time called MegaLiNe) available to registered brokers. This system allowed clients' risks to be monitored during the pre-trading phase, prior to the trades being performed. The mechanism (GTSLiNe) has been available since 2008 in the BM&F segment.[22]

Meanwhile, during this period, the stock exchange was modernized, and foreign investors started getting more technical facilities to operate in the country, but the domestic financial market technology companies did not have many specific solutions, programs or systems that were suitable for the new protocol, which required the banks and brokers to make more investments in new solutions adapted to their needs.

Between 2011 and 2013, a period which saw a massive entry of foreign capital into Brazil,[23] through a partnership started in 2008 with the CME Group (Chicago Stock Exchange) – that administrates four stock exchanges and is one of the world's biggest operators on the derivatives market – BM&FBovespa finished the production and full installation of a new trading system, that

---

22 After the Puma Trading System (2011 BM&F/ 2013 Bovespa) had been put into operation, and updated as the Line Entry Point platform, the system was in operation. The Line was developed by the Exchange itself and allows brokers to establish trading limits for clients with Direct Market Access (DMA) in modalities 3 and 4 (Direct Connection and Co-location, respectively), or clients that are classified as heavy users. Amongst its functions is the validation of the maximum size of an offer, limits for the long or short positions, and panic buttons, for which the final client is responsible. Since March 2013, use of the system has been obligatory for all investors classified as High Frequency Traders (HFTs).

23 During this period, the interest shown in Brazil by funds and HFT investors was such that two large conferences on the subject were organized in São Paulo, the first one in March 2011, and the second in March 2012: the 1st and 2nd Annual Algo and High Frequency Trading Latin America Summits. For more information on this, see: <http://quant-house.com/node/159>. Accessed on: Feb 15, 2017. To understand the recent growth of portfolio investment in Brazil, see Silva Filho (2015).

operated with a latency in the region of milliseconds. The new system, the Puma Trading System, fully updated with global state of the art for the sector, first replaced the old GTS in the BM&F segment (2011), and then the old Mega Bolsa at Bovespa (2013).[24] Since its implementation, the new system has surpassed successive records for the daily processing of transactions – from ~ 25 million in 2013 to more than 35 million in 2015.

The investments in this were great. According to information from the Stock Exchange itself, between 2010 and 2016, BM&FBovespa invested around R$1.6 billion in its information technology infrastructure, and in its functioning and operational risk, included in this sum being the construction of a data center[25] in Santana do Paranaíba (São Paulo), inaugurated in 2014. This was the biggest investment program in the history of the institution. Amongst other goals, one of the stated objectives of these investments was the development of an infrastructure that allows and supports the expansion of the activities of HFTs and other investors with high data processing needs that, in the view of BM&FBovespa, provides greater liquidity and, therefore, greater profit for the Exchange.

In August 2014, BM&FBovespa started operating the "BM&FBovespa Clearing" system, a new post-trading infrastructure that integrated the stock exchange derivatives and over-the-counter markets; fixed private income and shares; exchange spot transactions; and financial treasury bills, that up until then had used separate liquidation platforms.

As well as combining the liquidation platforms, something that had been planned since at least 2010 within the remit of the Post-Trading Integration Program (IPN), the same year saw the beginning of the operation of the system designed to manage risk in "almost" real time – CORE (Closeout Risk Evaluation). The new system is capable of monitoring tens of thousands of investors' portfolios with positions in stock and over-the-counter derivatives, and simulating thousands of possible paths of assets prices, contracts and guarantees contained in the investors' portfolios, using different modeling techniques that help each other in search of greater solidity in the calculation of risk. CORE[26]

---

24 For more information on the migration and features of the new system, see Circular Letter 017/2013-DP published by BM&FBovespa on February 25, 2013.

25 For more information on the new Data Center see <https://economia.ig.com.br/financas/investimentos/2014-03-19/novo-data-center-da-bolsa-de-valores-custou-r-200-milhoes-e-tem-sala-de-guerra.html> and <http://datacenterdabolsa.com.br/?utm_source=Bmfbovespa&utm_medium=Banner_home&utm_campaign=Banner_2colunas_BMFBOVESPA>. Accessed on: Feb 13, 2017.

26 The new "CORE" system of risk management was developed by a multi-disciplinary team made up of professionals specialized in risk management, statistics, mathematics and

also evaluates the market risks as well as those involved in the liquidity and cash flow of assets and contracts, allowing the integrated calculation of the margins of multi-market and multi-product portfolios.

Therefore, now fully up-to-date, the capitals market in Brazil can be considered to be operating in line with the global, state of the art technology for the sector. For systematization purposes, we have drawn up below a time line with the most significant technological advances in each of the segments of the current BM&FBovespa, accompanied by the respective important economic and institutional events to allow their interpretation within the context of the evolution of the Brazilian capitals market. This table will also be useful in the issue we will be addressing next, which concerns the results and consequences in the nature of the Brazilian capitals market with which these technological advances (Table 3) are related.

5.2   The Development of the ICT and the Transformations of the Brazilian Capitals Market: Elective Affinities

Brazil is the biggest financial marketplace in Latin America and one of the biggest in daily trading volumes amongst the emerging nations. As we have seen, after a process of concentration, in which the stock exchanges of São Paulo absorbed the other regional stock exchanges (of special importance being that of Rio de Janeiro, with greater volumes), the BM&FBovespa became the only stock exchange operating in the country. It has, therefore, despite the market only having been formally open since 2007, a virtual monopoly in the sector, since shares are traded exclusively on the stock exchange, as are the majority of the derivatives. Dark pools, Multilateral Trading Systems (MTFs) and/or alternatives (ATS), and the internalization of orders are not permitted.

In 2012, the market was informed of the creation of the Americas Trading System Brasil (ATS Brasil), a joint venture between the Americas Trading Group (ATG) and the New York Stock Exchange (NYSE), which, in June 2013, filed a request to the CVM for the creation a new stock exchange in Brazil. With its head offices in Rio de Janeiro, the company intends to operate in the market

computing, and included collaboration with international consultancies. With the implementation of the CORE platform, the Stock Exchange intends to provide a "processing capacity sufficient to support the growth of the markets over the next two decades and implement a more robust plan for the continuity of trading and recovery from disaster". For more details on this system, see: <http://en.resenhadabolsa.com.br/portfolio-category/clearinghouse-integration-and-core-closeout-risk-evaluation-bmfbovespas-new-risk-management-system/>. Accessed on Feb 13, 2017.

TABLE 3   Time line of technological innovations in the Brazilian capitals market

	Bovespa segment	BM&F segment	Economic/institutional changes
1992	Trading started to be performed by means of the Computer Assisted Trading System (CATS)		Start of the process of deregulation and liberalization of the Brazilian market
1997	Implementation of the Mega Bolsa electronic platform (based upon Euronext's NSC platform)		Start of the privatization program under the government of Fernando Henrique Cardoso
1999	Launch of the Direct Market Access (DMA) trading mode for the stocks segment. Implementation of the *Home Broker* interface.		End of the fixed exchange rate system
2000		Implementation of the Global Trading System electronic platform (based upon Euronext's NSC platform)	Launch of the "New Market" and the different levels of corporate governance
2002			Bovespa popularization program
2003	First ATs (*Algo Tradings*) used on the Brazilian stock exchange		
2004		Web Trading (WTr): first automated interface	Start of the so-called "era of IPOs"
2005	Start of the Operational Qualification Program (PQO) End of the open outcry trading system at Bovespa		
2007		New GTS: platform developed internally by BM&F, providing an FIX interface	Demutualization and IPO of Bovespa and BM&F

	Bovespa segment	BM&F segment	Economic/institutional changes
2008	New version of the Mega Bolsa platform (NSC v900), with FIX interface	Launch of the DMA trading mode for the derivatives segment (BM&F) and establishment of the routing agreement with the Chicago Mercantile Exchange (CME) Provision of the pre-trading risk management software "LINE" (Negotiation Limit)	Merger of the BM&F and Bovespa stock exchanges. Brazil receives investment grade status from the S&P ratings agency World financial crisis
2009	Implementation of the Mega Direct order entry interface (developed internally by BM&FBovespa) for the Mega Bolsa	End of the open outcry trading system at BM&F (where electronic trading had been dominant since 2007). Start of the Co-location mode	
2010	Start of the Co-location mode Provision of the pre-trading risk management software LINE (Negotiation Limit)		Start of the Post-Trading Integration Program (IPN)
2011		Replacement of the GTS with the Puma Trading System platform	
2013	Replacement of the Mega Bolsa with the Puma Trading System platform		
2014	Implementation of the BM&FBovespa Clearing system Implementation of the CORE (Closeout Risk Evaluation) risk management system Inauguration of the new Data Center	Implementation of the BM&FBovespa Clearing system Implementation of the CORE (Closeout Risk Evaluation) risk management system Inauguration of the new Data Center	Unification, within the sphere of the IPN, of four "clearings" that until then had been separate: stock and over-the-counter market derivatives; shares and fixed private income; spot currency exchange; and financial treasury bills

SOURCE: BM&FBOVESPA; OWN ELABORATION

as a new stock exchange initially focused on the trading of stocks, with the intention of expanding into other products in the future. The creation of the new stock exchange, according to information released by the ATS, is planned to take place in partnership with the company Risk Office and the post firm's pension fund, Postalis. The ATS Brasil will operate using trading systems developed and installed by NYSE Technologies, the NTSE technology department, which has already customized its trading platform for ATS Brasil: the Universal Trading Platform (UTP), a trading system used by stock exchanges belonging to the group in other parts of the world. The company is still, however, awaiting the approval of the Brazilian regulatory authorities before it can start its operations. In April 2016, in order to strengthen its position in relation to this competition even more, the BM&FBovespa announced that it would be merging with CETIP, the financial market and domestic capitals integrator that offers registration services, a central depositary, and trading and liquidation of assets and securities. In September 2016, the antitrust agency (CADE) opened an administrative inquiry to investigate a suspected infringement of the economic order by the BM&FBovespa.[27] The opening of this investigation is the result of a complaint filed by the ATS. According to a technical note issued by CADE, ATS Brasil provided evidence that, "asserting its monopolistic and vertically integrated position in the services markets related to the stock exchange, the BM&FBovespa has been adopting strategies to considerably raise the barriers designed to prevent the entry of potential competitors in the market". These strategies have included the refusal to provide clearing or central depositary services, or make any changes to the tariff policy, "that in turn will be tightening the margins of any entrants who are not vertically integrated".

Although it adheres to the regulations of the Brazilian Securities Commission (CVM), the stock exchange itself is responsible for the supervision and self-regulation of the markets in which it operates. The final beneficiary of the trading and post-trading chain is identified, and the over-the-counter operations must be registered, as must any loans of assets. The BM&FBovespa still acts as a central counterpart in all the trades negotiated within its spaces.

It should be noted that, in addition to the low level of penetration and the relatively small number of individual investors, few companies are listed on the exchange, with important sectors of the Brazilian economy not duly represented. Besides the fall in the number of operations involving companies going public in recent years, the majority of the volume traded is concentrated in a small number of stocks and instruments (42 percent in the 10 most-traded

---

27 Reuters. Available at: <http://br.reuters.com/article/businessNews/idBRKCN11X1OZ>. Accessed on: Feb 24, 2017.

stocks in the Bovespa segment, and 46 percent in the interest rate derivatives contracts in the BM&F segment). Due to the incidence of high interest rates over the last few decades, the portfolios of investors are highly concentrated in fixed income (government bonds),[28] something that additionally competes to also keep down the level of sophistication of pension funds and other institutional investors.

The Brazilian market, however, has, as has been noted, been shifting and modernizing rapidly over recent years, especially during the period at the end of the last decade, when, as we have seen, the demutualization, merger of the stock exchanges and acceleration of the process of technological modernization of the markets took place, with the end of the open outcry trading system and the enabling of fully automated trading structures in the BM&F and the Bovespa segments.

By looking at the history of the technical-operational and institutional development of the Brazilian capitals market with different numerical and accounting data, as well as information on the facts, background workings and details offered by various players (operators, investors, brokers and executives from BM&FBovespa, amongst others), it is possible to see a certain coincidence or elective affinity[29] between the process of development of the Information and Communication Technologies and the further development of the tendencies of consolidation of financial dominance, here expressed, at their genesis, in the very workings of the capitals market.

The development trajectory of the Brazilian capitals market over the last 20 years is notable for a certain technological advance that, although we cannot conclude that it is the only or most important factor in the conforming of its growth, is tightly bound to it in relation to the dimensions mentioned earlier – all reinforced by data and research, and including: (i) displacement of the space-time flows with the consequent increase in the number and volume of trades performed; (ii) additional difficulties for the process of market control and regulation; and (iii) the consequent concentration in different levels

---

28   More than 40 percent of all the assets in the hands of fund administrators is in fixed income, against an average of around 25 percent in other central markets (Weems and Tabb 2014).

29   "The passage taken by this term is rather curious: it goes from alchemy to sociology, moving though Romanesque literature. Its godfathers are Albertus Magnus (8th century), Wolfgang Goethe and Max Weber. In our use of the concept, we have tried to integrate the different meanings that the expression has assumed over the centuries. We designate 'elective affinity' as being a very particular type of dialectic relationship that is found between two social or cultural configurations that are not reducible to direct causal determination or 'influence' in the traditional sense" (Lowy 1989, p. 13).

of the market. Together, these factors operate, in the sphere of the technical-operational dynamics, to reinforce the general characteristics of financial dominance in the economies or make them more imperious. As can be seen in the graphs below, the data, in line with this theory, shows an affinity between the adoption of important technical-operational advances, above all through updates in line with the reality of the biggest and most advanced international markets, with subsequent periods of intensive growth in numbers, volumes and concentration in the Brazilian stock market. The same can be said in relation to the profile of the investors on the stock exchange.

But if these advances and updates can be seen, above all, as a response to global trends and needs, created in bigger and, at least initially, technically more sophisticated markets, in line with the increased presence of foreign investors in the Brazilian market, the *spiral of complexity of digitalized finance* (Figure 6), operating from out of its own particular contexts, has produced innovations, mechanisms and specific ways of working, in dialog with the reality of a more conservative and regulated market, as that in Brazil is recognized as being. Now totally updated, operating in line with the global state of the art technology specific to the sector, the operating dynamic of the Brazilian capitals market has become an international benchmark for risk and post-trading control and management.

This configuration is the product, as we have argued, not only of technological advances or direct consequences of the economic development of recent years, but of a dynamic of conflicts, disputes and the accommodation of interests of the different participants in the market: politicians and government authorities, regulators, different business sectors and the stock exchange itself – even though, ultimately, this process is oriented toward the striving for increased profits and connected to the global logics of the finance-led regime of accumulation; as we have stressed throughout this book. Whatever the case, even though it is not the primary objective of this work, we believe that if investigated from the theoretical perspective that we suggest, a reading of the events, processes and results of these disputes and accommodations could clarify a number of important factors, for which there is still no explanation, in relation not only to the capitals market, but to the Brazilian economy as a whole. This, pervaded as it is by multi-causal and complex processes, cannot be understood solely from a stack of numerical data, as though it were an exact science, but rather from an investigation performed through a careful reading of its political and social roots.

That said, by more specifically addressing the researched data concerning investor profiles, we can reach a number of conclusions. Following the relevant growth seen in 1999, motivated by the adoption of the Home Broker system that allows individuals to operate using personal computers connected to the

Internet, the percentage of participation by individuals in relation to the investors in the stock exchange as a whole, rose on average by just 0.7 percent per year between 2002 and 2006. After catching a bit more wind again between 2007 and 2009, when the percentage of participation of individual investors reached 30 percent of the total, it started falling again, until it closed 2015 with just 13.7 percent of the total number of investors in the Brazilian capitals market, a level close to that of 1999, prior to the consequences of the implementation of the mentioned system. In 2016, the figure rose to the still modest level of 17 percent.

If it is true that this drop occurred due to a series of factors that generally accompany the broader movements of euphoria and despondency in the economy, it seems evident that, additionally, the scenario of digitalized finance, that offers increasingly fewer chances of making gains to the uninitiated, reduces the direct investment of small investors, who, when they don't leave the capitals market altogether, start to outsource the management of their investments to large funds which are massive and growing presences. These small investors, as countless representatives of brokerage firms that we interviewed explained, despite doing their trading entirely over the Internet, using the Home Broker, rarely operate using ATs or HFTs. "There are more people going broke than making money in the market. The average lifespan of a small investor on the stock exchange is six months", Interviewee K, a manager at a large brokerage, specialized in attending to individuals, explained to us. It is possible to observe this tendency in the trajectory of the data.

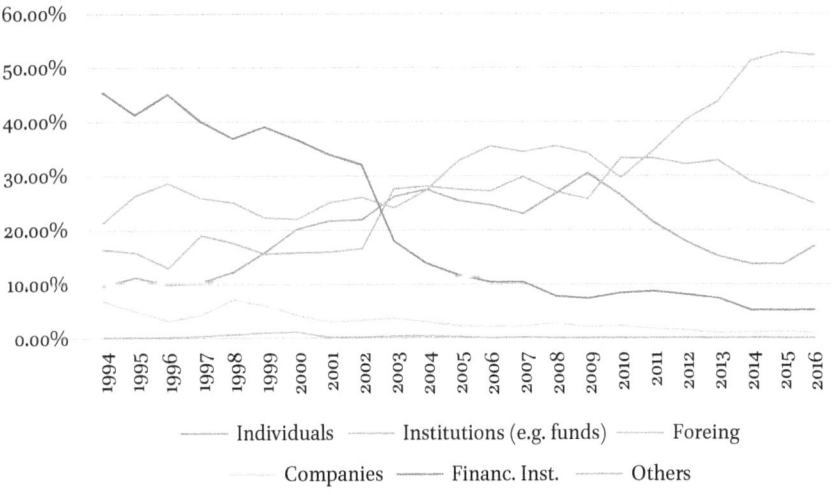

FIGURE 8 Participation by type of investor (volume of trades) – Bovespa segment.
SOURCE: BM&FBOVESPA; OWN ELABORATION

In 2010, a moment of great expectation in relation to Brazil on the international scenario, the BM&FBovespa hit its maximum peak of more than 610,000 listed investors. At this time, its president announced a target of 5 million individual investors by 2015, with an additional gain of 200 new companies with shares listed on the exchange by 2014. Contrary to the projections, however, the number of investors dropped, as did the number of companies with shares listed on the exchange (from 544 in 1994 to 363 in 2013).

Summing everything up, the scenario proved to be more favorable for large – above all foreign – institutional investors, who operate with advanced technological know-how, systems and solutions and great advantages in the computerized markets throughout the world. Demonstrating more or less sustainable growth between 1994 and 2016, the portion of the stock market in the hands of foreign investors more than doubled, jumping from 21.4 percent to 52.3 percent during this period, with steeper rises from 2005 and 2010, years that coincided precisely with the adoption of important technical-operational advances in the stock market: the start of the Operational Qualification Program (PQO), the end of the open outcry trading system at Bovespa, and the implementation of the Co-location system (2009 in the BM&F segment, and 2010 at Bovespa), that allowed for an increase of the penetration of ATs and HFTs in the Brazilian market. In the BM&F segment, between 2009 and 2016, the share of foreign investors in the volume of contracts rose from 19.3 percent to 37.9 percent (see Figure 9 below).

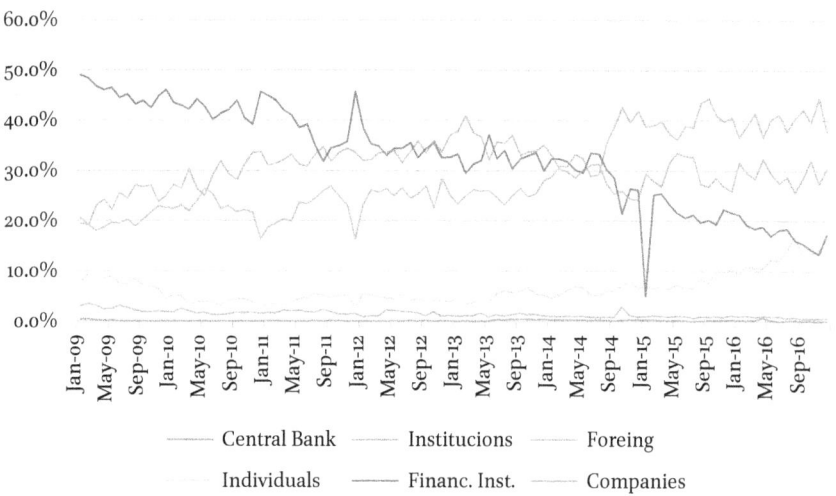

FIGURE 9 Participation by type of investor (contracts volume) – BM&F segment.
SOURCE: BM&FBOVESPA; OWN ELABORATION

The year 2005 that, as explained earlier, is also accepted as the year of note in the growth of the adoption of ATs and HFTs in the US markets due to changes in its legislation that opened up the scenario for this type of trading, has been noted in Brazil as the year that the number of brokerage firms operating in the market started to fall – from a total of 91 to 79 in 2016 (see Figure 10 below). Whilst this number fell, the percentage of purchases and sales of shares concentrated in the hands of the few rose. During this same period, the slice of the Brazilian stock market (daily volume of trades) concentrated in the hands of the five biggest brokerages jumped from 35 percent to 51 percent of the market (Figure 11), with special growth as of 2010, coinciding with the implementation of co-location in the Brazilian market (2009–2010). In 2005, of these five large brokerage firms, only two were foreign. Today four of them are foreign.

In a scenario characterized by the use of cutting-edge technology, in which the costs of trading on the markets have been reduced drastically, the brokers' profit margin has dropped. Many of those we interviewed for this book agree with the estimate that, of all the Brazilian brokers, only the 15 or 20 biggest are not currently operating in the red. As well as the concentration, the scenario points toward a complete reconfiguration of their role that, with the exception of those brokers who work for or are owned by large banks or domestic or international institutional investors, will probably assume the form of commercial representatives who will attract and manage new clients for larger brokers, or perhaps find themselves converted into "investment houses"

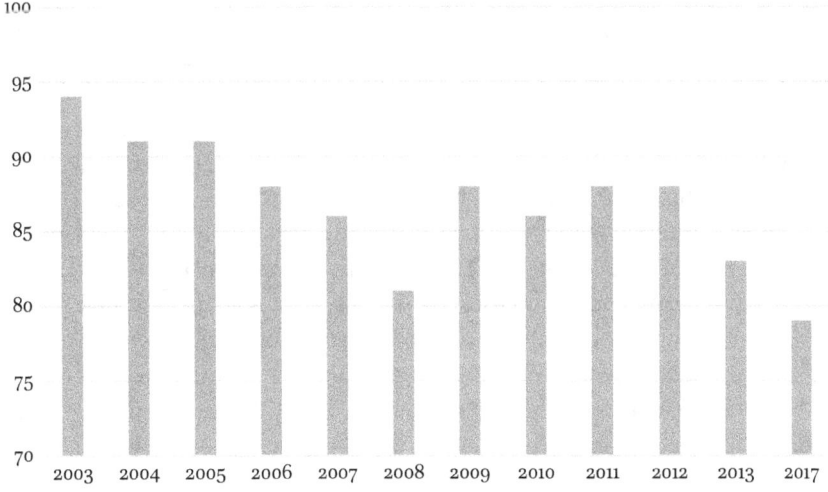

FIGURE 10   Number of registered brokerage firms operating in the stock market.
SOURCE: BM&FBOVESPA; OWN ELABORATION

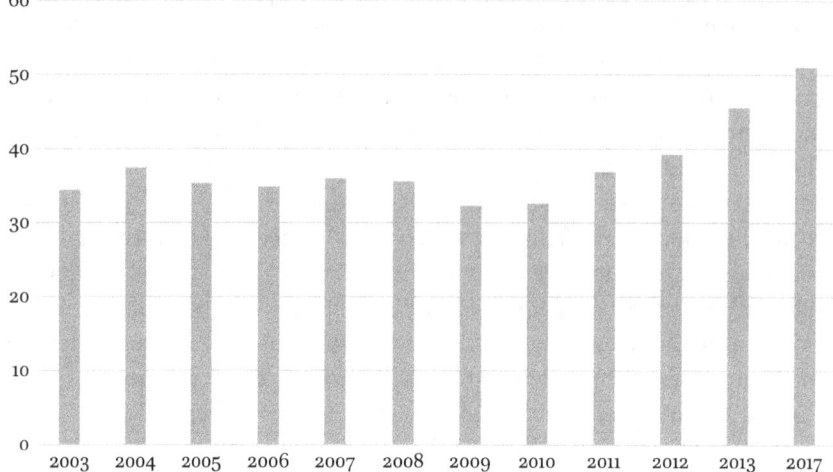

FIGURE 11   Share of the stock market in the hands of the five biggest brokerage firms (as a percent of the total).
SOURCE: BLOOMBERG TERMINAL, ROBOT TRADER PLATFORM; OWN ELABORATION

or "financial shopping malls". These, in addition to trading securities, fixed income and other commercial papers, also offer financial education and investment portal services, for instance (a model that is already operating in countries such as the United States).

Aware of the crisis being faced by the independent brokers due to the fall in the number of investors, as well as the high costs of technology, the BM&FBovespa developed and implemented a project to restructure the segment's trading model. The idea presented at the end of 2013, as a basic plan developed by an international consultancy firm contracted by the stock exchange, led to what came to be the categories of the "Participante de Negociação" (PN, Trading Participant, the brokerage responsible for serving clients by means of the account and order trading system) and those of the "Participante de Negociação Pleno" (PNP, Full Trading Participant, a brokerage that has all the technological structure necessary to execute the orders sent by the PN broker). Within this model, the PN is entirely focused on sending the orders for the PNP to execute, whilst the PNP is permitted to fulfill both functions.

In certain ways this new model reflects the different demands and forms of trading in the age of digitalized finance. Whilst in the market of large institutional clients what is required is solidity and speed, in the segment involving individuals, usability and automation are the more important factors. As

Interviewee K,[30] a representative of a brokerage specializing in meeting the requirements of small investors, such as individuals, explained to us, "our client wants ease of use. For the individual, faster technology doesn't make much difference; what is important is the service, the orientation".

In much the same way, and also following the trend toward concentration, the number of companies with shares quoted on the stock exchange fell 35.8 percent between 1994 and 2016 (from 544 to 349). The drop, however, cannot be explained by a so-called adverse economic scenario. At the same time as the number of companies trading shares on the stock exchange fell considerably during the period analyzed, the total sum capitalized on the exchange grew at an average rate of more than 20 percent per year. The same can be said of the volume and number of trades performed which, between 1994 and 2016, grew at an average annual rate of 20.1 percent and 27.1 percent respectively. As comparative gauge, the Brazilian Gross Domestic Product (GDP) during the same period grew at an average annual rate of 2.3 percent.

Advancing more intensely from 2005 on, the average daily number of trades performed rose from a little over 10,000 in 1994, to around 62,000 in 2005, when it started to rise dramatically until it reached more than 960,000 transactions made per day in 2016 (Figure 12), meaning a total accumulated growth

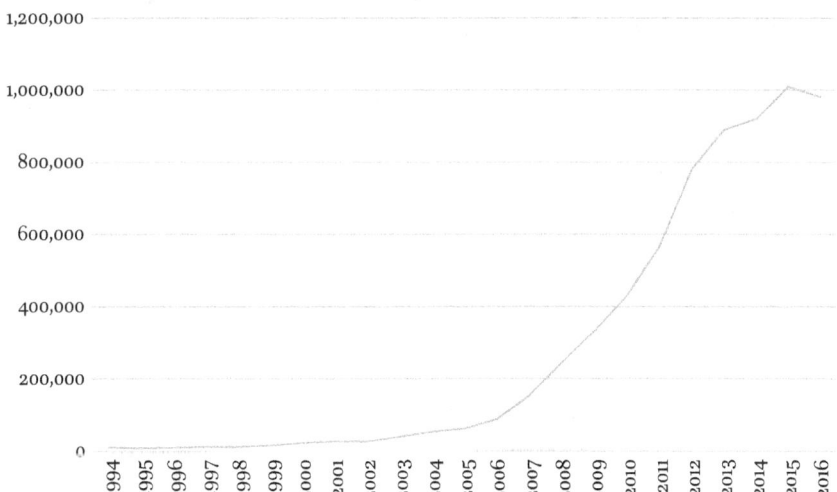

FIGURE 12 Average daily number of trades made in the stock market.
SOURCE: BM&FBOVESPA; OWN ELABORATION

---

30 Information obtained during an interview given on 06-Jun-2014, in São Paulo (DF). 1 file .mpeg4 (92min57seg).

of a staggering 9,600 percent during the period. It is worth noting that the growth in the number of trades is not, however, proportionally accompanied by a relevant growth in the financial volumes traded (with an increase of 30 times, from R$247.3 million in 1994 to R$7,416.5 million in December 2016), something that points to the growing fractioning-off of the contracts in the acceleration of trading.

The BM&FBovespa and its shareholders have more than enough reasons to celebrate these changes. If we concentrate on the period from 2009 to 2016,[31] within an adverse economic scenario, the increase in the volumes and, above all, the number of trades, has made it possible for the BM&FBovespa company to achieve an average annual operational margin in the region of 60.1 percent. During this same period, its net revenue grew by an average of 6.5 percent and its net profit by an annual average of 15.1 percent.[32] It was no surprise, therefore, that the stock exchange started encouraging the growing presence of ATs and HFTs in its markets, be it in the form of growing investment in infrastructure, or through discount and incentive policies for heavy users.[33]

In summary, according to the data outlined above, for the period analyzed, in reference to the Brazilian stock market, we can see that:

i) The number and volume of trades made grew at a highly accelerated rate, much faster than the Brazilian economy as a whole, with this increase taking place more during periods in which important technical-operational changes were adopted;

ii) Since then, despite being growing in terms of stock exchange capitalization, number and volumes of trades, the Brazilian stock market was being concentrated in the hands of a fewer number of companies listed on the stock exchange and increasingly fewer intermediation companies (brokerages) – and here also the more accelerated periods, both in the drop in the number of brokers and in the increased concentration of

---

31   Despite these figures, the same seven years (from 2009 to 2016) were notable for an average of falling amounts in IPOs (the exception being 2013), a drop in the number of brokers, a reduction in the number of companies listed on the exchange (from 385 to 349), and a modest increase in total stock exchange capitalization (from R$2,334.7 billion to R$2,467.0 billion), the result, largely, of adversities in the domestic macroeconomic scenario.

32   BM&FBovespa profit and loss statement. Available at: <http://ri.bmfbovespa.com.br/ptb/s-6-ptb.html?idioma=ptb>. Accessed on: Feb 20, 2017.

33   For more information on the BM&FBovespa's differentiated tariff policy for HFTs, see: <http://www.bmfbovespa.com.br/pt_br/servicos/tarifas/listados-a-vista-e-derivativos/tarifas-de-programa-hft/>. Accessed on: Feb 24, 2017.

the market in just a few of them, also coincided with the adoption of important changes in the technical-operational dimension of the markets;

iii) In the same period, the foreign presence on the Brazilian stock market grew, both in relation to the profile of the investors and to the leading brokers in the market, and this also coincided with the moments of technological change that were equally observed in the previous dimensions in relation to the more intense periods of growth;

iv) Finally, with the exception of the period corresponding to the adoption of the Home Broker technology, objectively directed to the attraction of investment from individuals in the capitals market, the participation of individuals in the market dropped considerably between 1994 and 2016, in opposition to the trend observed in the case of large foreign and institutional investors, with sharper drops also coinciding with the mentioned periods of important technological changes.

As far as the weakening of regulation of the financial market is concerned, despite a wide range of published materials, with powerful statements from those interviewed on this matter, some of which are published in this book, and observations concerning the day-to-day operations of the stock market performed in the field pointing to a substantial rise in the growing and additional difficulties for regulation, in line with the slow technological advance of some of the regulatory bodies and the growth of the restraints on the political power of the state institutions (along economic or institutional channels, or due to political cooptation) in the application of instruments of economic policy, and despite the observed tendency of growth and concentration in elective affinity with technological advances supporting this theory, it is not possible to understand it directly from the market figures. Whatever the case, even in that which relates to the previous situations, reducing them to simply graphs and figures would be extremely unhelpful in understanding a complex phenomenon with many different reasons.

That said, the tendencies, seen from the contribution of various sources of information, amongst which is numerical data, appear to us to reinforce our central and secondary hypothesis concerning the development of the ICT and the process of financialization of the economy, namely: even though we cannot affirm that it concerns the sole or most important explanatory reasons, the development of the ICT, the acceleration of which to a global level since the 1980s was not a coincidence, reinforces the financialization of economies, making it more pressing and imperative, as a constituent element of the finance dominated accumulation regime. This reinforcement, as we have attempted to explain, through the *cycle of operation of digitalized finance* (Figure 7), made up of a displacement of the space-time flows, increased difficulties of regulation and the consequent concentration in different levels. In order to organize and understand how this advance has taken place, anchored, from a technical-operational point of view, in the growing complexity of information technology, we developed the *spiral of complexity of digitalized finance* (Figure 6), that points toward the mutual reinforcement of institutional changes and technological advances in the shaping of the dynamics of operation and functioning of the markets.

Interpreted as such, the relationship between the development of the ICT and the shaping of the financial dominance in the global economy points to an elective affinity between these two dimensions, without direct identification or unidirectional motives, but as a dialectic relationship, pervaded as it is by various factors, social dimensions and particular causes depending upon its specific contexts, its movement, ultimately, however, being determined by its economic-material base.

CHAPTER 6

Final Considerations

The "revolutionary" transformations arising from technological development have advanced without precedent over the last few years. A founding element of capitalist development during its different historical phases, the compression of space and time has been greatly intensified through the rapid development of Information and Communication Technologies (ICT) that are central to this dimension. The unending instantaneous production, organization and presentation of data, information and news has become part of our day-to-day reality as a basic necessity for the production, commercialization and management of social life. Tied to this new reality, we have seen a countless number of economic, political, social and cultural transformations throughout the world.

As we have sought to show, behind these changes are important shifts taking place on the tectonic plates of society, that is, at its material base. Inspired by the works of the various authors and informed individuals mentioned in this book, we argue that within the structures of what is currently defined as globalization is, in reality, a process of internationalization of capital or, more specifically, of financial internationalization.

This scenario is a direct product of the crisis and vanquishing of the previous arrangement (regime of accumulation), the post-war Fordism-Keynesianism, also known as the "golden age of capitalism" in the developed countries. It is within this configuration, therefore, that we find the formative tie between the set of transformations that articulate the implementation of new organizational structures and technologies (amongst which are the ICT), that accelerate production, exchange and consumption times; the deterritorialization of production and the growth of the services sector; the advance in the exploitation of labor through outsourcing, deregulation and flexibilization; the predominance of the short-term as the hegemonic time period for decision taking in different spheres; the increasing concentration of capitals through mergers and acquisitions; and, above all, the growth and advance in prominence of the financial markets through their broad liberalization.

As such, out of the redisposition in the dynamic of capitalist accumulation, in response to the crisis of the previous arrangement, there emerges the regime of accumulation with the dominance of financial valorization, discussed in this book, and which, in simple terms, in relation to one of its fundamental elements, plans the predominance of financial valorization as a guiding axis for the globalized capitalist economy and interest-bearing capital as a center of gravity of this new scaling.

Under this flexible regime of accumulation, contrary to the previous rigidity, there emerge new forms for the valorization of value, through the simultaneous exploration of absolute surplus value (intensification of working days with a reduction of salaries) and relative surplus value (an increase in the organic composition of capital via technological development).

The desperate "setting-off of the future in the present", characteristic of the logic of operation of interest-bearing capital and fictitious capital in the financial markets replete with financial technologies and innovations, demands countless forms of protection from the risks that this unstable future can represent: deterritorialization of the manufacturing structures, outsourcing and different natures of securitization, etc. Establishing itself, thus, is the short-term mindset as the *tabula rasa* of this patrimonial capitalism that is increasingly exposed to risks and catastrophic crises, that expose the tragic disposability of the labor force in the capitalism of the 21st century.

With regard to the role of technological development in this process, and especially that of the ICT, we have sought to demonstrate that, induced in various aspects by financial valorization, these developments end up accelerating and strengthening the process of financialization of the economies or, more specifically, supporting the functioning of the finance dominated regime of accumulation that does not exist solely due to the development of the ICT, but which could not, within this scenario, be managed as such without their support.

By reducing time as a means of increasing the number and volume of operations in the markets, and thereby increasing their short-term gains, the development of the ICT signposts the way to a scenario that is more favorable to the maintenance and confinement of capitals in the financial sphere. This growth, as we have discussed, reinforces the trend toward the concentration of capitals. As such, with wealth being concentrated in the financial sphere, and with capitals enjoying full, institutionally and technically guaranteed freedom, it ultimately ends up amplifying the tendencies of detachment between the real and the fictitious economies (or better, the dominance of one over the other), in a scenario of growing financial instability and crisis. Displacement of the space-time flows, an increase in the technical vacuums between the regulator and those regulated, and a concentration of gains in the financial sphere, are complemented and mutually reinforced, therefore, in the creation of what we called the *cycle of operation of digitalized finance*.

By digitalized finance, we mean a particular form of technically managing the financial markets through operations characterized by low latency, highly intensive connectivity, and high-performance information technology, allowing the movements of arbitrage and high-frequency speculation to take place in milliseconds or even nanoseconds, being performed by "robots" that operate according to sophisticated mathematical patterns and models. This is a scenario that opens up a whole new set of events, risks and problems bound to this new operating logic. We also argue that we cannot overlook, without careful analysis, the fact that without the help of these technologies, a whole set of financial instruments would not exist or could not be traded as such, creating markets that are different from the current ones in terms of their qualitative and quantitative natures.

Within this highly sophisticated condition of valorization of capital, that sometimes appears to be straight out of a science fiction novel, the technological fetishism as a mimesis of the commodity fetishism, reaches paradigmatic levels. The belief in the infallibility of these robots and mathematical models, supposedly as neutral as simple technical artifacts, suggests, through increased mechanization, the overcoming of the problems caused by the "human factor" (different diversions, emotions and subjective factors) in the markets. Beyond the mere articulation of ends and means in view of a given objective, however, the insatiable striving for greater profits as a fundamental cognition of the operation of the markets bears the deeply ingrained marks of this "human factor", and has done since the beginning. What is a system if not the product of human (social) ingenuity, a prosthesis of thought to articulate its own objectives, primarily subject to this cognition? This is the most precise meaning of the idea presented in this work concerning the social content of technology.

After this look at the state of the art of the digitalized finance at a global level, that has found in the United States (not by accident, the biggest financial marketplace in the world) its most advanced stage, we have turned evaluation of its operation and history of evolution in the Brazilian context. Despite, as we have seen, having a history notable for its various particularities, the data analyzed reinforces our theories and arguments. The increasing electronification and automation of the Brazilian capitals market, that is advancing with enormous steps, is closely accompanied by an acceleration of processes, a substantial increase in the number and speed of trades performed, a concentration at different levels (investors, companies listed on the stock exchange, brokerage firms), an increase in the prominence of foreign investors and brokers, and a reduction in the participation of small investors in the market.

These occurrences, naturally, are tied to a set of social, and macro and microeconomic factors that we have sought to discuss, from our theoretical foundation to the verification of the data, throughout the book. More than factors that can be "isolated" by means of a simplistic approach using social investigation as a type of exact science (part of an epistemology that drains the complexity from the social factors, distorting our view of them), we have highlighted coincidences, affinities and tendencies in the sphere of the reality presented.

It is worth noting that, in relation to the central markets, the Brazilian stock exchange is considerably smaller in volume and number of trades and, as such, is more dependent on international liquidity, meaning that certain elements and tendencies perceived as being greater there are seen as being milder here. The influences of the demands coming from the central markets are, therefore, important. Today practically on a par with the global standard from the point of view of its technical sophistication, the impressive development of the Brazilian capitals market has taken place, above all, as a result of the economic opening that occurred in the form of the peripheral insertion of the country as a platform of valorization in the globalized finance (1992–1999).

As we have sought to demonstrate, the gradual but expressive development and technological sophistication of the Brazilian capitals market follows its own paths due to the dynamics, disputes, interests and demands of its particular context, that culminate in an operational logic that is equally unique to manage it, such being recognizably more conservative and self-regulated than the average.

However, even though the path and results of its trajectory of technical development are different due to its particular position in the international financial scenario, the general tendencies and consequences of the *modus operandi* of digitalized finance can be clearly inferred, as we have mentioned, from an observation of its operational data. Thus, ultimately, the broad economic foundation follows the global trends. Its unique model of development and functioning, accepted as being better regulated than others, has not prevented the rampant growth of the presence of High Frequency Traders (HFT), the marginalization of small investors (and the outsourcing of the management of their investments), the virtually total dominance of the market by large institutional and foreign investors, and the concentration observed at different levels.

Summing everything up, it becomes obvious that we are, in Brazil and globally, as the authors who have contributed to our understanding have suggested, facing a scenario in which the majority of the world's population, due to rapid technological development and increasing rates of mechanization, is becoming increasingly irrelevant from the point of view of capital that, as such, being alienated from the exploration of human labor as an essential component of the production of wealth, increasingly depends upon the circulation of fictitious forms of capital and the fetishized creation of wealth centered on money and on the credit system.

But if the truth is that this tightly bound web of finance, economic policy and production performance has acquired a certain automation, declaring that the financial expansion and all its consequences – that are social processes, the products of human action – are irreversible, is the same as playing with a naive form of historical determinism. As Chesnais (1998) has evaluated it, the appeal of the idea of irreversibility, accompanied by the common call for a supposed realism, is used as a resource of justification for the established order.

If we reject any form of mechanistic determinism, be it optimistic or pessimistic, in relation to the social reality, we would see it also as appropriate in the understanding of the technological phenomenon. Without accepting the naive celebrationism that reveals an "equality of conditions" between the different social sectors in the directing of technological development, in this book and in the evidence observed whilst developing it, we are reinforcing the relevance of a materialist rather than deterministic vision of technology, in the sense that it is understood as being non-neutral and partially autonomous, anchored ontologically in its "social condition", and overdeterminated, ultimately, by economic practice.

If the strategic importance of technical and cognitive control of the means of information and communication as elements of maintenance and reproduction of the established order are proven to be true, it is equally undeniable that such new technologies, especially the social ones, have anti-systemic potentials that can and should be explored, as could be seen in the rebellions that have been seen recently across the world. Even though these inroads, being the direct result of the serious social tensions that are present in our current form of social organization, have not been able to structurally redirect the hegemonic curse of the technological advances, they are a reality that requires close attention and examination.

The "magic" of technological development, regardless of its nature or direction, lies in its constant disruptive movement. As an anchor on the continual revolution of the means of production and the forms of organization of capitalist society, it is, as a phenomenon and object of investigation, constantly in movement, producing and being produced by new contradictions.

Be it through an approach that is more focused on the dynamics of the economic structure, or be it by an investigation of its configurations in the field of thinking and rationality, investigating technological change – where it is and where it is going – is an important key for the availability of the necessary effort to understand the capitalist society in our conjuncture.

In times of discussion concerning the potentials and consequences of the Information and Communication Technologies in social life, only a qualified evaluation of technics allows us to escape the traps of technological determinism that present technical progress as a direct synonym of social regression or progress.

References

Aglietta, Michel 1999, *A theory of capitalist regulation: The US Experience*, London: Verso.

Aldrighi, Dante, Luis Afonso, Guilherme Capparelli, and Ariovaldo Santos 2010, 'As ofertas públicas iniciais na Bovespa no período recente: Características das empresas, estrutura de propriedade e de controle, e desempenho', Salvador, XXXVIII Encontro Nacional de Economia ANPEC.

Althusser, Louis 1979a, *A Favor de Marx*. 2ed. Rio de Janeiro: Zahar.

Althusser, Louis 1979b, *Ler O Capital*, volume I, Rio de Janeiro: Zahar.

Althusser, Louis 1979c, *Ler O Capital*, volume II, Rio de Janeiro: Ed. Zahar.

Antunes, Ricardo and Ruy Braga (eds) 2009, *Infoproletários: Degradação Real do Trabalho Virtual*. São Paulo: Boitempo Editorial.

Aronowitz, Stanley 1978, 'Marx, Bravermann, and the logic of capital', *Critical Sociology*, 8 (2/3), pp. 126–146.

Arrighi, Giovanni 1994, *The long twentieth century: money, power, and the origins of our times*, London and New York: Verso.

Barcellos, Marta 2010, *Histórias do mercado de capitais no Brasil: depoimentos inéditos de personalidades que marcaram a trajetória das bolsas de valores no país*, Rio de Janeiro: Elsevier; São Paulo: Bovespa.

Bastos, Pedro Paulo Zaluth 2013, 'Financeirização, crise, educação: considerações preliminares'. *Text for discussion*. IE/UNICAMP, Campinas, n. 217, mar. 2013, available at: <http://www.eco.unicamp.br/docprod/downarq.php?id=3256&tp=a>. Accessed on: Jul 20, 2017.

Bector, Raj, Anthony Marrato and Chris Sparrow 2012, 'The hidden alpha in equity trading: steps to increasing returns with the advanced use of information'. *Oliver Wyman*, 6, available at: <http://www.oliverwyman.com/our-expertise/insights/2014/mar/the-hidden-alpha-in-equity-trading.html>. Accessed on: Jul 20, 2017.

Bicchetti, David and Nicolas Maystre 2012, 'The synchronized and long-lasting structural change on commodity markets: evidence from high frequency data', *UNCTAD Discussion Papers 208*, United Nations Conference on Trade and Development, Available at http://vi.unctad.org/devblog/506-%e2%80%a8-high-frequency-trading-contributes-to-deviate-commodity-prices-%e2%80%a8-from-fundamentals, accessed on: Jul 20, 2017.

Boyer, Robert 1990, *The regulation school: a critical introduction*, New York: Columbia University Press.

Braga, José Carlos 2009, 'Crise sistêmica da financeirização e a incerteza das mudanças', *Estudos Avançados*, 23 (65), USP, São Paulo.

Braverman, Harry 1977, *Trabalho e capital monopolista: a degradação do trabalho no século XX*, Rio de Janeiro: Zahar.

Brock, David (ed.) 2006, *Understanding Moore's law: four decades of innovation*, Philadelphia: Chemical Heritage Press.

Brunhoff, Suzanne de, François Chenais, Gérard Duménil, Dominique Lévy and Michel Husson, 2010, *A Finança Capitalista*. São Paulo: Alameda.

Bruno, Miguel, Hawa Diawara, Eliane Araújo, Anna Carolina Reis and Mário Rubens 2009, 'Finance-Led Growth Regime no Brasil: estatuto teórico, evidências empíricas e consequências macroeconômicas', In: *Encontro Nacional de Economia Política*, 14, 2009, São Paulo. Electronic records ... São Paulo.

Bukharin, Nikolai 1971, 'Theory and practice from the standpoint of dialectical materialism', In: *SCIENCE at the Crossroads*, London: Frank Cass.

Burawoy, Michael 1978, 'Toward a Marxist theory of the labor process: Braverman and beyond', In: *Politics and Society*, 8 (3/4), pp. 247–312.

Burawoy, Michael 1990, *The politics of production*, 3ed, London and New York: Verso.

Cardoso, Luís Antônio 2008. 'O conceito de racionalização no pensamento social de Max Weber: entre a ambiguidade e a dualidade', *Teoria e Sociedade*, n. 16.1, Jan/Jun. pp. 256–275.

Castells, Manuel 1999, A era da informação: economia sociedade e cultura; v.1, São Paulo: Paz e Terra.

Chesnais, François 1996, *A mundialização do capital*, São Paulo: Xamã.

Chesnais, François (ed.), 1998, *A mundialização financeira: gênese, custos e riscos*, São Paulo: Xamã.

Chesnais, François 2002, 'A teoria do regime de acumulação financeirizado: conteúdo, alcance e interrogações', In: *Economia e Sociedade*, Campinas, v. 11, n. 1 (18), pp. 1–44, Jan./Jun.

Chesnais, François (ed.) 2005, *A finança mundializada: raízes socais e políticas, configuração, consequências*, São Paulo: Boitempo.

Chesnais, François and Claude Serfati 2003, 'Ecologia e condições físicas de reprodução social: alguns fios condutores marxistas', In: *Revista Crítica Marxista*, São Paulo, v. 1, n. 16, pp. 29–75, Sept.

Cintra, Marcos Antônio Macedo 2016, 'A Crise econômica mundial e a Quarta Revolução Industrial', website of the magazine *Carta Capital*, 25. Feb, 2016, available at: http://www.cartacapital.com.br/blogs/blog-do-grri/a-crise-economica-mundial-e-a-quarta-revolucao-industrial, accessed on: 17. Feb, 2017.

Clark, Andy 2003, *Natural-born cyborgs: minds, technologies, and the future of human intelligence*, New York: Oxford University Press.

Cohen, Gerald 1978, *Karl Marx's theory of history: a defense*, Princeton: University of Princeton.

Crotty, James R. 1990, 'Owner-manager conflict and financial theory of investment stability: a critical assessment of Keynes, Tobin, and Minsky', In: *Journal of Post Keynesian Economics*, 12 (4): pp. 519–42.

Dantas, Marcos 1989, *O crime de Prometeu – como o Brasil obteve a tecnologia da informática*, Rio de Janeiro: Abicomp.

Dantas, Vera 1988, *Guerrilha tecnológica – a verdadeira história da Política Nacional de Informática*, Rio de Janeiro: LCT-Livros Técnicos e Científicos Ed.

Dawson, Michael and John Bellamy Foster 1998, 'Virtual capitalism', In: Robert W. McChesney, Ellen Meiksins Wood and John Bellamy Foster (ed.), *Capitalism and the Information Age*, Nova York, Monthly Review Press, pp. 51–67.

Dean, Jodi 2005, 'Communicative capitalism: circulation and the foreclosure of politics', In: *Cultural Politics*, Vol. 1, N. 1, pp. 51–74.

Dembinski, Paul, Carole Lager, Andrew Cornford and Jean-Michel Bonvin (eds.) 2006, *Enron and world finance: a case study in ethics*, New York: Palgrave Macmillan.

Diniz, Eduardo H. 2004. 'Cinco décadas de automação', *GV Executivo*, São Paulo, v. 3, n. 3, Aug./Oct.

Dussel, Enrique 1984, 'Estudio preliminar al "Cuaderno tecnológico-histórico"', In Karl Marx, *Cuaderno tecnológico-histórico*, México: Univ. Aut. De Puebla.

Eckhard, Hein and Till van Treeck 2008, 'Financialization' in post-keynesian models of distribution and growth – a systematic review, *IMK Working Paper*, n. 10.

Epstein, Gerald 2002, 'Financialization, rentier interest, and central bank policy', Paper prepared for *PERI Conference on "Financialization of the World Economy"*, December 7–8, 2001, University of Massachusetts, Amherst. This version, June 2002.

Epstein, Gerald (ed.) 2005, *Financialization and the world economy*, Northampton: Edward Elgar.

Farhi, Maryse and Daniela Magalhães Prates 2015, 'Playing it again: new financial innovations and renewed financial fragility', *Colloque "Gouverner la crise, gouverner dans la crise"*, Université Jules Vernes, CRIISEA, 7–9 décembre 2015.

Feenberg, Andrew 1991, *Critical theory of technology*, New York: Oxford University Press.

Feenberg, Andrew 1996, 'Marcuse ou Habermas: duas críticas da tecnologia', *Inquiry: An Interdisciplinary Journal of Philosophy*, v. 39. Available at: <https://www.sfu.ca/~andrewf/marhabportu.htm>. Accessed on: Jul 10, 2017.

Feenberg, Andrew 1999, *Questioning technology*, New York: Routledge.

Feenberg, Andrew 2002, *Transforming technology*, Oxford: Oxford University Press.

Fitzpatrick, Tony 2002, 'Critical theory, information society and surveillance technologies', In: *Communication and Society*, v. 5, n. 3, 2002, pp. 357–378.

Ford, Martin 2009, *The lights in the tunnel: automation, accelerating technology and the economy of the future*, United States: Acculant Publishing.

Foster, John Bellamy 2009, 'A financeirização do capital e a crise', *Outubro*, n° 18, 1st semester.

Freund, Julien 1987, *Sociologia de Max Weber*, 4.ed., Rio de Janeiro: Forense Universitária.

Gai, Jiading, Chen Yao and Ye Mao 2013, 'The externalities of high frequency trading', August 7, 2013, available at: http://dx.doi.org/10.2139/ssrn.2066839, accessed on: Feb 17, 2017.

Giffin, Karen Mary 2007, 'Financeirização do Estado, erosão da democracia e empobrecimento da cidadania: tendências globais?', *Ciência & Saúde Coletiva*, 12 (6), pp. 1491–1504.

Golub, Anton, John Keane and Ser-Huang Poon 2012, 'High frequency trading and mini flash crashes', *Working Paper*, 28 Nov, Available at: <http://arxiv.org/pdf/1211.6667.pdf>. Accessed on: Jul 20, 2017.

Goonatilake, Susantha 1984, *Aborted discovery: science and creativity in the third world*, London: Zed Books.

Guillén, Arturo 2014, 'Financialization and financial profit', *Brazilian Journal of Political Economy*, vol. 34, n° 3 (136), pp. 451–470, July–September.

Guttmann, Robert 1998, 'As mutações do capital financeiro', In: François Chesnais (ed.), *A mundialização financeira: gênese, custos e riscos*, São Paulo: Editora Xamã.

Habermas, Jurgen 1994, *Técnica e ciência como "ideologia"*, Lisboa: Edition 70.

Hagstromer, Bjron and Lars Nordén 2013, 'The diversity of high-frequency traders', May 18, *SSRN*, available at: http://dx.doi.org/10.2139/ssrn.2153272, accessed on: Feb 24, 2017.

Harvey, David 2005, *O novo imperialismo*, São Paulo: Loyola.

Harvey, David 2008, *O neoliberalismo: história e implicações*, São Paulo: Edições Loyola.

Harvey, David 2012, *O enigma do capital e as crises do capitalismo*, São Paulo: Boitempo.

Harvey, David 2013a, *Condição pós-moderna: uma pesquisa sobre as origens da mudança cultural*, São Paulo: Edições Loyola.

Harvey, David 2013b, *Os limites do capital*, São Paulo: Boitempo.

Hasbrouck, Joel and Gideon Saar 2013, 'Low-latency trading', *Journal of Financial Markets*, 16 (2013), pp. 646–679.

Haug, Wolfgang Fritz 2003, *High-tech-kapitalismus*, Hamburgo: Argument.

Heidegger, Martin 2006, 'A questão da técnica', In: Martin Heidegger, *Ensaios e conferências*, Petrópolis: Editora Vozes e Editora São Francisco, Coleções Pensamento Humano.

Hilferding, Rudolf 1981, *Finance capital*, London: Routledge Kegan Paul.

Hobsbawn, Eric 1996, *Era dos extremos*, São Paulo: Cia das Letras.

Horta, Isabela Botelho 2017, *O desenvolvimento da internet e os grandes bancos: um estudo a partir das iniciativas do Bradesco*, Masters dissertation presented for the

Post-Graduate Course in Communication, 177 pp, Faculty of Communication, University of Brasília (UnB).

Ianni, Octavio, 1994, 'Globalização: Novo paradigma das ciências sociais', In: *Estudos Avançados*, São Paulo, v.8, n.1, pp. 147–163, May/Aug.

Kaya, Orçun 2016, 'High-frequency trading: reaching the limit. Research Briefing: global financial markets', *Deutsche Bank Research*, May 24, available at: https://www.dbresearch.com/PROD/RPS_EN-PROD/PROD0000000000454703/Research_Briefing%3A_High-frequency_trading.pdf accessed on: Feb 23, 2017.

Kirilenko, Andrei A. and Andrew W. Lo 2013, 'Moore's Law vs. Murphy's Law: Algorithmic Trading and Its Discontents', *Journal of Economic Perspectives* (March 19), Available at SSRN: https://ssrn.com/abstract=2235963, accessed on: Feb 23, 2017.

Langley, Paul 2008, 'Financialization and the consumer credit boom', *Competition & Change*, 12 (2), pp. 133–147.

Lapavitsas, Costas 2011, 'Theorizing financialization', In: *Work, employment & society*, British Sociological Association, Los Angeles: Sage, v. 25, 4, pp. 611–626.

Lapavitsas, Costas and Paulo dos Santos 2008, 'Globalization and contemporary banking: on the impact of new technology', In: *Contributions to Political Economy*, n. 27, pp. 31–56.

Lapyda, Ilan 2011, *A "financeirização" no capitalismo contemporâneo: uma discussão das teorias de François Chesnais e David Harvey*, 223 pp, Dissertation (Masters in Sociology), Department of Sociology of the Faculty of Philosophy, Letters and Human Sciences of the University of São Paulo.

Lenin, Vladimir 2011, *O imperialismo: etapa superior do capitalismo*, Campinas: FE/UNICAMP.

Lévy, Pierre 1995, *As tecnologias da inteligência*, Rio de Janeiro: 34 Letras.

Lévy, Pierre 1999, *Cibercultura*, Rio de Janeiro: Editora 34 Letras.

Lewis, Michael 2014, *Flash boys: a Wall Street revolt*, New York: WW. Norton & Company.

Lojkine, Jean 2002, *A revolução informacional*, 3ed, São Paulo: Cortez.

Lowy, Michael 1989, *Redenção e utopia*, São Paulo: Companhia das Letras.

Marcial, Elaine C. (ed.) 2015, *Megatendências mundiais 2030: o que entidades e personalidades internacionais pensam sobre o futuro do mundo? Contribuição para um debate de longo prazo para o Brasil*, Brasília: Ipea.

Marcuse, Herbert 1979, *A ideologia da sociedade industrial: o homem uni-dimensional*, Rio de Janeiro: Zahar.

Marx, Karl 1971–1976, *Elementos fundamentales para la crítica de la economia política* (Borrador) 1857–1858, 3 vols, México: Siglo Veintiuno Editores.

Marx, Karl 2013a, *O Capital*, v. I. São Paulo: Boitempo.

Marx, Karl 2013b, *Grundrisse: manuscritos econômicos 1857–1858 Esboços da crítica da economia política*, São Paulo: Boitempo.

Marx, Karl 1987, *Miseria de la Filosofia*, México: Siglo XX.

Marx, Karl 1988, *O Capital*, v. III, tomo II. São Paulo: Nova Cultural.

Marx, Karl and Friedrich Engels 2010, *Manifesto do Partido Comunista*, São Paulo: Boitempo.

McLuhan, Marshall 1968, *As comunicações como extensões do homem*, São Paulo: Cultrix.

Mészáros, István 2002, *Para além do capital*, Campinas: Editora da Unicamp; São Paulo: Boitempo.

Minsky, Hyman P. 1986, *Stabilizing an unstable economy*, New Haven: Yale University Press.

Mollo, Maria de Lourdes Rollemberg 2011, 'Capital fictício, autonomia produção-circulação e crises: precedentes teóricos para o entendimento da crise atual', In: *Revista Economia*, Brasília, v. 12, n. 3, pp. 475–496. Sept/Dec.

Mollo, Maria de Lourdes Rollemberg and Adriana Amado 2001, 'Globalização e Blocos Regionais: Considerações Teóricas e Conclusões de Política Econômica', In: *Estudos Econômicos*, São Paulo, v. 31, n. 1.

Musse, Ricardo 2010, 'Introdução ao manifesto comunista'. In: Karl Marx and Friedrich Engels, *Manifesto Comunista*, São Paulo: Hedra.

Negri, Antonio and Carlo Vercellone 2008, 'Le rapport capital/travail dans le capitalisme cognitif', *Multitudes*, 2008/1 n. 32, pp. 39–50.

Netto, Coelho J. Teixeira 1983, *Semiótica, informação e comunicação*, São Paulo: Perspectiva.

Noble, David 1979, 'Social Choice in Machine Design' In: Adrew Zimbalist (ed.), *Case Studies on the labor process*, New York: Monthly Review Press.

Noble, David 2001, *La locura de la automatización*, Barcelona: Alikornio.

Novaes, Henrique Tahan 2010, *O fetiche da tecnologia: a experiência das fábricas recuperadas*, São Paulo: Expressão Popular.

Offe, Claus 1984, *Problemas estruturais do Estado capitalista*, Rio de Janeiro: Tempo Brasileiro.

Paulani, Leda Maria 2006, 'Capitalismo financeiro e estado de emergência econômico no Brasil: abandonando a perspectiva do desenvolvimento', In: *X Jornadas de Economia Crítica*, Barcelona, 2006, available at: http://www.egov.ufsc.br/portal/sites/default/files/anexos/26185-26187-1-PB.pdf, accessed on: Jul 20, 2017.

Paulani, Leda Maria 2009, 'A crise do regime de acumulação com dominância da valorização financeira e a situação do Brasil', In: *Estudos Avançados*, vol. 23, no 66, available at http://www.scielo.br/scielo.php?script=sci_arttext&pid=S0103-40142009000200003, accessed on: Jul 20, 2017.

Paulani, Leda Maria 2016, 'Acumulação e rentismo: resgatando a teoria da renda de Marx para pensar o capitalismo contemporâneo', In: *Brazilian Journal of Political Economy* 36 (3), pp. 514–535.

Pires, Hindenburgo Francisco 1997, 'Reestruturação inovativa e reorganização das instituições financeiras do setor privado no Brasil', *Geouerj*, n.2, Rio de Janeiro, pp. 65–79.

Plihon, Dominique 1999, 'Au nom des entreprises', In *Le Monde Diplomatique*, Feb, p. 4, available at: https://www.monde-diplomatique.fr/1999/02/PLIHON/2759, accessed on: Jul 20, 2017.

Pollin, Robert 2007, 'The resurrection of the rentier', *New left review*, v. 46, Jul/Aug, pp. 140–153.

Puliti, Paula 2013, *O juro da notícia: jornalismo econômico pautado pelo capital*, Florianópolis: Insular, 2013.

Rezende, Pedro 2009, Comparando modelos de confiança para segurança, Working paper. Available at: http://www.cic.unb.br/~pedro/trabs/outrasconfiancas.html, accessed on: Jul 20, 2017.

Romero, Daniel 2005, *Marx e a técnica*, São Paulo: Expressão Popular.

Rüdiger, Francisco 2011, *As teorias da cibercultura: perspectivas, questões e autores*, Porto Alegre: Sulina.

Saad-Filho, Alfredo 2010, 'Crisis in neoliberalism or crisis of neoliberalism' In: Leo Panitch, Greg Albo and Vivek Chibber (eds.), *Socialist Register*, 47, pp. 242–259.

Santos, Milton 1992, 'A aceleração contemporânea: tempo mundo e espaço mundo', *Conferência de abertura do Encontro Internacional O novo mapa do mundo*, Departamento de Geografia, Universidade de São Paulo, 1 Sept 1992.

Scharff, Robert and Val Dusek (ed.) 2003, *Philosophy of technology: the technological condition: an anthology*, Oxford: Blackwell Publishing.

Schiller, Dan 2000, *Digital capitalism*, Cambridge: MIT Press.

Schwab, Klaus 2016, The fourth industrial revolution, Cologne/Geneva: World Economic Forum.

Sell, Carlos Eduardo 2011, 'Máquinas petrificadas: Max Weber e Sociologia da Técnica', *Scientiae Studia*, São Paulo, v. 9, n. 3, pp. 563–583.

Sell, Carlos Eduardo 2012, 'Racionalidade e racionalização em Max Weber', *RBCS*, v. 27, n. 79, June 2012, pp. 153–172.

Sell, Carlos Eduardo 2013, *Max Weber e a racionalização da vida*, Petrópolis: Vozes.

Serfati, Claude 1998, 'O papel ativo dos grupos predominantemente industriais na financeirização da economia', In: François Chesnais (ed.), *A mundialização financeira: gênese, custos e riscos*, São Paulo: Editora Xamã.

Shorter, Gary and Rena S. Miller 2014, 'High-frequency trading: background, concerns, and regulatory developments', *CSR Report*, Congressional Research Service, June 19, available at: https://fas.org/sgp/crs/misc/R43608.pdf, accessed on: 23. 23, 2017.

Silva Filho, Edison Benedito da 2015, 'Trajetória recente do investimento estrangeiro direto e em carteira no Brasil', *Boletim de Economia e Política Internacional* – BEPI, n. 19, IPEA, Jan./Apr.

Smith, Reginald D. 2010, 'Is high-frequency trading inducing changes in market microstructure and dynamics?' In: *Cornell University Library*, available at: http://arxiv.org/abs/1006.5490, accessed on: Jul 20, 2017.

Stiglitz, Josef 2001, 'Information and the change in the paradigm in economics', *Nobel Prize Lecture*, December 8, 2001, available at: https://assets.nobelprize.org/uploads/2018/06/stiglitz-lecture.pdf, accessed on: Jul 20, 2017.

Stockhammer, Engelbert 2000, 'Financialisation and the slowdown of accumulation', *Working Paper*, n° 14.

Tabb, Larry, Robert Iati and Adam Sussman 2009, *US equity high frequency trading: strategies, sizing and market structure*, Tabb Group, available at https://research.tabbgroup.com/report/v07-023-us-equity-high-frequency-trading-strategies-sizing-and-market-structure, accessed on: Jul 20, 2017.

Taleb, Nassim Nicholas 2010, *The black swan: the impact of the highly improbable*, 2nd Edition, Random House Trade, New York.

The Government Office for Science 2012, *Foresight: the future of computer trading in financial markets*, Final Project Report, London, available at https://www.gov.uk/government/publications/future-of-computer-trading-in-financial-markets-an-international-perspective, accessed on: Jul 20, 2017.

Therborn, Goran 1980, Science, class and society, London: Verso.

Trigueiro, Michelangelo Giotto Santoro 2008, *O conteúdo social da tecnologia*, Brasília: Embrapa Informação Tecnológica.

Trigueiro, Michelangelo Giotto Santoro 2009, *Sociologia da tecnologia: bioprospecção e legitimação,* São Paulo: Centauro.

UBS Union Bank of Switzerland 2016, 'Extreme automation and connectivity: the global, regional, and investment implications of the Fourth Industrial Revolution' *UBS White Paper for the World Economic Forum*, Annual Meeting 2016, January 2016.

Weber, Max 2004, *A ética protestante e o "espírito" do capitalismo*, São Paulo: Companhia das Letras.

Weber, Max 1994, *Economia e sociedade*, 3. ed., Brasília: UnB.

Weber, Max 1980, *História geral da economia*, 2. ed., São Paulo: Abril Cultural, pp. 121–178 (Os Pensadores).

Weems, Marlon and Alexander Tabb 2014, *Eletronic trading outlook for Brazil: trading faster, trading smarter*, Tabb Group. V12: 061, October.

Index

acceleration   3, 11, 55, 56, 58, 60, 88, 101, 133, 140, 141, 145
accommodations   34, 134
accounting   13, 15, 16
accumulation   8, 9, 11, 12, 18, 19, 21, 23, 24, 28, 33, 92, 105, 143, 144
advancement, technological   65, 66, 85
affinities, elective   133, 141, 142
agency   92, 125
agents   1, 4, 29, 34, 50, 64, 66, 93
algorithms   64, 73, 95
American markets   89
annulment of space across time   55
apparatus
   regulatory   18
   technological   43, 44
applications   65, 67, 93, 101, 120, 141
approach, post-Keynesian   22
arbitrage   14, 84, 85, 93, 98, 108, 144
articulations   5, 24, 58, 59, 145
artifacts, technical   47, 54, 55, 64, 145
artificial intelligence   65, 101, 103
assets   1–2, 11, 14, 19, 20, 63, 64, 65, 98, 106, 108, 110, 129, 132, 133
   productive   105
assets markets   119
   financial   116
asymmetries   76, 103
ATs   77, 80, 88, 129, 132, 135
ATs and HFTs   86, 96, 108, 126, 136, 137, 140
ATS Brasil   129, 132
auctions   97, 116
automated capitals market   114
automation   9, 15, 40, 64, 65, 73, 100, 101, 138, 145, 146
autonomization   1–2, 42, 43
autonomy   2, 25, 28, 37, 46, 56, 92, 99
   circulation-production   37

banks   22, 23, 24, 28, 29, 30, 74, 79, 81, 102, 103, 108, 110, 111, 127
   large   61, 100–101, 110, 112, 137
banks and brokers   61, 127

Barcellos, M.   107, 113, 114, 115, 117, 118, 119, 123, 124
barriers   11, 28, 49, 52, 109, 132
Bats Global Markets   82
behavior   64, 101, 108, 110
belief   42, 85, 88, 99, 145
biotechnology   101, 119
blocks   29, 108, 116
Bloomberg   61, 76
BM&F   110, 120, 122, 123, 125, 126, 127, 130–31, 133
BM&F Bovespa   16, 17, 71, 72, 77, 89, 108, 109, 121, 128, 129, 131, 132, 135–36, 138, 140
   technology area of   66
BM&F segment   72, 110, 119, 122, 127, 128, 130, 131, 133, 136
boom   122, 123
Bovespa   71, 72, 107, 110, 113, 114, 116, 117, 118, 122, 123, 125, 126, 130, 131, 136
Bovespa segment   71, 77, 110, 114, 119, 130, 131, 133, 135
Brazil   15, 17, 61, 76, 81, 106, 107, 109, 111, 113, 116, 120, 125, 127, 129
Brazilian capitals market   68, 69, 85, 86, 94, 95, 96, 97, 98, 112, 113, 118, 129, 133, 146
Brazilian Context   105, 107, 109, 111, 113, 115, 117, 119, 121, 123, 125, 127, 129, 131, 133
Brazilian derivatives market   119
Brazilian economy   105, 106, 123, 132, 134, 140
Brazilian investors and brokers   112
Brazilian market   99, 107, 109, 110, 113, 114, 119, 121, 123, 126, 130, 133, 134, 136, 137
   central   108
Brazilian stock brokers   111
Brazilian stockbroking   68
Brazilian stock exchange   17, 72, 107, 108, 117, 120, 124, 126, 130, 146
Brazilian stock market   118, 119, 123, 134, 137, 140, 141
brokerage firms   10, 118, 121, 124, 126, 135, 137, 145
brokerages   69, 72, 115, 117, 121, 138, 139, 140
   biggest Brazilian stock   79
   five biggest   118, 137

INDEX

brokers 79, 81, 85, 107, 108, 109, 117–18, 121, 122, 125, 127, 137, 138, 140, 141
Brunhoff, S. 29
Burawoy, M. 4, 47
businesses 35, 53, 62, 73, 86, 93, 100, 102, 121
business models 61, 69, 75, 115

capital 7, 9, 11, 12–14, 20–21, 24, 25, 26, 27, 29, 34, 37, 51, 52, 55–56
   accumulation and valorization of 92, 99
   accumulation of 1, 4, 6, 9, 18, 20, 21, 22, 33, 55
   bank 2, 23, 24, 28
   commodity 24
   concentrated 33
   crisis of over-accumulation of 9, 19, 21, 23, 30, 58
   expanded reproduction of 12, 33, 51, 53
   fictional 17
   fictitious forms of 106, 146
   flow of 31, 32
   foreign 113, 127
   function as 25
   globalization of 2, 14, 29
   individual 12, 35
   industrial 23, 28
   interest-bearing 2, 4, 24, 25, 26, 29, 32, 36, 106, 143, 144
   interest-producing 25, 27
   money 2, 24, 27, 29, 34
   monopolistic 28
   open 110
   organic composition of 50, 144
   over-accumulated 107
   potential 25
   private 32
   processes of centralization and concentration of 51, 93
   productive fixed 105
   real 2
   regulating 32
   reproduction of 20, 34, 55
   valorization of 52, 92, 99, 145
capital and society 14, 40, 41, 43, 45, 47, 49, 51, 53, 55, 57, 59
capital as a whole 4
capital base 55

capital demands, pronounced 74
capitalism 7, 8, 18, 19, 21, 22, 23, 28, 29, 30, 37, 46, 55, 56, 62
   cognitive 3
   communicative 3
   contemporary 21
   digital 3
   finance-led 105, 106
   financial 60
   high-technology 3
   informatics 3
   informational 3
   industrial 12
   imperialistic 23
   modern 35, 62
   patrimonial 34, 143
   virtual 3
capitalism's tendencies 56
capitalist accumulation 5, 6, 19, 21, 31, 40, 143
capitalist economy 2, 4, 8, 12, 39, 41, 50, 52, 64, 93
   central 30
   global 92
   globalized 63, 143
capitalist endeavor 53
capitalist exploitation 8
capitalist mode 11, 28, 35, 49, 50, 58, 94
capitalist property relations 47
capitalist relations 8
capitalists 4, 5, 18, 28, 33, 35, 50–55
   financial 28
   single 52
   small 35, 54
capitalist system 1–2, 18, 21, 94
capitalization 24, 26
capital management 28
capitals market gains 106
capitals market regulator 90
capitals markets 40, 75, 76, 77, 85, 91, 92, 109, 110, 111, 112, 121, 122, 123, 126
capitals markets demand 66
capitals markets technology company 62, 67
CATS, system 114, 115, 130
centralization 12, 21, 36, 50, 51, 52, 56
centralization and concentration of capitals 12, 34, 51, 52, 92

INDEX

centralization of capitals 29, 51, 52
CFTC 78, 99
Chesnais, F. 1–2, 4, 7, 8, 14, 19, 21, 23, 28, 29, 30, 32, 33, 34, 36, 38, 52, 119
Chicago 73, 114
Chicago Stock Exchange 108, 114, 127
circulation 1–2, 9, 10–11, 27, 28, 37, 52, 54–55, 60, 61, 66, 146
circulation of capital 9, 29, 30
class struggle 48, 49
clients 61, 67, 69, 74, 79, 89, 108, 110, 116–19, 121, 122, 127, 138, 139
CLOB 96
Closeout Risk Evaluation 128, 131
closure 63, 97, 98
cognitive capitalism 3
co-location 70, 71, 72, 109, 110, 127, 137
co-location mode 131
co-location service 70, 71, 72
commodities 1–2, 7, 20, 24, 25, 26, 27, 28, 33, 34, 35, 37, 54, 55, 72, 75
commodity capital forms 2
Commodity Markets 91
Communication Technologies 3, 6, 7, 9, 12, 13, 16, 56, 57, 58, 60, 62, 64, 143, 147
communicative capitalism 3
companies 23, 61, 67, 69, 100, 111, 112, 119, 120, 122, 123, 125, 126, 132, 140
  traded 123
company shares 26, 36
competition 10, 12, 35, 37, 50, 51, 52, 53, 66, 70, 85, 87, 107, 109, 110
competitiveness 10, 63, 68
competitors 14, 51, 52, 62, 73, 80
complexity 17, 36, 40, 41, 53, 61, 85, 86, 87, 88, 93, 103, 134, 142, 146
  growing 86, 87, 142
compression 11, 54, 57, 58, 63, 143
computers 40, 60, 61, 64, 73, 74, 81, 84, 95, 103, 114, 130
Computer Science 15, 16, 74
concentration 10, 12, 13, 34, 50, 51–52, 93, 107, 111, 112, 137, 139, 144, 145, 146
concept 3, 4, 22, 23–24, 28, 29, 33, 34, 44, 46, 48, 51, 53, 117, 119
configuration 13, 14, 23, 29, 31, 32, 41, 44, 48, 56, 63, 74, 134, 143, 147
conflicts, social 13, 87, 88

conformation 13, 23, 34, 42
consequences 3, 19, 41, 62, 75, 77, 81, 87, 90, 91, 101, 129, 135, 146, 147
consequent 9, 29, 36, 37, 101, 133
consolidation 3, 55, 111, 118, 133
consumption 1, 18, 27, 30, 31, 33, 53, 54, 56
content, social 6, 13, 17, 40, 48, 49, 59
contexts 11, 13, 15, 17, 19, 35, 36, 37, 39, 45, 47, 76, 85, 86, 112
  economic 107, 109
contracts 78, 120, 128, 129, 133, 136, 140
contradictions 39, 45, 46, 48, 49, 50, 52, 103
contributions 4, 17, 23, 43, 46, 47, 141
control 8, 9, 10, 13, 29, 32, 34, 35, 43, 44, 46, 47, 85, 115, 119
  technical 44, 109
core 5, 128, 131
corporate governance 35, 119, 120
costs, high 10, 54, 73, 106, 138
countries 8, 9, 10, 34, 67, 90, 91, 105, 106, 107, 108, 111, 112, 113, 127
creation 6, 10, 18, 24, 27, 33, 35, 38, 40, 53, 54, 116, 119, 129, 132
creator 44, 45
credit 2, 12, 22, 25, 26, 29, 52, 105, 106, 112, 117
credit system 24, 25, 29, 33, 37, 53, 146
crises 5, 7, 9, 10, 18, 27, 28, 29, 30, 34, 36, 37, 105, 143, 144
  fiscal 32
critique 46, 47, 48
Crotty, J.R. 22
culture 42, 43, 48
currencies 2, 11, 14, 29, 102, 105–7, 110, 120
CVM 17, 99, 113, 121, 123, 129, 132
cycle, of operation of digitalized finance 11, 13, 50, 92, 93, 141, 144

data
  primary 3, 15
debt 32
demutualization 125, 130, 133
deregulation 10, 30, 32, 34, 40, 104, 107, 130, 143
  financial 30, 32
derivatives, over-the-counter market 131
derivatives market 106, 110, 127

determinants   49, 66
deterritorialization   143, 144
development   2, 3, 5, 6, 12, 13, 14, 52, 58, 87, 88, 91, 133, 141, 144
   capitalist   2, 47, 143
   economic   19, 134
   intense technological   6
   rapid technological   146
   technical   3, 11, 54, 62, 85, 146
diagnosis   21, 32, 41, 52, 58, 59
dialectic relationship   3, 4, 133, 142
dialog   54, 56, 58, 134
digitalized finance   11, 50, 60, 61, 63, 65, 66, 67, 91, 93, 94, 99, 101, 103, 112, 135, 138–39, 142
digitalized financial markets   86
dimensions   9, 43, 49, 50, 51, 61, 62, 64, 65, 67, 68, 92, 93, 142, 143
   technological   41, 67, 81
Direct Market Access   108, 116, 127, 130
disjunction   27
dispossession   21, 33, 34, 53
   accumulation by   33
disputes   4, 17, 18, 48, 76, 120, 134, 146
distances   66, 70, 87, 102
dominance   13, 14, 29, 31, 38, 118, 143, 144
domination   8, 39, 42, 44, 47
dot com companies   100, 119
Dow Jones Industrial Average, DJI   80, 82, 84
dynamics   6, 16, 33, 36, 39, 54, 63, 64, 83, 142, 146, 147

economic crises   5, 10, 12
economic history, General   44
Economic/institutional changes   130, 131
economics   15, 16, 32, 75
economic scenarios   68, 139, 140
economists   60, 64, 84, 85
economy   1–5, 8–9, 21, 22, 23, 30, 31, 36, 41, 42, 49, 50, 99, 134, 141
   fictitious   11, 13, 15, 41, 144
   global   1, 9, 31, 40, 69, 93, 102, 116
effects, unfolding   21, 22
elaboration   71, 72, 77, 88, 93, 98, 131, 135, 136, 137–39
electronic system   115–16, 120, 124
empowerment, increasing technological   41
environment, technological   87
Epstein, G.   1, 22

errors   65, 80, 81, 85
establishment   1, 26, 40, 47, 51, 64, 87, 95, 96, 116, 121, 131
Europe   78
European markets   78
European Securities and Markets Authority   90
evaluation   4, 5, 13, 22, 25, 42, 59, 145
events   40, 62, 80, 81, 82, 113, 123, 134, 145
   adverse/extreme market   103
evolution   13, 22, 28, 29, 35, 42, 64, 66, 78, 99, 115, 129, 145
   technological   99–100
Exchange Commission   90, 98, 99
exchange rate   31, 32, 33, 106, 110
exchanges   78, 80, 81, 98, 99, 107, 108, 109, 125, 126, 127, 128, 136, 139, 140
execute   64, 96, 97, 116, 117, 138
execution   16, 67, 68, 70, 90, 106
expansion   3, 4, 6, 12, 22, 33, 34, 36, 51, 52, 64, 81, 83, 119, 128, 147
   capitalist   12
exploitation   7, 11, 18, 33, 34, 40, 42, 50, 52, 76, 80, 84, 110
   economic   76, 79
exploration   10, 40, 62, 65, 70, 76, 146
exposure   109, 110

factors   31, 32, 44, 48, 49, 51, 52, 64, 65, 66, 67, 74, 84, 133, 134, 146
   economic   14, 48
   human   64, 65, 85, 145
   technological   14
factory   44, 45
Feenberg, A.   4, 47, 48
fetishism   1, 47, 48
   technological   38, 47, 145
feudalism   55
fiction   26
fictitious   24, 25, 100
fictitious capital   1–2, 4, 12, 19, 23–27, 29, 34, 36, 37, 40, 53, 57, 92, 144
   development of   27, 37
fictitious nature   37
field   14, 15, 53, 54, 58, 59, 61, 66, 67, 94, 147
finance   7, 8, 9, 22, 23, 27, 28, 32, 34, 35, 38, 99, 100, 144, 146
financial accumulation   1, 14, 20, 21
financial assets   15, 19–20, 57, 64, 91, 105

INDEX

financial capital   1–2, 24, 28, 29, 30, 34, 56
  definition of   28, 29
  international   32
  valorization of   1, 11, 32
financial crisis   15, 23, 25, 27, 29, 36, 64, 74, 78, 110, 131
financial dominance   4, 9, 27, 32, 60, 63, 69, 81, 91, 92, 106, 116, 133, 134, 142
financial gains   10, 11, 40, 64, 87, 93
financial globalization   1, 30, 32, 35, 38, 52, 54, 60, 94
financial institutions   10, 13, 16, 23, 32, 38, 40, 79, 85, 99, 103, 110, 111, 112
financialization   1–4, 7, 13, 18, 21, 22, 23, 29, 32, 34, 35, 91, 93, 105, 106
  processes of   22, 24
  process of   3, 4, 5, 12, 15, 17, 19, 22, 23, 41, 50, 90, 93, 141, 144
financial market history   84
financial marketplace
  advanced   145
  biggest   129
financial marketplaces   11, 38
  fewer global   32
  global   9, 92, 125
  international   36
  large   10
financial markets   11, 13, 15, 16, 34, 52, 56, 57, 61, 63, 64, 75, 81, 94–96, 111, 144
  connected   40
  domestic   30
  modern   62
financial sphere   1, 5, 9, 12–14, 19, 30, 34, 91, 93, 101, 144
financial system   3, 4, 5, 9, 34, 37, 53, 56, 103, 111, 119
financial technologies   52, 102, 144
  Virtu   74
financial valorization   19, 27, 29, 30, 31, 32, 36, 38, 56, 116, 143, 144
financial volumes   17, 72, 77, 118, 140
FIX interface   126, 130–31
Flash Boys   73, 79, 90
flash crashes   80, 83, 84, 90
flexibility   31, 56, 57
flexibilization   10, 30, 31, 38, 56, 81, 143
flow   32, 34, 41, 65, 76, 106
foodstuffs market, global   91
food supplies   91

forces, productive   3, 46, 47
Fordism-Keynesianism   30, 32, 58
Fordist capitalism   22
foreigners   127
Foreign Exchange Market   83
foreign investors   99, 109, 113, 121, 126, 127, 134, 136, 145, 146
  large   73, 122
Fourth Industrial Revolution   101, 102
fractions   25, 26, 80, 87, 95
freedoms   13, 30, 36, 42, 44, 106
freeing   1, 19, 21
frontiers   6, 10, 11, 33, 40, 63, 66, 70, 116

game   86, 93, 113
Game Theory   64
Gateway   117
geography   17, 58, 73, 74
globalization   1–2, 14, 33, 38, 52, 143
globalized capitals markets   65
Globalized Finance   18, 19, 21, 23, 25, 27, 29, 31, 33, 35, 37, 39, 146
globalized financial marketplace   38
GDP   106, 120, 139
GNP   20
golden age of capitalism   143
golden years   19, 30
goods   2, 14, 20, 25, 26, 45, 47, 54
governance   13, 86, 87, 119
governments   9, 10, 32, 58, 85, 88, 93, 99, 102, 119, 120, 121, 130
growth   21, 22, 56, 72, 85, 86, 93, 112, 113, 120, 133, 134, 140, 141, 143
GTS   74, 119, 131
guides   14, 15, 52, 53

Harvey, D.   4, 8, 14, 21, 23, 29, 30, 31, 32, 33, 50, 52, 56, 57–58
heart   9, 19, 34, 36, 48, 54
Hegel, G.W.F.   48
hegemonic capitalist formations   22
heuristics   73, 80
HFTS   65, 71, 72, 76, 77, 78, 84, 88, 89, 90, 95, 96, 108, 109, 140
  participation of   78
  trading share of   71, 77
High Frequency Trading   63, 65, 90, 100–101
Hilferding, R.   8, 23, 24, 28, 29, 35
Home Broker   116, 117, 118, 119, 130, 135, 141

human factor 64, 65, 85, 145
human interference 117

Ianni, O. 58
ICT 3, 4, 5, 12, 13, 14, 41, 50, 57, 101, 129, 141, 142, 143, 144
ideology 47, 48, 49
imposition 32, 33, 90, 96
income, fixed 61, 133, 138
increasing 10, 12, 13, 20, 27, 33, 50, 63, 70, 84, 86, 87, 91, 92, 144
increasing concentration 125, 143
independence 44–45
index 80, 82, 84, 110
individuals 10, 42, 113, 117, 119, 122, 134–35, 138–39, 141
industries 8, 27, 29, 35, 54
informational revolution 9
information technologies 3, 15, 16, 38, 74, 100, 103, 111, 142
   high-performance 9, 144
infrastructure 67, 68, 103, 106, 117, 126, 128, 140
   technological 40
innovations 10, 34, 37, 45, 51, 53, 54, 55, 65, 67, 68, 88, 109, 144
   technological 57, 130
instabilities 18, 81, 85, 87, 94, 103
institutional changes 118, 121, 124, 126, 142
institutional investors 30, 113, 119, 133, 136, 141
instruments 43, 44, 76, 85, 95, 98, 99, 132, 141
integration 19, 38, 55, 101, 113, 114, 115, 123, 126
intelligence, established 45
intensification 3, 5, 30, 36, 42, 84, 144
interaction 3, 13, 39, 40, 126
interconnection 38
international business market 16
international capitals market 123
international derivatives markets 122
international markets 108, 119
   advanced 134
Internet 9, 15, 74, 76, 101, 116, 117, 118, 122, 135
interpretation 7, 23, 55, 57, 129
Interviewee 62, 66, 67, 68, 72, 76, 81, 85, 86, 109, 111, 121, 122, 125, 126
   explained 108, 109, 121
interviews 14, 15, 16, 62, 66, 67, 68, 71, 72, 73, 74–75, 84, 85, 110, 111

interweaving 49
investigation 4, 5, 6, 9, 12, 13, 15, 16, 17, 38, 41, 80, 132, 134, 147
Investment Grade 125, 127
investment in research and development 54, 87, 88
investments 51, 52, 53, 54, 69, 70, 73, 74, 79, 85, 86, 88, 100–101, 106, 128
   productive 51
investor profiles 17, 134
investors 15, 63, 65, 67, 70, 79, 80, 85, 87, 89, 92, 93, 95, 97, 109, 128, 135
   categories of 63, 89
   financial 14, 35, 91
   individual 54, 132, 135, 136
   large 69, 79, 80, 89, 91, 98, 101, 108, 111, 113, 116
   new 107, 109, 117
Investors Exchange 90
IPO 82, 122, 123, 125, 126, 130, 140

joint-stock companies 26, 29

Knight Capital 82
knowledge 46, 52, 64, 65, 76, 91, 99

labor 7, 19, 21, 30, 31, 32, 33, 42, 43, 44, 46, 47, 48, 50, 51
   control of 30, 42, 43, 51
   exploitation of 7, 28, 30, 36, 143
   new forms of 7
   world of 7
labor markets 31, 56
labor time 51
languages 15, 76
Lapavitsas, C. 6, 22, 23
latency 66, 67, 70, 128
layering 89
Lenin, V. 2, 8, 23, 24, 28, 47
liberalization 10, 14, 30–31, 40, 63, 112, 130, 143
liquidation platforms 128
liquidity 20, 21, 27, 32, 35, 65, 87, 88, 89, 96, 128, 129
logic 1, 4, 5, 6, 9, 20, 37, 40, 63, 64, 69, 75, 88, 92, 106
logical-cognitive antecedents 64
Long-Term Capital Management 88
losses 52, 79, 88, 108

INDEX

low latency market   70
lucrative   87, 91, 92

machines   9, 43, 44, 45, 70, 71, 84, 108, 114
   inanimate   45
machine-tool revolution   9, 10
management   4, 11, 31, 34, 52, 54, 62, 85, 86, 118, 119, 134, 135, 143, 146
manufacturing capital   26
manufacturing process   20, 21, 24/25, 31, 34, 50, 75
market activities   52, 53
market agents   94
market behavior   69
market conditions   95
market control   133
market data   70, 89, 109
market economy   75
market eventualities   50
market figures   141
market imbalances, potential   116
marketing   122
market jurisdictions   112
market-maker   95, 98
market manipulations   90
market microstructure   83
market movements   108, 126
market operations   91
market participation   78
market penetration   83
marketplaces   52
market players design   65
market prices   51, 80, 124
market risks   129
markets   10, 12–14, 64, 65, 66, 70, 80, 85, 86, 87, 89, 90, 91, 92–98, 99–101, 109–18, 141
   blocked   97
   central   107, 108, 133, 146
   commodities   72, 91
   computerized   136
   conservative   110
   crossed   97
   digitalized   66
   domestic   67
   electronic   96, 109
   emerging   37
   equity   83
   foreign   115
   futures   57

   global   15, 38, 125
   globalized   11, 115
   liberalized   36
   lucrative   86
   over-the-counter   110, 128
   parallel   85, 108
   public   97–98
   regulated   134
   secondary   2, 19
   share   71, 84
   single   107
   spot   84, 115
   technological-solutions   87
   total   78
   unconsolidated   107
Markets Authority   90
market stress   95
market structure   63, 78
market trader   89
market value   26, 125
Marx, K.   2, 4, 8, 11, 12, 18, 24, 25, 27, 28, 29, 35, 42, 43, 44, 45, 46, 48, 49, 51, 52, 54
Marxist   2, 19, 47
Marxist tradition   24, 28, 46
Marx's formulations   28, 50
mathematical models   64, 87, 99, 145
mathematicians   60, 61, 64, 80
mechanisms   10, 15, 27, 32, 33, 34, 36, 80, 85, 90, 94, 103, 127, 134
Mega Bolsa   114, 115, 117, 130, 131
members   13, 67, 99, 100, 113, 119, 121, 125
mergers   8, 10, 28, 35, 51, 110, 125, 131, 133, 143
Mészáros, I.   4, 47
middleware   74, 75
Mifano, G.   107, 115, 117, 118, 119, 120, 124
model   40, 45, 64, 65, 85, 91, 109, 116, 125, 138, 145
modernization   55, 112, 118, 121
   technological   69, 133
Mollo, M.   1, 19, 25, 26, 27, 28, 29, 37
money   24, 25, 26, 27, 28, 52, 55, 56, 60, 63, 118, 121, 125, 126, 135
movement   8, 11, 28, 30, 31, 32, 35, 37, 56, 58, 95, 98, 99, 142, 144
multi-market   129

Nasdaq   81, 82
negotiation   26, 63, 64, 65, 67, 95, 124
Negotiation Limit   131

neoliberalism   14, 23, 29, 30, 31, 32, 37, 99
networks   3, 9, 16, 66, 67, 71
New Market   31, 118, 120, 121, 123, 130
new technologies   44, 53, 56, 88, 118, 147
New York and Chicago   73, 114
New York Stock Exchange   80, 81, 82, 83, 84, 129
New York Times   81, 100
Noble, D.   4, 47, 48
NSC   114, 115, 131
NYES   82, 83, 129

object   5, 10, 13, 43, 147
objectification   9, 10, 39
Obligations   95
OECD   119
opacity   36, 85, 86
opaque   86, 87, 103
open outcry trading system   116, 120, 121, 123, 124, 130, 131, 133, 136
operators   15, 16, 34, 67, 80, 84, 85, 109, 114, 115, 117, 124, 133
orders   18, 19, 36, 49, 50, 79, 80, 82, 96, 97, 108, 109, 111, 117, 138
  economic   132
  established   147
organization   15, 23, 29, 31, 41, 49, 52, 75, 143, 147
outsourcing   57, 112, 143, 144, 146
over-accumulation   9, 19, 21, 23, 30, 33, 57, 58
  crisis of   22, 23, 33, 57
owners   24, 27, 33, 51, 72, 79, 109, 125, 126
ownership   20, 31, 119
  private capitalist   31

panorama   13, 14, 86, 100–101, 123
Paris Stock Exchange   114
participants   16, 65, 66, 89, 126, 134
participation   119, 135, 136, 141
Participation by type of investor   135, 136
paths   11, 41, 128, 146
patterns   31, 33, 64, 86, 110
Paulani, L. M.   19, 21, 28, 105, 106
payments   26, 30, 37, 89, 102, 108
pension funds   35, 133
perspectives   4, 17, 35, 42, 43
PF (productive forces)   3, 46, 47
phases   2, 15, 19, 23, 55, 56, 57, 78

phenomenon   2, 3, 4, 5, 6, 17, 41, 48, 147
  technological   17, 41, 147
phrases   62–63
pioneers   51
platform, electronic   119, 130
players   4, 9, 10, 11, 19, 35, 62, 63, 66, 102, 104, 109–10, 112, 116, 118
portfolios   14, 69, 128, 133
power   8, 26, 29, 31, 32, 33, 34, 45, 48, 67, 99
PQO   121–22, 130, 136
practices, technological   3, 14, 40, 45
predominance   18, 43, 56, 143
president   99, 113, 115, 121, 136
  former   115, 123, 124
price limits   96, 97
prices   26, 35, 53, 65, 69, 71, 97, 98, 111, 116
  best purchase   97
  best sale   97
  market trading   116
  new   79, 80
primitive accumulation   21, 33
private companies   41, 61
privatizations   3, 21, 31, 33, 37, 112
privileged information, obtaining   76
problems   5, 29, 42, 43, 63, 80, 81, 82, 84, 100, 103, 108, 124, 145
processing   6, 53, 63, 64, 65, 66, 70, 102, 110
production   7, 8, 18, 24, 25, 26, 27–28, 35, 37, 42, 49, 51, 54, 55, 143
  capitalist   12, 18, 21, 40, 46, 47, 55
  economic   93, 112
  mode of   3, 43, 49
  real   20, 25, 27, 28, 37, 56
  Social Relations of, SRP   46, 67
  technological   49
production and circulation of information   60, 61
production factors   20
production process   46, 52
productive activities   18, 20
productive capacity   37
productive capital   4, 12, 24, 35
  industrial   8
productive forces. See PF
productive process   1, 21, 22, 37, 42
productivity   35, 50
profits   2, 8, 19, 28, 30, 36, 37, 48, 50, 52, 57, 78, 81, 92, 98

INDEX 165

progress   12, 42, 147
   technological   50, 55
projections   78, 79, 101, 136
protocol   126
   new   127
provision   14, 67, 95, 131
proximity   70, 109
public debt   26, 34, 106
Publicly Traded Companies   120
Puma Trading System   110, 127, 128, 131

race   35, 53, 68, 70, 73, 74, 127
   technological   10, 102, 109
rates   30, 53, 91, 96, 105, 106
   annual   139
rationalization   30, 42, 43, 45, 47
R&D   54
real time   38, 40, 57, 60, 91, 128
real time information   92
reconfiguration, socio-technical   88
reduction   3, 29, 31, 36, 52, 57, 65, 67, 68, 74, 90, 117, 140, 144, 145
references   4, 14, 16, 17, 21, 140
   theoretical   4, 11
regime   9, 14, 18, 23, 27, 31, 38, 143
   accumulation   6
   finance-dominated accumulation   6, 12, 17, 19, 29, 40, 50
   Fordist   9
   of accumulation 19   143
   of accumulation with the dominance of financial valorization   118
   of flexible accumulation   8
regions   9, 10, 55, 58, 86, 128, 140
regulation   10, 13, 18, 81, 93, 94, 95, 96, 98, 103, 104, 132, 133, 141, 142
regulators   13, 16, 80, 85, 88, 90, 93, 94, 95, 99–100, 103, 134, 144
relationship   3, 4, 5, 11, 14, 17, 18, 23, 25, 28, 29, 43, 44, 50, 51
rentier   22, 35
Replacement   131
reproduction   1, 19, 20, 33, 54, 147
   capital-extended   2
reproduction logic   4
research   2, 8, 9, 13, 14, 15, 41, 53, 88, 92, 110, 133

researcher   62, 66, 67, 68, 72, 73, 74, 75, 84, 85, 91, 111
resistance   19, 104, 117, 120, 124
resources   16, 32, 33, 37, 62, 63, 70, 93, 117, 147
restraints, structural   21, 48, 49
return   23, 24, 26, 51, 79, 87, 92
revenue   20, 27, 36, 37, 76, 78, 92, 98, 107
   technological   102
Rio de Janeiro   107, 129
Rio Stock Exchange   107
risk control   88, 95, 96, 98, 109
risk management   87, 128, 131
risks   80, 81, 84, 85, 86, 87, 88, 94, 100, 109, 110, 116, 127, 128, 144, 145
   systemic   85, 87
robots   64, 72, 73, 78, 79, 80, 81, 89, 101, 108, 110, 111, 145
routes   70, 71, 73
rules   77, 120

sale orders   69, 74, 96, 97, 116, 117
sales   2, 37, 56, 60, 64, 97, 116, 137
São Paulo (SP)   66, 67, 68, 72, 73, 75, 76, 91, 107, 110, 111, 127, 128, 129
São Paulo Stock Exchange   110
scale   19, 35, 36, 54, 93
scenario   10, 11, 12, 13, 62, 63, 87, 92, 93, 94, 98–99, 106, 110, 112, 137, 144
   technological   127
science   46, 47, 78, 94, 146
sectors   29, 54, 55, 57, 91, 92, 103, 105, 110, 111, 126, 128, 129, 132, 134
   external pre-capitalist   55
   financial   6, 22, 34, 35, 102, 111
   individual investors   112
   productive   20, 57
securities   9, 11, 19, 36, 37, 61, 91, 98, 99, 114, 132
servers   67, 70, 71
   stock exchange's   71
services   1, 9, 14, 20, 21, 32, 44, 60, 73, 81, 102, 118, 121, 122, 139
   technological solution   67
services markets   132
Shanghai Stock Exchange   82
shares   27, 30, 35, 77, 78, 98, 108, 110, 116, 128, 129, 131–32, 136, 137, 139
   companies trading   139

shares markets 78
shortening 9, 50, 92, 93, 101
shortening time 12
small investors 85, 122, 135, 139, 146
  participation of 122, 145
social action 42, 43
socialism 46, 47
social life 1, 18, 19, 41, 44, 49, 54, 64, 101, 143, 147
social relations 29, 46, 48, 101
society 2, 3, 4, 9, 10, 13, 14, 40, 41, 43, 45, 47, 48, 49, 55
  capitalist 45, 56, 58, 147
  post-capitalist 46
Sociology 15, 16, 21, 46, 133
socio-technological systems 101
software 16, 51, 65, 66, 67–68, 73, 74, 75, 76–77, 80, 82, 85, 103, 126
software development 53, 103
solutions 29, 65, 68, 69, 70, 107, 111, 112, 115, 120, 126, 127, 136
sophistication 63, 64, 133
  technological 146
Source 20, 71, 72, 77, 83, 88, 93, 98, 125, 131, 135, 136, 137–39
SP. See São Paulo
space 7, 11, 44, 52, 55, 57, 58, 70, 72, 73, 98, 116, 132, 143
space-time 58
space-time boundaries 21
space-time flows 9, 11, 13, 50, 54, 92, 93, 133, 141, 144
space-time frontiers 4
specialists 3, 13, 14, 15, 67, 69, 70, 94, 119
speculation 1, 9, 11, 19, 20, 26, 29, 30, 53, 57, 63, 70, 87, 144
speeds 9, 36, 58, 60, 65
spending 31, 111
spheres 19, 22, 35, 49, 50, 52, 54, 55, 58, 118, 119, 131, 134, 143
  productive 19, 36
  social 42, 43, 56
  technological 44
spiral 37, 86, 87, 88, 134
  of complexity of digitalized finance 86, 88, 103, 134, 142
spoofing 89
stability 68, 88, 90, 113, 119

standards 30, 35, 110, 113, 115
start 22, 23, 30, 55, 93, 100, 126, 130, 131, 132, 135, 136
Stiglitz, J. 75, 76
stock brokerage firms 16, 68
stockbrokers 69
stockbroking companies 69
stock exchange
  first 81
  largest 125
  new 129, 132
  single 107
stock exchange building 70
stock exchange capitalization 140
stock exchange derivatives 128
stock exchange directors 13, 15
stock exchanges 69, 70, 73, 82, 84, 107–10, 114, 115, 120, 122, 125, 126, 127, 129, 132
  advanced 109
  modern 114
  regional 129
stock exchange's system 108, 117
stock markets 26, 93, 100, 119, 136, 137–39, 141
  world's 84
stocks 2, 9, 19, 21, 26, 30, 98, 105, 114, 116, 118, 128, 130, 131, 132, 133
  global 19
  most-traded 132
  multiple 83
  sales of 2, 116, 118
  selling 35
structures, technological 82, 138
subject 3, 4, 13, 15, 21, 24, 26, 46, 48, 59, 64, 91–92, 127, 145
subsumption 44, 45
superstructures 48, 49
supremacy, technological 84
surplus value 7, 18, 24, 25, 33, 42
  relative 46, 50, 53, 57, 144
symbols 76, 123
systemic fragility 36
systemic risks 85, 87
systems, new 33, 119, 128

technics 3, 14, 17, 39–41, 43, 45, 47, 48, 49, 51, 53, 55, 57, 59, 147
technological artifact 87
technological base 117

INDEX

technological changes 141, 147
technological determinism 3, 41, 42, 147
technological development 3, 4, 5, 6, 12, 13, 17, 46, 48, 50, 51, 54, 101, 144, 147
Technological Development and Financialization 50
technological dissemination 102
Technological investments 8, 93
technological operation 15
technological products 54
technological resources 64, 67, 80, 92, 117
 automated 11
technological solutions 67, 69, 76, 126
technological strategies, new 70
technological thinking 46
technology 16, 41–44, 46, 47–49, 51, 52, 53, 59, 63, 86, 87, 102, 109, 111, 112
 advanced 89, 110
 advanced trading 123
 cutting-edge 102, 110, 137
 highlight military 54
 modern 42, 43
 social content of 48, 49, 145
 supplying 122, 125, 126
technology acts 54, 92
technology companies 13, 16, 69, 72, 79, 81
 domestic financial market 127
 international 75, 111
 large international 86
technology market 54, 111, 125
technology sector 81, 86
tendencies 9, 10, 11, 12, 13, 51, 54, 55, 60, 93, 94, 133, 135, 144, 146
terminals 61
thinkers 8, 45, 46, 47
time 7, 11, 12, 27–28, 31, 41, 55, 57, 58, 63, 66, 109, 114, 115, 124
time difference 62, 73
time is money 62
time period 71
 hegemonic 56, 143
time priority 97
time-space 57
 compression of 58
time-space flows 101
tools 11, 43, 44, 63, 70, 102
Toronto Stock Exchange 114
Tokyo Stock Exchange 90

trade orders 70, 84, 108
trades 22, 23, 60, 61, 62, 63, 64, 65, 66, 69, 70, 71, 72, 78, 81, 90, 91, 96, 98, 108, 118, 133, 139, 140
trading 83, 84, 85, 103, 107, 108, 113, 114, 115, 116, 120, 124, 130, 132, 137
 high-frequency 74, 83, 89, 90
trading floor 73, 115, 123, 124
 open outcry 115
trading floor operators 124
trading spaces 69, 72, 86
trading stocks 115
trading systems 82, 95, 98, 111, 114, 130, 132
 automatic 84, 90, 114
 electronic 115, 116, 120
 stock exchange's 116
tradition 43, 46, 47
transactions 1, 9, 10, 26, 34, 40, 57, 63, 72, 74, 78, 102, 113, 128, 139
transformations 3, 4, 5, 6, 19, 21, 23, 38, 43, 56, 68, 119, 122, 124, 129
 accelerated technological 85
 economic 2, 92
 structural 4, 5, 41

United Nations Conference 91
United States 22, 69, 74, 78, 79, 86, 102, 106, 116, 138, 145
United States' Public Securities Market 74
University 7, 21, 74, 84, 91
US 23, 86, 107, 108, 116, 125
US capitals market 86
US elections, recent 100–101
US markets 68, 78, 80, 81, 99, 137
US stock exchanges 90

valorization 11, 19, 24, 25, 26, 27–29, 33, 36, 37, 50, 55, 63, 92, 105, 106, 118, 146
 productive 19, 34
value 7, 25, 27, 33, 34, 35, 46, 68, 70, 75, 105
 global stock 20
 theory of 7
 valorization of 11, 27, 28, 56, 144
verbal information 2, 4, 7, 8, 73, 75, 77, 79, 80, 84, 85, 86, 100, 110, 113
volatility 65, 80, 83, 84, 90, 91, 103
volumes 11, 12, 65, 66, 78, 90, 91, 112, 113, 114, 116, 125, 126, 132, 140

wealth   13, 27, 31, 33, 34, 58, 106, 123, 146
  fictitious   19–20
Weber, M.   42, 43, 44, 45, 62, 63, 133
Web Trading. *See* WTR
western rationalism   42, 43
work   3, 5, 16, 17, 41, 42, 44, 46, 55, 65, 66, 92, 99, 100, 101

workers   21, 31, 42, 44, 46, 47, 50, 51, 52
world economy   1, 3, 4, 5, 8, 15, 19, 20, 81, 91, 105
world stock   20

www.ingramcontent.com/pod-product-compliance
Lightning Source LLC
Chambersburg PA
CBHW071202070526
44584CB00019B/2885